D0539243

MONTY'S TURN

MONTY'S TURN
TAKING MY CHANCES

MONTY PANESAR

with Richard Hobson

HODDER &
STOUGHTON

First published in Great Britain in 2007 by Hodder & Stoughton
An Hachette Livre UK company

1

Copyright © Mudhsuden Singh 'Monty' Panesar 2007

The right of Monty Panesar to be identified as the Author of the Work
has been asserted by him in accordance with the Copyright,
Designs and Patents Act 1988.

A CIP catalogue record for this title is available from the British Library

Hardback ISBN 978 0 340 93620 7
Trade Paperback ISBN 978 0 340 95289 4

Typeset in NexusSerif-Regular by Palimpsest Book Production Limited,
Grangemouth, Stirlingshire

Printed and bound by Clays Ltd, St Ives plc

Hodder & Stoughton policy is to use papers that are natural,
renewable and recyclable products and made from wood grown in
sustainable forests. The logging and manufacturing processes are
expected to conform to the environmental regulations of the country
of origin.

Hodder & Stoughton Ltd
A division of Hodder Headline
338 Euston Road
London NW1 3BH

www.hodder.co.uk

CONTENTS

ACKNOWLEDGEMENTS

There are too many family and friends to thank in person for the friendship and help they have given over my life and career. Firstly, they offered encouragement, now they keep my feet on the ground. They know who they are, but I must give special thanks to my mother and father and to Hitu Naik, the man who taught me the game I quickly grew to love. He remains a rock of support.

At Northamptonshire, Nick Cook, David Capel and David Ripley have always been especially helpful with their wise words here and there. And at England, I must say thanks to the players and management who made me feel so welcome when I joined the squad for my first senior tour to India. A few months earlier these same people had won the Ashes. Straight away, they treated me like one of their own.

Off the field, Mike Martin at Paragon Sports Management and Dave Parsooth, a trusted family friend for many years, have managed my business without any hitches. Their work allows me to focus on my cricket without worrying about anything off the field.

For the book, I am indebted to Richard Hobson, of *The Times*, for his patience and help in articulating my thoughts in a readable way. Roddy Bloomfield, at Hodder & Stoughton, gave me the opportunity to tell my story and Hannah Knowles has worked tirelessly through the editing process.

And finally, I want to say particular thanks to all of you out there who have cheered me on, downloaded Monty masks and turned up at games wearing false beards and the rest. Few players are lucky enough to enjoy that level of support. You make me happy.

Photographic Acknowledgements

The author and publisher would like to thank the following for permission to reproduce photographs:

Bedford Modern School Archives, Hamish Blair/Getty Images, Shaun Botterill/Getty Images, Philip Brown, Graham Chadwick/ *Daily Mail*, Nigel Chinneck, Mark Dadswell/Getty Images, David Davies/PA Photos, Anthony Devlin/PA Photos, Patrick Eagar, Mike Egerton/PA Photos, Paul Ellis/AFP/Getty Images, Mike Finn-Kelcey/Getty Images, Stu Forster/Getty Images, Paul Gilham/ Getty Images, Alastair Grant/AP/PA Photos, Laurence Griffiths/ Getty Images, Tom Hevezi/AP/PA Photos, Mike Hewitt/Getty Images, Bryn Lennon/Getty Images, Indranil Mukherjee/AFP/Getty Images, Rebecca Naden/PA Photos, Max Nash/AFP/Getty Images, Pete Norton, Jason O'Brien/Action Images, John Oliver/the *Luton News*, Nick Potts/PA Photos, Ben Radford/Getty Images, Aijaz Rahi/AP/PA Photos, Rex Features, Clive Rose/Getty Images, Aman Sharma/AP/PA Photos, Tom Shaw/Getty Images, Jon Super/AP/ PA Photos, Dave Thompson/AP/PA Photos, Rui Vieira/PA Photos, Chris Young/AFP/Getty Images, Richard Young/Rex Features.

All other photographs are from private collections.

1

MY HERO, MY VICTIM

To say that Sachin Tendulkar was my boyhood idol barely hints at the admiration I had for the great little batsman. In my teens, increasingly drawn to cricket, I had a picture of him on my bedroom wall. And the first time I paid to watch a day of county cricket, in 1996, it was really just to see him in action. By a stroke of good fortune India's tour of England included a game against Northamptonshire at Wardown Park in Luton, a mile or so from home. A group of us decided to put our education on hold, take a day off school and go along to cheer our hero. We had a great time and must have made an impression during his innings because when he reached his inevitable fifty Tendulkar waved his bat in our direction. That sent us into a frenzy of singing and dancing, as if we were not excited enough already.

I had taken along my own precious cricket bat. Precious, because it was a gift from an inspirational man called Hitu Naik, whose name will crop up regularly over these pages. He had brought it back from India as a present and the first time I used it I made a mark on the back against a stump by accident. I was devastated, but he told me not to worry. This time I was determined to get marks of a different kind on that piece of willow. I ran around collecting autographs and the highlight of the day came when Tendulkar himself signed his name in pen. I still have that bat, and I always find it funny as a

Northamptonshire player myself to think that I didn't see fit to ask any of my future team-mates for their autographs that afternoon.

Ten years later I was to get Tendulkar's signature a second time – in circumstances I could not have dared imagine. By now that bedroom wall was decorated with his image. In 2000–01, when I was picked to tour India with England Under-19s, I went into every sports shop I could find to add to my collection of posters. With all his promotional work he is such a presence in India that I returned home with a very good collection. I even feel proud that our birthdays are so close together – his is on 24 April, mine a day later. So when I was told by Andrew Flintoff that I would be making my England debut in Nagpur on the eve of the First Test in March 2006, one of my first thoughts was 'I'll have to bowl to Sachin'.

My plan was simple: concentrate on line and length, bowl to a standard field and don't, at any price, try to do something special. This is one of the greatest batsmen who have ever lived and he will notice it before it leaves my hand. Bring him forward, gently, and try to get him to drive. At least with the field set I might get away with a dot ball and if by some piece of magic it happens to turn I may even beat the bat. Then, on the day itself, a ball hits his pad. 'Wow, that's close,' I think to myself. Geraint Jones appeals from behind the stumps, and I join in. A couple of seconds later, umpire Aleem Dar raises his finger and Tendulkar heads back to the pavilion.

If you want to know where and when my exuberant wicket-taking celebrations began, then I know the exact place and date: Nagpur, 3 March 2006. I have never felt the same release of energy before or since that incredible moment of triumph. A first Test wicket is a treasured memory in the life of any bowler, but when the victim happens to be your hero, the player you have worshipped since the age of ten, then . . . well, I think you're entitled to go on a bit of a run and a leap and exchange a few high fives. I felt like an exploding volcano with an incredible release of energy from the inside. It was only when Tendulkar was about three-quarters of the way back that I thought, 'My God, what have I done?'

At the end of the India innings one of the England management asked the umpires for the ball for me to have as a keepsake. The game ended in a draw – we were on top for quite a lot of the time but ended up having to repel a thrilling counter-attack – and the Indian physio, John Gloster, suggested that I ask Tendulkar to sign it. I wasn't sure. I thought it might come across as taking the mickey if I asked him to autograph the very ball that had brought his demise. It could have been misinterpreted as being disrespectful. But Gloster obviously knew him far better. He said that Tendulkar would not think anything of the sort and after the presentation ceremony went away on my behalf. A couple of minutes later he returned with the ball, mission duly accomplished.

Tendulkar had written in black marker pen: 'Once in a blue moon, never again, mate.'

I didn't know whether to laugh at the message or cry in joy at the whole experience. As a memento of a Test debut it is something I will always cherish. I don't know how much that ball is worth on the open market, but to me it is absolutely priceless. A little later I spoke to Tendulkar. He asked me if I'd got the ball back and I thanked him for the message. He is a really nice, quiet, humble guy, but to me he remains there on a pedestal. Talking to him, I felt like a kid around his favourite pop star or footballer, not really knowing what to say but never wanting the conversation to end.

In every sense it seemed a world away from our first fleeting meeting at Wardown Park.

2
HAPPY DAYS

M y father, Paramjit, came to England to visit his brother in 1977. He decided almost straight away to emigrate, knowing that he might struggle with the language in those early days. He was 19 and a carpenter by trade. His family lived in and around Ludhiana, a city in the Punjab region of north-west India with a population of around a million people. I've heard it described as the Manchester of the East because of its industry, though the state as a whole is largely based on agriculture. His distant ancestors had settled in the region having come from Lahore many years earlier, long before the partition of India and Pakistan.

Gursharan, my mother, also has family roots in the Lahore area. As a child she lived in Haryana, which is immediately to the south of the Punjab. She arrived in England in 1979 and, like my father, she came initially simply to visit friends. The pair of them met at the Sikh temple in Coventry. They both used to go there on full-moon days and after the formal introductions they married within about three months. I think there was a degree of arrangement about it but, from what I can gather, romance also blossomed. I was the first of three children, born by Caesarean section on 25 April 1982.

They decided to call me Mudhsuden Singh Panesar. It comes from Madhusudanah, one of 108 names of the god Krishna. All of them have different meanings and legend holds that

Madhusudanah slayed the demon Madhu. He was a strong man, and my parents told me that they settled on Mudhsuden because I looked so solid myself, weighing in at a bouncy nine pounds. My dad says that he remembers an alertness in my eyes in those first few minutes. Apparently, once I'd stopped crying, I kept looking around the room, trying to take everything in. That curiosity is still there, because I am always asking questions in the England dressing room today.

On the subject of names, about a year ago I read on a website that mine happens to be an anagram of 'huge spin dashed man's run'. So maybe my parents had some foresight. But it was not until my early teens that the majority of people abbreviated that to Monty. It seems that one of my aunts gave me the nickname before I was very old, but it didn't stick properly until I started to play club cricket. Some of the players found Mudhsuden a bit long and difficult to pronounce, so they wondered if I would accept an alternative. After a while it just became easier to intro-duce myself as Monty in the first place. When people call me Mudhsuden nowadays they tend to be taking the mickey.

I grew so quickly in my early days that on one of my check visits to the clinic the doctor told my mother that I needed to lose weight. At six months I topped the scales at nearly two stone. My hands and feet were always bigger than normal for my size. In the first case, that has since worked to my advantage because I can get a really good grip around a cricket ball. My weight soon settled down. I was always healthy and never suffered serious illness. I still had an appetite but my favourite foods were oranges and bananas, and I preferred fruit juice to fizzy drinks.

Although I avoided coughs and colds, I did cause my parents a great deal of stress on one occasion when I was three years old. We used to live in a tall house in a part of Luton called Stopsley.

At the time, my father worked night shifts at the Vauxhall car plant, so he slept during the day. My mother was putting some washing out to dry and somehow I managed to clamber down the stairs and through the door without her noticing. The road is usually very busy but there could not have been any traffic on that occasion because I wandered across to the other side and then down another couple of streets. When my mum went back indoors and noticed I had disappeared panic quickly set in. To lose a child is a parent's worst nightmare and she soon shook my dad awake to add an extra pair of eyes and legs to the search. Fortunately, a woman some three blocks away – who wasn't known to the family – had sensed that something was wrong when she saw me wandering around lost, and made sure I was safe. Apparently the two women were both very upset when they met some 15 minutes later. I was returned to my rightful owner, oblivious to the chaos I'd created.

Stopsley was a mixed area rather than a Sikh community. As a family we still tend to speak Punjabi first, but outdoors we soon switched to English. My brother, sister and I are all equally fluent in both languages. We followed the normal principles of Sikhism. I have never eaten meat, tasted alcohol or cut my hair. We said prayers daily and visited the temple where my parents met in Coventry once a month. I think of religion as being a part of me. I have never known life without it or rebelled against it. I am proud to wear a patka when I play cricket or go out, just as my father wears a turban, but I am not making a statement and would not persuade anybody to follow our particular faith. Religion has helped to guide me but has never taken over completely. I have friends of all faiths and some who do not follow religion at all. That is their freedom. I have always had English as well as Indian friends and have always tried to understand everybody's point of view.

At the age of four, I went to India for the first time. According to my mother, I did not like the country because I struggled with the heat and the flies. I was also frightened of the cows in the streets. Apparently, my dad took me closer to the animals to confront that fear and I soon felt at ease. My only vague memory is of listening to my grandfather tell amazing stories about battles and warriors from the Sikh history. I was fascinated by those tales, but I also upset him when I knocked all his books down from a shelf in my excitement. My grandfather did not know how to control me, but fortunately my dad entered the room before I could run further amok.

We took family holidays to India on several other occasions to see different parts of the country as well as visiting relatives. I remember in particular a trip to Rishikesh, a holy Hindu city in the north on the banks of the River Ganges. It became famous in 1968 when the Beatles visited and is now popular with trekkers. The sight of so many small temples near the water with the beauty of the Himalayas in the background left a lasting impression – perhaps because this is where Madhusudanah was said to have killed Madhu. On a less profound note, my mother says that I got most excited that day when I saw a Chinese boy crying and wanted to take photographs of him.

Education was always important to my father. He began to study part-time almost as soon as he arrived in England because he saw the road to prosperity through good qualifications. In between work he took A levels in maths, biology and zoology. He was always scientifically minded and, looking at my generation of the family, it seems that his kids inherited the love of numbers in the genes. I can't imagine how hard he must have worked in those early days here; I found A levels hard enough years later and that was without the considerable worry of having to bring

7

home a wage for the family. Effort such as that deserved reward. He eventually managed to set up his own business broadly based in construction, which he still runs as tirelessly as ever today.

There always seemed to be a very relaxed atmosphere inside our house. It is probably for others to say, but I like to think I have been brought up to be polite, respectful and well mannered, and to understand the difference between strength and weakness. We always knew that my father was in charge as the head of the household, but he never needed to be particularly strict. He was keen on our schooling right from the start. I remember the smile on his face when I arrived home one day, beaming with pride, to announce that I had won a handwriting competition in class. I was six. He thought that neat writing was a way of making a good first impression. These days, my brother Isher, sister Charanjit and I spend quite a lot of time away from home either studying or, in my case, playing cricket. But it always feels special when we sit around the table together to sample my mum's cooking. Only four years separate the three children. Given all the travelling, I would say we are as close as we can be.

To be honest, cricket did not occupy much of my early life. In fact it was hardly there at all. My dad had played a bit in India, along with hockey. When he decided to join the Luton Tech team his driving force was to make new friends and build up a network in the new country rather than simply to bat and bowl. He was a true all-rounder who bowled a decent medium pace and batted somewhere in the middle order. His technique wasn't great – I grew to realise there was a lot of bottom hand in his shots – but he had so much power that when he hit it from the middle of the bat the ball would travel for miles. That, at least, is the way it seemed at the time. He always enjoyed trying to take on the spinners, so perhaps it is a good job I never came across him in his prime.

A lot of my spare time after school and in the holidays would be spent playing football and swimming. My biggest passion was wrestling. I used to love the WWF events shown on TV, such as the Royal Rumble and Summer Slam. After watching a few moves I enjoyed trying to put them into practice against my brother and cousins. They were just as enthusiastic. The Sikhs are known as a warrior race and, yes, we did hurt each other from time to time – accidentally, I ought to stress straight away. There was never anything nasty intended and it doesn't take long now before we burst out laughing when we remember those friendly bouts in the living room. Snooker and pool also became popular pastimes. Jimmy White was my favourite player, I think because he was left-handed the same as me. I used to think I was all right at potting balls – until I started on a full-size table and found it rather harder.

Christmas was always a very joyful time at home. We celebrated in the same way as most other people, with lights outside the house and a tree with decorations indoors. Being vegetarian, we drew the line at turkey. Mum would cook a special Indian dish and I remember one year having a lovely pizza with vegetables, a big treat. According to my mother, if I thought that my brother or sister had been given a better present I would start fighting them, thinking that it would embarrass my parents into buying something more expensive for me next time. I'm not sure. That doesn't sound like me at all!

It was only when I sat down to think about this book that I went back through those early years with my mother and father. I have learned things that I never knew. When my mum told me I could be a bit of a dictator, I didn't believe her. Apparently, though, I was always making my brother or sister pick things up off the floor if the place was untidy, picking up the phone when somebody rang or rearranging things in the kitchen.

There is a Sikh celebration called Rakhi which takes place on the full moon of our month of Shraavana, the fifth in our calendar. It commemorates the relationship between brother and sister. The sister ties some sort of decorative band onto the wrist of her brother, who then pledges to look after her and buys her a gift or offers some money. But when Charanjit gave me the band I would untie it, give it back and say, 'There – that's your present.' My parents thought this was very funny, even if little Charanjit wasn't impressed.

There was always a steady flow of English families from the neighbourhood through our door. I used to enjoy teaching the children words of Punjabi. The funniest thing was to watch them eat our food. There is quite of a lot of chilli and spice in Indian cooking and I can remember people smearing paste onto their samosa or pakora as though it were mild ketchup. Those of us who knew would just dip a corner in very gently. To see their faces turn red as their mouths started to burn made me laugh. Nobody would make the same mistake on a second visit. Generally, people couldn't get enough of my mother's curries and dhals.

I first picked up a cricket bat at the age of nine. Hitu Naik, who worked in the same Vauxhall factory as my dad and became a family friend, had started to run Sunday-morning coaching sessions for youngsters at the Luton Indians club where my father now mixed. Quite a few members of the team had children of roughly the same age and Hitu, whose own kids were still too young to start playing, saw the opportunity to nurture interest. I can't imagine what he made of me that morning when he saw me grip the bat – I remember it was a big Duncan Fearnley –

with my hands crossed the wrong way around. If he thought there was a bit of work to do, then he was certainly right. But from this most unlikely of starts, he was to become the biggest influence on my cricketing life.

Hitu is approaching his 50th birthday but he could still pass for being nearer to 40. He is a Hindu who was born in Tanzania and went to Gujarat in India with his brother because his parents, who stayed in Africa, thought it would be a better place to study. His family came to England in 1976, when he was 18. By then his time in India had instilled a deep love of cricket. He jokes that his mother knew more about the sport than his father, but Hitu has enough knowledge for a whole family. Ironically, given my own subsequent problems, he liked fielding more than batting or bowling. He once told me that his favourite player growing up was Eknath Solkar because of the brilliant catches he took for India in the bat-pad position. It was Hitu who gave me my first bat, a Centurion, for my tenth birthday.

Once I had picked up the basics, I was hooked not only on playing but on following the Test matches on television. The 1991 series between England and West Indies grabbed my attention and never let it go. I can picture now the way that Viv Richards was caught by Hugh Morris for 60 in his last Test innings, even though I didn't appreciate at the time just how fine a batsman he had been. These were the first games that Mark Ramprakash played for England and I became fascinated at the way he would get into the twenties and then get out. As the summer wore on I would sit in front of the television when he was at the crease, just willing him to reach 30. I tried to figure out why he always fell short even when – to my untrained eyes – he seemed to be batting beautifully.

I started to go along to my father's matches and my debut arrived when the team was a man short. Somebody suggested that a ten-year-old lad was better than nobody in the field. No doubt people will find it funny that my first appearance came as a specialist fielder. I don't remember batting and bowling, but I did chase the ball enthusiastically.

The 1992 World Cup made a lasting impact. When Wasim Akram dismissed Allan Lamb and Chris Lewis with successive balls in the final I decided to model myself on the great Pakistani fast bowler. I just wanted to be Wasim, with his whippy left-arm action and that mysterious ability to swing the ball at the last moment. I even wanted to copy the way he walked in slightly splay-footed fashion. He was the first player I really imitated, though when it came to supporting a country my allegiance remained with England and India. No, it doesn't embarrass me to say that I had an affinity for both countries.

As for my own game, I had started to progress quite nicely. My early experiences were at Hitu's sessions working with the other kids rather than with the adult sides. I did, though, enjoy scoring for my dad – I think it was my fascination with numbers coming through again. Eventually I made what I think of as my proper debut for the men's team – not just to make up the numbers – and even took two wickets with my left-arm seam. I remember my dad feeling very proud when he paid my match subs for me. The important thing was that I really enjoyed batting and bowling. Hitu made the practice sessions fun, but they were also demanding. That was important because it meant our attention never wandered. He also stressed the importance of practice, practice, practice.

As the months went on, Hitu became more and more of a driving force. He quickly established junior and youth teams at

Under-11, Under-13 and Under-15 level. It was not too long before he saw his efforts rewarded as we brought trophies to the club. Those achievements might seem small in the bigger picture but they fuelled his passion. Guys like Hitu rarely get the credit they deserve for putting in all those hours of their spare time. There is no personal reward except the quiet satisfaction of watching their boys progress, discover a love for the game and make the best of their ability. I sometimes wonder how many players who have gone on to enjoy careers at county and even international level would have been lost without the energy and commitment of the Hitu Naiks of this world. I know for sure that I wouldn't be where I am today but for him.

One of my earliest breaks came when Hitu found out about trials for the Bedfordshire age-group sides through a boy called Dipesh Patel. He was a really good all-rounder, the star of our junior side and a much more gifted player than me. I was physically strong, but Dipesh had real flair. I was a bit concerned that I would be way out of my depth but Hitu pushed his group to test ourselves against the others in the county and stressed that it was a big opportunity to get ourselves noticed. It was my first taste of what then seemed like a very high standard of cricket. My own left-arm seam was developing and I was no mug with the bat. I tended to go in at number three and saw myself as an all-rounder. The experience itself really was something new. The trials always took place at Bedford Modern School and the boys from Bedford Modern all seemed to be so much better. They just looked more polished with their sound, well-coached techniques and the latest gear, including helmets. I did my best and remember being very happy when one of the selectors said that I reminded him of Wasim Akram.

On the way back in Hitu's van we relived every ball in great excitement, but none of us really felt confident of making the cut. But then, a few days later, came the most surprising news of my life to that point. Five of the Luton Indians juniors had been chosen for the Under-12 or Under-13 sides. Hitu could see that his work was starting to pay off and the fact that a few of us were in there together meant that we wouldn't shrink into ourselves when the games began. We did not go to a private school or have a highly qualified coach to show us exactly how things should be done. For us, it was a case of hitting as many balls as we could in the way that came naturally. Hitu's approach was that as long as we put in the hours we were sure to improve, and I have never lost that belief.

He could be a tough taskmaster. Once, when I'd not scored many runs for the county Under-13s, he saw me walking around the boundary with an ice cream. 'You don't deserve that,' he said, taking it from me. But he also backed his kids and had great faith in us. He told us a story about a conversation with another coach in a bar. With every pint of beer, his predictions had become more and more extravagant. Finally, he told this guy that one of his boys, as he called us, would go on to play for England. 'So make sure you work hard,' he said. 'I don't care which of you it is, but I don't want to be proved wrong.'

The junior section of Luton Indians was very much his area. He had a dream, and his drive and passion to fulfil it was just incredible. Sometimes I would walk home from school thinking, 'God, I hope Hitu doesn't come around again tonight.' There was even the odd Sunday morning when I asked my dad to tell him that I couldn't make it when he came to pick me up. 'You tell him,' my dad said. 'You should have the courage to say so if you don't want to play.' Once I got there, of course, I loved those sessions.

The club played a big part in my life. Facilities were not lavish but they were good enough. Over the past couple of years I have seen a few articles in which friends describe how I used to go down there to practise even in the winter as snow or frost lay on the ground. Well, that did not happen very often – probably only once or twice – and I know most kids like to go out and play whatever the weather. But it is typical of Hitu's commitment that even in those conditions he saw a space of time where he thought I could put in some extra work to improve. A lot of the time he would be there himself, as if to show that he would not ask us to do anything that he wasn't prepared to work on himself.

One summer Gordon Greenidge, the great attacking opening batsman from the West Indies, visited the club to promote a mock World Cup tournament being staged in Luton between sides representing England, India, Pakistan and West Indies. He showed me how to play a forward defensive shot that involved twisting the back leg to help balance the body weight. I considered myself to be pretty quiet and shy in most areas, especially around people I didn't really know. But cricket was different. I always asked lots of questions if I thought the answers would give me that little something extra, that little tip to take me a couple of steps forward. I bombarded Greenidge that day and I always remember his final piece of advice. 'As soon as you stop enjoying the game, you should give it up,' he said. 'Try to play with a smile on your face all the time.'

Round about this time, I had my first taste of captaincy, in an Under-14 game. Dipesh Patel was the usual captain. In junior sides you tend to find that the best player takes charge, and Dipesh was still some way in front of the rest of us. I can't remember our opponents that afternoon, but I do remember how we bowled well enough to get them all out for 41. Hitu suggested that to make all of us feel involved I should reverse the batting order. That sounded very fair, but unfortunately we lost some early wickets, the other side gained confidence and bowled us out for 11. I haven't captained a side at any level since.

When I was 14 we moved house to a quieter part of Luton. This was ideal for me because it meant I could play cricket in the back garden. The previous owners had built a patio area but before too long my brother and I had ruined the brickwork with the constant thud of the ball. Within a week we also managed to accidentally smash one of the greenhouse windows. Dad replaced it, but when it was broken again just a few days later he decided, for the sake of his wallet, to wait until his boys had left home before ordering yet another pane of glass.

Hitu not only encouraged us to play for our own age group but challenged us to make the next one up. That way we could get involved in more games as well as push ourselves against older, more experienced boys. A gang of us grew up and learned together: Dipesh Patel, Nitin Parsooth, Hemal Randerwala, Ankur Desai, Sanjay Sidar and myself. Nitin, like Dipesh, stood out in those early days. He bowled left-arm wrist spin, like Brad Hogg, and spun the ball miles. But for a knee injury he could have been a really good player. These days he is probably my best mate. We played for the county Under-13 and Under-15 side one season, then for the Under-14s and Under-17s the next. The biggest leap came when I represented the Under-15s and the Under-19s, by which time I was also playing regular adult cricket. I think it is a good idea to try to play against the best you can, even if it takes a while to feel confident.

Looking back, I can see that I was a very naive cricketer as a boy. Things would happen that I just didn't understand. For example, I could swing the ball in to the right-hander but I hadn't a clue how I did it. A lot of my wickets came by bowling batsmen through the gap between bat and pad as they pushed outside the line of the ball. Those hours of practice stood me in good stead, because I soon became very accurate and had the strength in my shoulders to be able to bowl long spells. In boys' cricket especially I think a few wickets probably came when batsmen started to get bored waiting for a ball they could hit. For all that, however, my days as the next Wasim Akram were drawing to a close.

There is probably a sound reason why so many spinners began as seam bowlers. Shane Warne and Ashley Giles are among those who have made the switch and gone on to achieve great things. The seed was first sown in my mind by Paul Taylor, the Northamptonshire and England left-arm bowler, who was doing some coaching for Bedfordshire during the off-season in 1994–95. I don't think he was very impressed with my seam and swing. During a break I bowled a few spinners away from the nets just to pass the time. Taylor had seen me out of the corner of his eye and suggested I give it a go properly. Even at the age of 12 I had relatively big hands and long fingers, which helped me to get a good grip on the ball. I already had the accuracy and I liked the sensation of watching the ball come out of my hand and mysteriously change direction off the pitch. Taylor seemed to be a bit more impressed and told me I ought to think about switching. Personally, I was a bit sceptical.

But the next time I saw Hitu I told him what Taylor had suggested. We couldn't just ignore advice from such an experienced bowler, especially one who bowled left-arm himself. He knew the game far better than we did, so we decided to give it a go. What was there to lose? Even then the change was a gradual process, to the extent that I did not bowl spin exclusively for another couple of years or so. I would bowl seam at the start of the innings and then switch to spin midway through. I actually enjoyed that arrangement because it meant I bowled more overs. Looking back, I can see why I made the ball turn sharply. It wasn't that I had a lot of craft and guile but rather that pitches were wet and grassy, enabling the ball to grip against the surface. But with every game that passed, it increasingly felt the right way to go.

I remember the day when I finally decided to switch once and for all. It was an Under-15 game between Bedfordshire and Worcestershire. Having been told to concentrate entirely on spin, I managed to take 7 for 35, and on the back of that performance I was selected to play at the prestigious Cambridge Under-19 Festival. This is one of the biggest events in the annual junior cricket calendar. I would guess that almost all the leading players in England have been there at some point in their development. If there were still doubts that spin rather than medium pace was my forte, they had been wiped away inside 24 hours.

The gradual change required a few alterations to my action. I had been given a book called *MCC Masterclass*, which featured split-second photographs of Bishan Bedi working through his delivery stride. Bedi was also a Sikh who enjoyed a good career as an overseas player for Northamptonshire. Maybe that influenced me to a point, although at that stage I had no connection with Northants. What mattered was the action itself. Bedi had been a great bowler and I could see why; he looked so well balanced and light on his feet. I stood in front of my bedroom mirror imitating each picture in sequence. The next step was to stitch the movements together so that my arms and legs flowed smoothly. Even after a few minutes I thought I had found a natural, economical way to bowl.

By this time I was probably playing an average of three times a week. I had made it into the Luton Indians 1st XI and, on Hitu's advice, I decided to join Dunstable CC as well. They played in the Hertfordshire League at a slightly higher standard. Past players included Tim Robinson, who enjoyed great success opening for England in the 1985 Ashes series. I was not being disloyal to Luton Indians. I still think of them as my club and I go back there as often as I can to support the men's team and help out the younger players with little bits of coaching. It is great to see the way that our junior sections are really thriving these days. In any case, the two clubs played in different leagues, so it was not as if I was playing against my mates.

Perhaps my highlight for Dunstable came when I scored 127 in a 40-over game for the second team. Apparently, since I played for England the club have been trying to find the original score-book logging the innings. I actually have my own record. A very kind man at Dunstable, Brian Chapman, who helped to coach the juniors, took the trouble to write out a scorecard in proper ink. I soon had it framed at home and still count it among my proudest possessions. I went in at my usual number three position and I think I hit 15 fours. So, yes, you could say it is a pretty strong memory! At the time I was a genuine all-rounder. Unfortunately my batting started to fall behind as I moved through the grades.

The problem was at Bedfordshire, where they saw me first and foremost as a bowler, and sent me in at nine, ten or eleven from Under-15s upwards. I guess that with the way my career as a spinner has developed that might have been the right approach, but it meant that I rarely enjoyed the opportunity to learn how to build an innings rather than swing at a few balls towards the end. If I had gone in even at six or seven I might be a bit better now because of the extra practice. But who knows? Hindsight gives everyone a great advantage. Maybe my bowling would not have developed if I had concentrated on both areas.

I will admit that my fielding did get neglected. Looking back, I probably ought to have spent more time on throwing and catching balls. When it became a talking point with England I went back to Hitu to ask what my fielding was like. He was honest, as ever, saying, 'You were pretty bad at throwing and collecting the ball, but your catching was all right.' I used to bowl so much – for my club sides it wasn't unusual to start off at one end and continue for most, if not all, the way through. At the end of an over I would wander down to fine leg or third man and think of the next three minutes or so as the chance for a breather. My focus was usually on how I might take a wicket when it was my turn to bowl again.

We tended to play rather than watch, although Hitu did take us to see the India side when they came to Luton and also to see the final of the Under-15 World Cup between India and Pakistan. That was my first visit to Lord's and the place was just incredible. Mohammad Kaif was the vice-captain of India and Taufeeq Umar opened the batting for Pakistan. Both have gone on to play Test cricket. I couldn't believe the standard. It seemed awesome and I had never seen anyone – man or youth – hit the ball as hard as Taufeeq. By that stage Luton Indians were winning all the trophies at junior level, but these boys were just in a different league. I suppose that was natural – by definition they were the best in the world.

The game ended with a crowd invasion. The organisers had clearly underestimated the interest in the game and the stewards could not cope with people running onto the outfield. I remember hearing the police sirens screaming as their van arrived through what I now know are the famous Grace Gates. They had to form a guard to stop supporters invading the pavilion. Hitu whispered to me, 'They'll never get in there without a jacket and tie.' We just stayed in our seats and watched, hoping things would die down. One way or another, we had plenty to talk about when we got home.

Although cricket occupied more and more of my time, I always took my education seriously. In fact I was probably a bit of a geek. I don't remember getting into serious trouble at school. The odd detention came my way but only for minor offences, such as late homework or not paying attention in class. I think I was quite popular and used to impersonate one particular teacher who waved his hand in a very conspicuous way when he called somebody to the front or asked them to stand up. It must have taken a lot of courage because I was very shy – and still am until I get to know somebody. Fortunately I enjoyed most subjects, especially maths, geography and the sciences.

Probably thinking back to his own experiences, my dad never wasted an opportunity to stress the importance of being well qualified. For a while he thought I was spending too much time on cricket and was convinced that my schoolwork would begin to suffer. Fortunately, he knew Hitu well enough to trust his honesty and judgement. Once he realised that I was making progress and starting to become quite useful, he let me go. He bought me the equipment I needed and helped by giving me lifts to games. But if my reports were ever slightly down or it seemed as though I was rushing homework, he made his point. 'The balance has to be right,' he would say. He used to reward me if I scored a fifty or took five wickets and it was the same with my reports: if he was satisfied he would give me some money or we would go into town to buy something I wanted. When I came home after scoring that hundred for Dunstable he was genuinely thrilled. 'You are talking about it so much I feel as though I was there to see it,' he said over dinner that evening.

My brother, sister and I are the first generation of our family to be born in England. It was not like being in India, where there would have been a strong network of friends and family to help us into work if we needed that leg-up. Dad just wanted us to give ourselves the best opportunity to secure good jobs when we entered the big wide world, and that meant getting good school reports and decent results in our exams. As it turned out, all three of us have made it through to university, and I know he is very proud of that.

I found time to swot up for my GCSEs and came away from Stopsley High School – whose former pupils have included the actor Rodney Bewes and Scotland footballer Bruce Rioch – with four As, four Bs and two Cs. They say that schooldays are the happiest of your life. Well, I've had some pretty good ones since, but I still look back fondly on that period. Stopsley was a good school with all the facilities you would need, including a grass cricket pitch. Teachers were prepared to run teams outside their hours. I represented the school at football as well as cricket, but although I'd say I was a reasonable left-back there was never any suggestion of going up to a higher level. Then, as now, I supported Luton Town and Arsenal, and I went through a phase of avidly collecting those Panini stickers of all the players and swapping them with mates.

When I got to 16 I faced a difficult decision. Most of my friends had also secured good grades and were moving on to the local sixth-form college. But quite a few of my team-mates from Luton

Indians were already at Bedford Modern, an independent school in the area. They told me that the education was good but, more important as far as I was concerned, the facilities were fantastic. There would be more cricket matches in the summer, and of a better standard. I began to set my heart on going, so I wrote to the school explaining my ambitions in cricket. They said they would accept me on a sports scholarship, which meant that my dad did not have to pay for those two years.

In my second season there, we established a new school record by winning as many as 13 games. There were three Minor Counties players in the side, Kelvin Locke, Jamie Wade and myself. In 1999 we went on a cricket tour to Barbados for a fortnight. One evening I happened to spot Brian Lara in a bar. I couldn't believe it was really him, even after checking his face from all angles to confirm the identification. A friend of his came over and said, 'You're beginning to worry him; do you realise how loud you are?' I apologised and the guy started to smile. 'Look, come over and have a word,' he said. I plucked up the courage and started a conversation. I told Lara about my teams and the fact that I bowled spin, then tried to pump him for all the information I could. Finally he said, 'Good luck, it's been nice to meet you. Maybe we'll play against each other one day.' It was very kind of him to give up the best part of 30 minutes and I hope I didn't put him off his evening.

By that time I felt as though I was making serious progress up the ladder towards what had become my ambition of playing for England. David Mercer, the Bedfordshire coach, had always been happy to push me forward at county level. The ECB had begun to organise the coaching side of the game, so each of the Minor Counties had their own development officer to work in the region. Mercer worked with me from quite early on and helped

to introduce me to a few subtleties of the game. I began to understand not only what was happening on a cricket field, but why.

Hitu Naik, though, remained my biggest influence. If I did well
in the Under-19 side in an away game I always rang him as well
as my mum and dad to talk about the wickets I had taken and
go through how I thought I had bowled. One tip he gave me was
to put in a really big effort when we played against teams from
the first-class counties. He reasoned that one of their players or
coaches might be watching and put in a good word. Like all of
his advice, it made a lot of sense to my young ears and the advice
paid off in a big way when we went to Essex for an Under-17
match.

To be honest, I can't remember my figures or even how many
wickets I took that day. I do remember delivering a lot of overs.
Next morning, John Childs approached me to ask about my
bowling. Childs ran the Essex youth academy and had been a left-
arm spinner himself. He is best known for making his England
debut against West Indies in 1988 at the age of 36. In fact he was
also called into the squad four years after that, but didn't quite
make the XI. It was only later that I looked up the specifics of
his career, but I did know that he had been a very good bowler
in his day and soon worked out that he wielded some influence
at Essex.

He asked whether I fancied coming to the county nets for what
amounted to a trial. Did I fancy it? That one took me all of a
couple of seconds to answer. Essex were known as a good county
with a reputation for producing excellent young players, including Nasser Hussain, who was a regular in the England team and
within a year of being appointed captain. They were good footsteps to try to follow and when the letter plopped onto the doormat
confirming that I had been invited to Chelmsford I could barely

contain my excitement. Although the butterflies were flying around my stomach as I made my way to the ground, I really thought that as long as I held my nerve and bowled as well as I thought I could, then I had a chance of winning some sort of recognition.

Keith Fletcher, the former England captain and a real stalwart of Essex cricket, was there to welcome me and go through what I would be doing. I started in the indoor nets, but things got off to a bad start when Graham Napier, a young but talented all-rounder, came down the track and hit one so hard that as the ball crashed into the palm of my outstretched hand I thought it was about to turn into a bagel with a giant hole in the middle. It took all my effort to pretend that I wasn't feeling any pain; at least I knew things could only get better. And they did. We went outside and I had much more luck on the proper grass pitches. There was an encouraging word from Peter Such, another Essex and England spinner, and by the end of the day I thought I might have done myself justice after all.

Essex were sufficiently impressed to offer me terms, but by now Northamptonshire had also begun to show an interest through their link with Bedfordshire. Once again, I was invited along for a trial. Nick Cook, the 2nd XI coach, supervised proceedings and we hit it off almost immediately. Over the next few years we would work very closely together. Like Childs, he had bowled left-arm spin for England and as such was somebody I could only look up to. I remember that David Capel, who had various roles at the county after retiring as a player, also watched and took note.

Capel, an England all-rounder in his day, suggested that they might be able to offer something and Steve Coverdale, the chief executive, eventually said that a summer contract was mine if I wanted it. That took me completely by surprise. How could they offer me something like that when I had not even played for them in a proper game? It appeared an enormous risk on their side, but it didn't seem wise to ask too many questions in case they had second thoughts. I remember Coverdale asking me what I wanted in life; I told him my ambition was to play cricket for England. That might have sounded a touch big-headed, but at least it was the truth.

I asked Hitu which would be the better county: Northampton-shire or Essex? It was a tough call. Essex had John Childs, but then Northamptonshire had Nick Cook. I could learn equally well from either. The facilities looked fantastic at both counties and their first teams were full of names I recognised from the score-boards printed in the newspapers. In the end we decided that Northants would be the better option, purely because the County Ground at Northampton was closer to home than Chelmsford. I still see Childs from time to time and we joke about what might have been at Essex.

As if hearing about a first proper contract was not enough good news that summer, I also made my full debut for Bedfordshire. It came against Cambridgeshire at Luton and I arrived on the morning of the game to read an article in the local newspaper saying that I was about to become the youngest player ever to represent Bedfordshire at senior level – aged 16 years and 113 days. Until then I hadn't thought anything of it, but I soon discov-ered the improvement in standard as Simon Kellett, the former Yorkshire batsman, hit us for 223 not out. I didn't think I bowled too badly in the circumstances, considering that it was my first effort and I was extra nervous. My figures read 30–6–75–0. We lost quite heavily – all out for 190 against their 403 – but it seemed amazing to think I was actually playing in a two-day game with and against guys who made their living from cricket. Andy Pick, a fast bowler who made it as far as England A level, was also playing for Cambridgeshire.

Wayne Larkins was our most famous player. He is still a legend at Northamptonshire even though he left more than a decade ago. His nickname was Ned and on the county circuit there used to be a word, 'Nedded', to describe bowlers who had come in for punishment at his hands. A few people with long memories have told me that he was one of the most naturally gifted players to represent the county. I can quite believe that, given the way he used to tear Minor-County attacks to pieces even though he was past his 40th birthday. I would love to have bowled to him in practice but, unlike most batsmen, he didn't bother with nets. He just went into the middle and smacked the ball around as though it was the most natural pastime in the world.

In fact, he went against convention in more ways than one. It is common knowledge that he didn't mind a drink or a cigarette – quite a contrast to the new boy in the team. He was the first superstar that I played with and an inspiration in his own way as my first captain. I can remember being twelfth man for a game against Norfolk at Lakenham, and that they were practising intensely before play while we were just chilling. Most of our side were still tucking into the breakfast they had picked up from McDonald's on the way. We were a very relaxed team and I think the approach worked more times than it failed. There was a great atmosphere in the dressing room.

Although our lifestyles were completely different, Larkins never tried to push me into areas where I felt insecure. That has held true throughout my career in every one of my teams. Sometimes after a good win a guy might suggest I have a beer, but as soon as I say that I'm sticking to soft drinks we move on without any fuss. While on the theme, I ought to say that I've never encountered prejudice in any dressing room. Quite the opposite. I think players like the idea of being in the same team as somebody from a different culture. I often get asked about my background and beliefs. People seem to be genuinely interested.

My team-mates at Bedfordshire quickly respected me as both a player and a person. In my second game, against Hertfordshire, I opened the bowling and sent down 61 overs in a row through the day to finish with 3 for 127. My memory is a bit hazy about all those balls – they probably merged into each other after a while – but I do recall Larkins paying me a huge compliment at slip when he said that my action reminded him of Bishan Bedi. Larkins ought to have known because he actually played with Bedi at Northants in the 1970s. I was pretty tired after that effort, but the next day I made sure I got up early so I could bowl in the nets before play. Whenever I was there on my own I simply dropped a handkerchief on a length and tried to hit it. A few of the guys were surprised at my stamina, but the odd sore muscle never disrupts a strong work ethic or the exuberance of youth. I thought that my progress was down to bowling, bowling and bowling. Nothing was going to stop me now.

3

BREAKING THROUGH

I may have taken Steve Coverdale by surprise when I told him I wanted to play for England, but right from the start I saw county cricket as a stepping stone on the path towards the Test team. If anybody thought I was being big-headed then I can only apologise. I never meant it that way. But I didn't understand then and don't really understand now how any young player coming into the game can want to settle for anything less. Looking back, I can see it was my innocence coming through, being so open about my ambition. There were some experienced guys in the dressing room and fortunately they all took me the right way. They had been in my position once and knew how I felt.

In some ways a teenage spin bowler is a peculiar contradiction. At that age you want things to happen now – if not sooner. Slow bowling, however, requires patience. Slowly, slowly catches the monkey, as the old saying goes. But I couldn't see why, having signed me, Northamptonshire didn't put me in the first team. Why bother giving me a contract if I wasn't going to play? It didn't dawn on me that there were at least 25 other players on the staff, and most of them with better claims than my own. It was obvious to everybody except me that I had been taken on because of potential. I didn't appreciate just how much time it would take to work my way through the system and build towards Championship standard.

Northants already had three very good spinners on the staff in Graeme Swann, Jason Brown and Michael Davies. All of them were around England squads at some point in their career, and none of them were anywhere near the veteran stage. In fact, it looked as though Brown and Swann, who was a genuine all-rounder, might form the spin partnership for the next decade. Northants were very honest about where I stood in the pecking order and the way they saw my career developing. It would be a while before I challenged for the first team. I relayed this to Hitu Naik and my parents, and we all agreed that the best thing was to continue studying for A levels. That way I would have an education behind me if for some reason I didn't go as far as I wished in the game. And it wasn't as though I detested school after all, particularly with all the cricket at Bedford Modern and being able to concentrate on my favourite subjects.

So, like probably 99 per cent of young players, my first experience for the county was in the 2nd XI. Before that, however, I was chosen to play for a representative Minor Counties Under-25 team in a friendly against Middlesex at Milton Keynes. This would be unremarkable except for the fact that I came across Andrew Strauss for the first time. I wonder what odds you could have got back then that a few years down the line we would be playing together for England. We met again in a 2nd XI game later in the season; this time he scored a hundred. Amazingly, Middlesex included three players that day who would become team-mates at the 2007 World Cup, with Ed Joyce and Jamie Dalrymple there alongside Strauss. Northants lost that one by an innings and 170 runs, and I'm not surprised, with the talented young batsmen in the opposition's side.

Studies meant that I couldn't play all that often in the early part of the 1999 summer. My second-team debut finally arrived in July, in a 50-over game against Warwickshire at Leamington Spa. Wayne Larkins, my Bedfordshire captain, lived in the town and came along to watch and offer some vocal support. We lost by five wickets but I took a wicket and felt more relaxed than I imagined I would, perhaps because my position on the staff meant there would be further opportunities no matter what. Mal Loye, who had scored a staggering number of runs the year before, played for us during a break from the first team and I remember Dougie Brown, who had almost made the England World Cup squad a couple of months earlier, playing for Warwickshire.

My first three-day game seemed more important. That was against Surrey at Milton Keynes about a week later. Perhaps I have fonder memories because we won – by seven wickets – and I was allowed a good long bowl. This was the first time that I worked in harness with Jason Brown for any length of time. The pitch started to turn and I bowled 41.3 overs in the second innings to finish with 5 for 114. Brown took 4 for 76 at the other end. Rob Bailey, a good batsman who is acknowledged as one of the nicest men in the game, stood at slip for most if not all of my spells and at one point I overheard him say to another close fielder, 'This kid could be in our first team even now, bowling like that.' That gave me a lot of encouragement and looking back I wonder if he intended it to be heard for that reason.

I must have looked like a real outsider. In those days I didn't even have a proper cricket coffin. I stuffed all my kit in the kind of big plastic bag you might take to school on a PE day, and carried my bat in the other hand. I still wore buckle pads rather than the light, Velcro ones that professionals and even good club players had been using for several years. The funniest thing was my helmet. In those days they were not compulsory at junior level, so I'd spent most of my career with nothing on top of my patka. When I did find a helmet it was a very old-fashioned white thing better suited to riding a motorbike than facing fast bowling. The visor was too big, so I had to peer out of a gap about a centimetre wide to see the ball. Taking guard, I heard one of the Surrey fielders clap his hands and shout, 'Come on, let's get the starship trooper out.'

Although, as the club hinted, I didn't make the first team, I did get to know some of the players. The odd one featured for the 2nd XI either after injury or to rediscover form between four-day matches. We all practised together at nets when we were not involved in games. It soon became apparent that professional players were a class above most of those I had come across at Bedfordshire. I suppose that is inevitable because they have more time to practise and more intensive coaching. If I overpitched even slightly in the nets I would feel the ball coming straight back my way, while balls that I thought were perfectly reasonable would somehow find the middle of the bat.

My attitude towards nets is straightforward. I am there to get the batsman out, not to give him practice. Most batsmen prefer it that way too; I know that I don't want to be treated lightly when I bat. How can you improve like that? Besides which, Hitu Naik told me that batsmen soon notice young bowlers who are causing them trouble. Was it too much to think that one of them might have a word with the coach and suggest I go into the first team? Another thing Hitu suggested was to bowl to the leading batsman in the team as often as I could. That may sound a bit sadistic on the surface but, as I said earlier, you have to challenge yourself against the best. I guess it comes down to trying to leave the most favourable impression you can.

On the same note, Nick Cook, the 2nd XI coach, gave me some very good advice when he stressed the importance of winning the confidence of the captain. He pointed out that if your first few overs went for a few boundaries then the captain may feel tempted to whip you out of the attack. So I didn't mind having an in-out field in those early stages with a couple of men back until I felt in control of the game. Even as great a bowler as Shane Warne likes to make sure his first few balls land on the right spot before trying anything adventurous – not that I can ever imagine his captains being reluctant to let him bowl long spells!

I have heard stories from other counties where the odd senior player starts to look over his shoulder if a youngster begins to threaten his position. But I never came across anything like that at Northants. They were all very encouraging, even if I was a bit shy when it came to mixing in with the banter you always get in dressing rooms. My best friends were Toby Bailey, who had a great view of my bowling from behind the stumps as the second-team wicketkeeper, Mark Powell and Rob White. We were all striving to win a place in the first team. Mal Loye was also a good mate. He had more experience and there was an age gap between us, but we grew to know each other as I spent time bowling to him in the nets. He warned me not to think about cricket, cricket, cricket all the time because he thought I might get fed up. There was no danger of that, but I know what he meant.

Having Nick Cook around was a big help. He could see when things were not working and was always very honest with every-body, though not in a dour, negative way. He never felt that he had to point out a little mistake every game to justify his posi-tion or to give me something to work on. Cricket is very close to my heart and if I had a bad day it could really get me down. I would look into situations in matches and analyse them in my own mind far too deeply. Sometimes it is better just to move on, accept that a batsman is entitled to play well or have a bit of luck, and appreciate that things even themselves out over the course of time.

Cook had a good sense of humour. More important, he knew the right time to make a joke. He would ease me out of my disappointment and when something really wasn't quite right he would store it at the back of his mind and bring it up when I was in a more receptive state. He had been a young spinner himself and he had a good idea of the way I felt. I was still only in my teens so those occasions when I did go back to my bedroom and sulk after things had not gone my way were probably part of the growing-up process. Sometimes I forgot that I was a human being first and a cricketer second.

In those days I used to come between the umpire and the stumps when I bowled round the wicket, which has always been my Plan A to the right-hander. My feet were a little wide apart and there was a crossover in the approach, but because my front arm and shoulder were really strong I could get away with it. Basically it was a good, solid action that just needed some fine-tuning. It wasn't really different from the way I bowl today. My biggest asset was being able to turn the ball on most pitches. Cook used to reassure me about my action when I started to worry after a long spell had gone wicketless. He understood that I had not had a lot of formal coaching and the way I bowled was the way that felt natural. He thought I was fine, and that when I did have an off day there was no deeply rooted problem. Even when you know that deep down, it is good to hear it from somebody else.

Further encouragement came my way in 2000 when I was picked for an England side for the first time. Up to then I had not even been chosen for the Midlands regional team – perhaps being at a Minor County was a disadvantage in my younger days

– but suddenly here I was lining up for the national under-19s. It was just the tonic I was looking for after slogging through A levels. I managed three Bs in chemistry, physics and maths, but they were hard work and had kept me away from cricket until July. Once they were over, I considered myself a full-time player for the first time. University remained an option – I had a place available at Loughborough – but I wasn't prepared to make a firm commitment at that stage. Better, I thought, to weigh up the situation at the end of the season.

The first time I was chosen for the Under-19s was for a warm-up game against Middlesex. I don't know if there had been much communication between the England hierarchy and Nick Cook and David Capel at Northants, but for me the call came completely out of the blue. I asked Cook what was happening, because it baffled me. He said that I had been chosen on merit and shouldn't feel any less deserving than the rest of the squad. So I travelled down to Southgate and bowled, I think, something like 31 overs at a cost of around 50 runs with two wickets. I know that I bowled economically and they must have liked what they had seen because I was then chosen to play against Sri Lanka.

Ian Bell, our captain, made an immediate impression. Some young players are streets ahead at junior levels and go on to fulfil their potential. Others fall by the wayside for different reasons, and a few, like myself I suppose, are recognised later in the system. Bell already had a great reputation as a sound, unflappable batsman and was a regular in the Warwickshire first team. His technique looked so solid, he had a wonderful temperament and he just seemed to understand the game better than the rest of us. My plan was basically to pitch the ball on leg stump and hope it hit the top of off stump; his went much deeper. No doubt some of Bell's maturity could be put down to the fact that he had simply played more matches of a good standard. But I also think he was born with the character to succeed. He was confident in his own ability but not in a showy, big-headed way. Even to my untrained eye he looked a very obvious England player in the making.

Among the others who played that summer were Kabir Ali, Jamie Dalrymple, Chris Tremlett and Gary Pratt, who was to enjoy an unusual place in the spotlight as England's twelfth man in the 2005 Ashes. Initially, as I had said to Nick Cook, I did wonder whether I should have been there. But as the series got under way and my bowling figures held up, I realised there was nothing to worry about. I took five wickets in the First 'Test' at Trent Bridge and three in the next at my home ground, Northampton. We stood 1–1 going into the final game at Worcester, where we lost by two wickets on a real green-top. Just how green should be clear from the fact that I bowled only four overs in the match. It had been an interesting few weeks, although being with England effectively removed any slight chance I may have had of making my debut for Northants.

One way and another, I did not have too much to do at the county that summer and unfortunately never managed to play with Matthew Hayden, our overseas player from Australia. When I saw him for the first time I had to take a deep breath, he was so big and powerful. His strength – if not his physique, I should stress – reminded me of some of the wrestlers I used to watch on TV. I did bowl to him in the nets and remember the aura that surrounded him like plated armour. He had incredible self-belief and used to like practising his sweep shot against me. By the law of averages I suppose I must have got him out, but I can't actually remember doing so.

Towards the end of the season I was named in the England Under-19 squad for the winter tour to India. It seemed too good an opportunity to turn down and I think I would have deferred my entry to university wherever the destination of the trip. Clearly, though, the idea of playing in India was extra special because of my family background. I think that my father and Hitu Naik felt even prouder than I did. As for university, I had no idea whether I would ever take up that place. By now cricket was obviously going to be my career – for a few more years at least – and I didn't want to jeopardise it by rejecting any opportunities that came along.

Before the tour we had to go to Lilleshall for preparation and training. This was my introduction to the detailed planning and standards of fitness required at England level. Having been to India a few times and with my roots over there, I became a source of information for the rest of the squad, even though they had far more experience as cricketers. India is certainly different and I know that it can overwhelm people for the first few days. I tried to explain that it would be a culture shock, with the beggars, the bustling and the unrelenting sound of car horns. I think my best piece of advice was to be careful crossing the road. But for anybody with an open mind it is a wonderful experience. The funny thing was that I hadn't actually been to any of the venues for the matches. There is a big difference between the Punjab I knew in the north and Chennai on the south-west coast, just as there is between Durham and Cornwall in England.

What I hadn't banked on was the interest of the Indian media in me as a cricketer. I received all sorts of requests for interviews and photographs and I didn't really know what to say. I don't think it was anything to do with being a Sikh, simply that my parents are Indian. Being a slow bowler added to the story they had in mind to write because of the great spinners to come from India, my hero Bishan Bedi included. Harbhajan Singh, another

Sikh, had started to establish himself in the national side and in some cases I think they wanted to draw comparisons between us. Before then my only contact with the media had been the occasional phone call from somebody on the local paper in Luton and a feature in the *Sun*, who picked me out as one of their Millennium Kids for 2000 and beyond. I never thought I would make it on to the back page of that particular paper.

Once all that was out of the way, I could concentrate on the cricket. And what a learning curve it proved to be. The First 'Test' took place at the Wankhede Stadium in Mumbai and although the ground was some way from being full, the crowd was large enough to produce a huge din whenever one of the India players struck a boundary. It grew even louder after Sivaramakrishnan Vidyut hit me for the biggest six I could remember, a straight hit that soared over my head into the stand. What you are told on these occasions is to avoid the trap of spearing in the next ball a bit quicker, because that is what the batsman will expect. It is the natural act of self-preservation – you've been hit hard and don't want it to happen again. The quicker the ball, the less time he has to get through his shot. Well, that's the theory. I did exactly what Vidyut should have anticipated least, floated it down slowly – and turned round to see it disappear even higher and farther.

This was a fine all-round game for Vidyut, a left-arm spinner like myself. In our second innings he opened the bowling and took eight wickets including a spell of 18.3–15–6–7. In contrast, my match figures were 2 for 134 from 31 overs. We were not a bad side, but the scores reflected the difference in experience on those types of pitches. You definitely need to adjust in India, which is why our performance in drawing the full series in 2005–06 was such a fantastic effort. The young Indian batsmen played me very differently from English players back home. They looked to attack almost immediately and I had never met that level of aggression before. I was being hit straight or over extra cover, but they were equally quick to cut if I dropped a little bit short. Their footwork was so quick it seemed they could read my mind and know in advance where I would pitch. The surfaces were lower and slower than in England and I had to adjust my length to go a bit fuller.

We actually started well in the next game at Chennai, where I will never forget the smell of the sewers outside the ground. Unfortunately we couldn't build on our first-innings advantage when we made them follow on. Second time around, their openers, Gautam Gambhir and Vinayak Mane, put on 391 for the first wicket in 76 overs. Gambhir has gone on to play for the full India side and Mane, I believe, has come close. They were a formidable partnership and I remember dropping an early catch off Chris Tremlett at third man when one of them went to cut a short ball. Somehow I just missed it and the ball hit my chest. That was the first time people really picked up on my fielding. I was dropped for the Third 'Test' and I suppose, deep down, I could see it coming.

I hope I haven't painted the picture of a disappointing trip. It was anything but. That kind of experience in different conditions is priceless and it stood me in good stead when I returned with the full England team five years later. There was also a special highlight away from the pitch when I managed to meet Bishan Bedi. Tim Boon, our manager and coach, knew him from his playing days and set up a visit to his Academy in Delhi. After delivering a few balls, I looked at Boon and said that I couldn't believe how much the ball was turning. 'Don't be surprised,' he replied. 'These are Bishan's own pitches.'

It soon became obvious that Bedi is a bubbly, joyful personality and a great talker, especially about spin. He has strong opinions about most things. He went into a lot of depth but basically the message was very encouraging: don't change the way you bowl, because you don't need to. I was pleased that he saw a little bit of himself in the action. He told me to keep the front arm strong and gave me a few additional tips for certain situations. I was quite in awe of him and that hour or so was enough to make the tour worthwhile on its own. When we returned to England, Boon told me to keep working on my action, to try to get a bit higher in delivery and think about a slightly straighter approach to the wicket.

It wasn't long before my next trip overseas. For 2001, Northamptonshire had signed a fast bowler, Lesroy Weekes, but he was forced to pull out of a pre-season trip to Grenada in the West Indies because of a complication with his passport. Bob Carter, the first-team coach, called me into the squad and stressed that I wasn't going out there to make up the numbers. The aim of those two weeks was to prepare for the long summer ahead, but I managed to take four wickets in one of the games to make an impression on Carter. Opportunities sometimes come when you expect them least and I felt that I'd taken advantage of this one. The message from Carter was to keep up the good work because I was getting close to a first-team chance and needed to be prepared.

For all that, I spent the next four months in the second team, just trying to work on the areas that had cropped up during the winter. I kept taking wickets and as the season ran into mid-August I wondered if I would have to wait until 2002 to make my first-team debut. However, after I'd taken seven wickets in the first innings of a second-team game against Middlesex at Uxbridge, Nick Cook sidled over for a quiet word and suggested

I might have a chance for the 1st XI the following week. I told him to stop teasing me because I didn't want my hopes built up for no reason. But he said that he was serious, and by that stage I knew him well enough to know when he was joking and when he was being straight.

The news I'd been waiting for came the day before our game against Leicestershire. Carter said that he expected the pitch to turn – it was Northampton, after all – and that he wanted the insurance of a third spinner. Not only would I be making my debut, but conditions were likely to give me every assistance. I rushed home, told my mum and dad, Hitu Naik, everybody else I thought would be interested and a few who probably weren't! You can't be expected to keep news like that to yourself at 19 years old. And it turned out to be one of the most amazing games in the Championship all season.

In their first innings Leicestershire scored 484 with the brilliant Pakistan batsman Shahid Afridi blasting 164 from 121 balls. He tapped at a couple from me and then just tried to belt the rest. No amount of preparation and planning can prepare you for an assault like that. You simply have to keep doing what you think is right and believe that over time it will work out. I tried quicker balls and slower balls, the patient and the attacking game. But to no avail. Fortunately I had a bit more luck against the rest and in the circumstances I drew a lot of satisfaction from figures of 35–5–120–4.

By the final day there was no chance of even Afridi playing that way again. As expected, the pitch had started to crumble and Leicestershire started to go into their shell. I tried to bowl a little bit quicker, which suited the surface, and the hours of landing the ball on that handkerchief paid off as I settled into just the line and length I wanted. The fact that batsmen were trying to survive rather than go for the win played into our hands, because it meant we could set attacking fields. They were only three down at tea on the fourth day but in that final session we took the last seven wickets for 18 runs. I operated in tandem with Graeme Swann; he finished with 5 for 34 from 17.1 overs while my figures were 20–16–11–4. I couldn't get over my success as a never-ending line of people wanted to shake my hand or pat me on the back. Nick Cook let me enjoy the moment – I think he was very proud because of his input into my development – but he also warned me that pitches would not always offer as much help.

Life has an amazing way of evening itself out and my second appearance could not have been more different. It was as though somebody wanted to ensure my feet remained on the ground. We played Somerset at Taunton, a ground known as being as helpful for batsmen as Northampton is for spinners. In the first innings they scored 650 and I had major difficulties with the wind blowing towards the Pavilion End. Their second innings turned into a run chase, so my role was to be more restrictive. Unfortunately I fell into exactly the trap I talked about earlier, of pushing it through quicker and quicker as they started to get on top. I think I panicked because I felt I was letting my team down by not doing the job they expected. In a tight situation with experienced batsmen against a novice bowler there would only be one winner and Somerset duly came through by four wickets. My 18.3 overs this time cost 107 runs.

All in all it became a difficult season for the club as we were relegated from the First Division in the Championship and the 45-over league. This was despite a great effort from Mike Hussey, our overseas player. You had to go back to 1952 to find a player who had scored more runs in a season for Northants than the 2,055 he accumulated in 2001. Watching him at first hand was a great experience because it confirmed the value of hard work. I spent hours bowling to him in the nets, never thinking that a few years later I would be doing the same for real in an Ashes series in Australia.

When training finished, everybody would pack their bags but I liked to do a bit extra on my own if necessary and Hussey had the same mindset. It made sense to pair up so he could bat and I could bowl. Sometimes those sessions would go on for another couple of hours and Nick Cook, who could see us from his window, had to come out of his office to order me to stop. When I got that call I felt like the unhappy kid who is playing in the street when his parents call him in for bedtime. Practising with Hussey always carried a bit of an edge. We made it as competitive as we could. I would tell him my imaginary field and we worked out little scenarios where he needed so many to win from so many balls. The problem came if he hit one, say, uppishly into the leg side of the net. I would say midwicket had taken the catch but he might claim it had fallen to his left or right or fallen short. He was a wonderful player, very intense in games and practice, but a lovely person off the field.

I think the county had deliberately waited until we had a really turning pitch for my debut so that it would help my confidence. They were thinking longer term than that one game, even though it carried a lot of importance in the context of the season. Had I only played at Taunton, then I might have worried through the winter, without that earlier success to fall back on. I also played in another England Under-19 game, this time against a West Indies side including Devon Smith, Carlton Baugh and Jermaine Lawson, who have all gone on to Test cricket. Unfortunately the last day was washed out so we had to settle for a draw.

Around this time I met Bishan Bedi again. He brought a touring side from India to Bedford, which is only 20 minutes away from Luton. Northamptonshire had helped to organise some of the games because he still has links with the club. When I heard about this I decided to go to one of the matches and invite him over to our house for dinner. Yuvraj Singh's father was an official on the trip – manager, I think – and he came along as well. As always seems to be the case with Bishan, we did a lot of listening. He held court as he talked about spin bowling, his time at Northampton, the way the city had changed since he first started to play county cricket, and life in general. He took a lot of pleasure from my progress and really felt that I was following in his footsteps with the county, which remains dear to his heart.

Bedi was a legend in our family and I think my father was as pleased as I was that he came to see us. When Dad talks about him he always calls him by his full name of Bishan Singh Bedi.

The respect was clearly mutual because I read somewhere that Bishan was pleased that 'I had been brought up the Indian way'. I think he saw that my mum and dad had raised us to adhere to and respect the Sikh traditions while allowing us to blend in with the English culture. Although Bishan himself is quite western-ised in many ways, he agrees with my father that families should remember their roots. I think he was pleased by the balance that our household has managed to strike. My mum was a bit concerned and when he rang to confirm what time he would arrive she warned him that we did not drink alcohol or eat meat. 'You mustn't worry,' he reassured her.

As far as the current Northants spinners went, it was inevitable that Jason Brown and Graeme Swann should become two of my best sounding boards in the team. Although they are both off-spinners they approached the job in completely different ways, which is why they enjoyed a lot of success together. Brown used variations of flight and pace while Swann liked to rip the ball as sharply as he could. In some ways their styles reflected their characters. Brown was quiet, preferring to think about things and gradually lure a batsman into his trap, whereas Swann was one of the loudest people in the dressing room. Some people might have found him a bit much after a while, but he always made me laugh with his little stories and funny comments. Even though he was still relatively inexperienced, he had bags of confidence and was popular with the members because he was Northamptonshire through and through.

Neither of them played a Test match but Brown had been to Sri Lanka with the England squad while Swann went on Duncan Fletcher's first tour as coach, to South Africa, and played in a one-day game. The fact that they didn't manage to go on and become regular players in the side worked to the county's advantage, as they were important to our strategy. Ashley Giles was beginning to establish himself in the England team and, with the policy of greater consistency of selection, it could be hard for those on the outside to take that next step. Of course, it also meant that I continued to face a hard task to break into the Northants side, despite those eight wickets on debut. But as a young spinner I still thought it was a great place to learn my trade.

It is understandable if people think that bowling on a turning pitch is straightforward: just put the ball on somewhere close to the right spot and wait for it to spin and spit. In reality it isn't anywhere near as simple. The key, as with any pitch, is to work out the most effective pace, and there are a few variables to take into account. At normal speed on a flat pitch the ball may turn too slowly to be dangerous. On a turning pitch you can try to push it through a bit quicker, but then the trajectory may not be quite right and you may not get the bounce to trouble the batsman.

That works the other way too: you may be able to get bounce but not the amount of turn you really need. The perfect ball will turn and bounce – and sometimes, remember, it is possible to spin it too much, so you don't get the edge you're looking for. This might sound a bit complicated to a young bowler starting out, but don't worry! With practice everything will start to come very naturally. And if you can make the ball spin, then you always have a chance of taking wickets.

As a general rule, opposition spinners are nowhere near as successful when they come to Northampton. There is a certain skill required to exploit Northampton's pitch and they do not have the same degree of experience on it. Perhaps, too, they feel the pressure of expectations, as if to say, 'Oh no, it's Northampton; I must take five wickets or I'm not doing my job.' Even then, you can know what you are trying to do but just not quite manage to execute it on a given day. I always think it is interesting to see how teams take us on. Some go for an extra batsman to stack up the runs, others for an all-rounder to try to cover both bases.

In those days I didn't think too deeply about the wider game, as long as I was bowling well myself. So how did I feel at the end of the 2001 season? In some ways I suppose it could be viewed as a breakthrough year because I had made my debut. But to me it was more of a taster. I had been given a very small helping and wanted a larger piece in 2002.

4
UNIVERSITY TO ACADEMY

Towards the end of the 2001 season I began to wonder about the winter. What were the options, and which was the best? Basically, it came down to a choice of two. I could either go to somewhere like Australia to play grade cricket and keep building up experience, or accept the place that was still being held for me at Loughborough University. In the end I opted for university, but I took a lot of advice before finally making the decision. Northamptonshire thought it was a good way of mixing cricket and learning, because the ECB had launched its Centre of Excellence at Loughborough and the facilities were very good. My parents also emphasised the fact that I could have the best of both worlds and pointed out quite rightly that if I deferred studying again, the chances were that it would never happen. It wasn't something I was likely to do at, say, 25, because by then I would have other commitments.

The responsibility of having to cope for myself away from home seemed exciting but daunting at the same time. And the course in computing and management proved to be as interesting as I hoped and expected. Over the three years I learned to do some basic programming as well as investigating developments in software and computer languages and learning how international businesses operate and raise funds. I am not sure what I will do when I stop playing – fingers crossed, that won't be for a number of years yet – but the knowledge I managed to pick up ought to stand me in good stead.

Our coach at Loughborough was the former England, Kent and Worcestershire fast bowler Graham Dilley. For a time he also worked as a part-time bowling coach for England under Nasser Hussain and Duncan Fletcher, so he was obviously somebody who was very highly regarded. Loughborough has a great reputation for sport, going back to the days when Sebastian Coe was a student. We had some good young cricketers during my time there, such as John Francis, Mark Powell, Rob White and Steve Selwood. By university standards, it made for a strong line-up and we had a lot of success.

The highlight of my first year with the team arrived when I played at Lord's for the first time, where we took on and beat Oxford in a one-day competition. It was far calmer than when I had come as a spectator for the India v Pakistan Under-15 final, but it is impossible not to be impressed by the ground even on days when it is a long way from being full. You can almost smell the atmosphere and traditions in the buildings. Walking through the famous Long Room and into the dressing room for that first occasion was an experience I will never forget. I tried to take in all the pictures, paintings and old prints of the great players from the past who seemed to be staring down at us from the walls. We were put in the opposition dressing room. On the wall are two honours boards listing all the players who have scored hundreds and taken five wickets against England in Test matches at the ground. It is an amazing roll call that can only inspire anybody who ever changes there. At one point before the start I went on to the balcony on my own just to take in the view quietly. Lord's is only about 30 miles from the ground at Luton Indians, but in another sense it is a world away.

As well as Loughborough, I managed to make it into the British Universities team, which brought in players from all over the country. It was an interesting mix of personalities and backgrounds and I thought for a while there might be a split. The Oxford and Cambridge players seemed to have posher accents, while those of us from Loughborough were a bit more streetwise. I tend to be a bit shy when I meet people for the first time in any case, but there was nothing to worry about as we soon mingled together. I enjoyed the company of the other guys and it soon dawned on me that when you cut through everything else we were no different from any other representative side. From my experience cricket is a great unifying force. Whatever our differences, we also had plenty in common: we all loved the game and desperately wanted to beat whoever happened to be the opposition.

I believe that those matches offer invaluable experience for young players, which is not always easy to acquire at county level. For example, I remember playing against a Sri Lanka touring team that included Sanath Jayasuriya, Kumar Sangakkara, Marvan Atapattu and Aravinda de Silva. I managed to get Atapattu caught on the drive and bowled de Silva around his legs, although I think he'd had all the practice he needed by then and was starting to mess about. He had played some amazing shots against Rob Ferley, our other spinner, whom I'd first come across at Minor Counties level. De Silva swept him from around the wicket behind square, then reverse-swept in front when he went over the wicket. I remember thinking to myself, 'Oh my God, this man is such an amazing player.' For a 20-year-old like me to have the opportunity to bowl to a batsman as good as de Silva – whatever the result – was simply priceless.

I really enjoyed the student experience. There were plenty of organisations to get involved with, such as the Indian Society, a taekwondo group and a rhythm and blues club. It was nice to be able to mix with people from the different cultures you find on campus and I was always bumping into somebody I knew already or had heard of through friends and relatives. We had some good nights at the Students' Union and I think back now on a joyful time all round – even if I never did quite master the domestic side. The washing machine wasn't a problem, but after a few days of beans on toast and pasta I decided to end the self-catering lark and buy a special swipe card, which allowed you the run of the canteen. Having said that, I do remember having some fun occasionally when groups of us got together to knock something up in the kitchen. They say you learn about yourself when you go away. One thing I learned is that I'll never be a chef.

The downside of university life is having to sit exams. On my course we had six in January and six in June, which meant a lot of work and cramming sessions, trying to learn and digest facts. Looking back, I can't think how I did it. Anybody who has ever been through the situation will know that the two weeks before an exam make for a very nervy period. Loughborough was like a ghost town for those fortnights. The Students' Union would be almost empty and the libraries stayed open late to cope with the extra demand. I remember trying to get hold of old exam papers to predict what the questions might be, but second-guessing the examiner could be as difficult as second-guessing a batsman. I had colour codes in my mind to help remember information, but although I have a pretty well-organised mind there were nights when I got very little sleep as I wondered what might crop up.

At least in cricket if you are struggling, the captain can take you off and bring on another bowler. With an exam you just have to keep going on your own. I always found the first few minutes the worst, when you look through the paper and always seem to focus on the bits you don't know. I found the mental stress enormous and after the three hours or so were up I would always go straight back to my room for a long, long sleep to make up for all the lost hours when my head was buried in books. Thankfully, I passed everything as I went along and was really happy when I found out that I had been awarded a 2:1. The thought of resits brings me out in a cold shiver even now.

Once my first year at Loughborough was over, it took some time to switch back into full-time cricket mode. I spent the first month at Northampton in the second team before I was lucky enough to go back to Lord's to play for the first team against Middlesex – and watch Phil Tufnell, one of my favourite spinners. It wasn't a great start, as we were well behind on the first innings before the game was cut short by rain, but Phil Tufnell's loop and variations in flight were at least something for me to take from it. Our next match, against Gloucestershire at Bristol, was memorable for an unbeaten 310 by Mike Hussey and I can claim to have played a small part in helping him to reach his landmark. He was heading towards 300 when I came in as last man. I was determined to hang on for long enough to make sure he got there. Out in the middle he said that he didn't doubt me, although I did wonder when he struck two sixes almost straight away! When he finally raised his bat he looked so happy and excited. We declared not long afterwards and as we walked off, I said to him, 'I bet I don't have too many chances to bat with you.' It was an amazing effort of his to open the innings and stay in for so long. In all we scored 746 for 9 with my own more modest contribution an unbeaten two. Incredibly, Jack Russell did not concede a single bye through the innings.

At the end of the season Hussey gave me the pads he'd worn

for that innings. I still have them at home in my small collection of mementoes. The only downside of the game was that we couldn't seal the win and I felt annoyed that I didn't take a wicket despite bowling 40 overs. As a spinner, you are there to go through teams in the second innings, especially towards the later stages of the season when pitches as a rule are more helpful. At least I didn't go for more than two runs an over.

Up to then, I had been picked in four-day cricket only, but my one-day debut arrived against Essex in August. The limited-overs game is usually about entertainment, but this one must have been awful to watch on a difficult pitch at Colchester. We scored only 167 for 8 and lost by four wickets. But I do recall hitting a six against the off-spinner James Middlebrook, and I like to point out that with Will Jefferson fielding at long-on it couldn't have just scraped over the boundary: at 6 ft 10 in, Jefferson is the tallest person I have ever seen – and not just in cricket. I remember hearing some very strange laughter from the dressing-room balcony and turning around to see the rest of the Northamptonshire team cheering me on.

It can really lift a team when a lower-order player scores runs late in the innings, but we knew that we were probably short. This was the first time I had bowled to Andy Flower and as he came in to bat our wicketkeeper Toby Bailey turned to me and said, 'This guy is the best player of spin in the world.' All I could say was, 'Thanks, mate. You know how to give your bowlers confidence.' I managed to beat Flower a couple of times, but he soon started to knock the ball into gaps. He was actually very orthodox, but what stood out was his ability to place the ball between fielders. Flower is one of those batsmen who always seems to have more runs than you think, because he picks up the ones and twos that go unnoticed.

My own batting must have made an impression on our coach Bob Carter because he asked if I fancied being nightwatchman at Durham late in the season. I said that I'd give it a go. I don't like to turn any opportunity down in cricket, but I hadn't reckoned on facing Steve Harmison late in the day with the light starting to fade. At that stage I didn't know much about Harmison and had never faced him before, but I did wonder what I had let myself in for as I heard some of the Durham players say 'good luck' as I started to take guard. The first ball pitched back of a length and I was not quite through with my textbook backward defence when I felt the ball whistle past my ear. Up to then I hadn't faced anything as quick and even five years on it must rank as one of the swiftest balls I've had to deal with. At least I survived the rest of the over.

Unfortunately there isn't much by way of chapter two for this particular story: I got out almost immediately the following morning. At least I had done my job. The experiment, though, proved to be short-lived. I was called into service again in our next game, against Gloucestershire, after Rob White and Mark Powell put on 375 for the first wicket. Another of the batsmen, Jeff Cook, had kept telling me 'get forward, get forward', so as Mike Smith ran in to bowl I was determined to plant my front foot well down the pitch. Unfortunately, while I managed to get forward I still missed the ball – and turned to see my off stump out of the ground. Some things are just not meant to be.

More important, we won the game by an innings and I was happy to end on a good note with match figures of 7 for 114 from 50.3 overs. But it had been a disappointing season for the county. We finished seventh in Division Two of the Championship and failed to win promotion in the National League. Despite the results, I was surprised to get a text message a few weeks later from Bob Carter to say that he was leaving Northants and wishing me good luck with my cricket in the future. I had played in five four-day matches that season, had begun to develop a relationship and was looking forward to continuing under him in 2003. The club did not take the decision to sack him lightly, because he had been a good servant for many years as player then coach. Towards the end of a season players talk among themselves about things like contract offers, whispers from other counties and who may or may not be around in 12 months' time. Most of this seemed out of my league, so I didn't pay much attention. I certainly didn't expect Carter to go, even though everybody could see we were languishing in the lower half of the tables.

By then I had received some happier but equally unexpected news. I knew that I was on the shortlist for the England Academy but it still came as a huge shock to be told by Nick Cook that I'd been chosen in the actual squad. Because I was at university I didn't think I was in serious contention; as I was only playing half a season at a time I did not even think of myself as a full-time cricketer. My guess was that I had been put on the short-list more as encouragement for the years ahead and as a way for the selectors to say they had noticed me on the county circuit. I thought I had done reasonably well in 2002 and was definitely getting better, but there is a big step between that and being named in what people tended to describe as an England A squad. Selection meant that I had to put my studies on hold yet again, in effect taking a year off. But there was no way I could turn down the chance to go to Australia with some of the best players in the country and learn from great coaches. And with the full England squad out there as well, trying to regain the Ashes, it was going to make for a very interesting winter.

During those weeks in Adelaide I worked harder than I ever

thought possible and when I got back just before Christmas I was fitter than I had been in my life. On most days, work would begin at seven in the morning with cross-climbing and vertical-climbing machines. After breakfast we concentrated on cricket sessions working on our skills, followed by lunch, gym work, dinner, perhaps a bit of yoga and sleep. We were too tired to do much else afterwards. For me those climbing sessions could be agony. All sportsmen are used to building up muscles and endurance but a lot of my fitness had come through actual bowling. All those overs delivered one after another for Hitu Naik as I was growing up gave me the strength I needed – or so I thought.

Rod Marsh took charge of the programmes. He had a reputation as being quite a fearsome character. I thought of him as the man who had made the Australia team because he had run their Academy for many years and all the leading players in the Test side had passed through at some stage. He had been one of the all-time great wicketkeepers in his playing days, so when all of this is put together he was clearly a man with a lot to offer. More than anything, I wanted to discover what it was about the Australians that gave them a competitive edge. He also had a physical presence about him, not tall or even stocky but with a distinctive bristly moustache and brushed back hair. To start with, I listened rather than spoke much, but soon I got to like him and realised he enjoyed nothing more than talking about cricket. He was very honest and was one of the first people who really made me understand what bowling spin is all about.

He told me that I needed to get a better appreciation of batsmen and fielding positions. At that point my method was not very subtle. I tried to bowl what I think of as magic balls that would pitch on leg stump and hit off. That must sound like the best way to go – obvious, in fact. Well, it would be fine in a perfect world. Unfortunately life isn't like that and pitches don't always provide the help that you want. If it doesn't turn, you can easily give the batsman a ball to hit. Marsh explained that I needed more options, that magic balls were not the way forward and that I needed to plan dismissals. He suggested I think about different lengths and paces to bowl. And that was the big word for him: think. I am still inexperienced now compared to a lot of international spinners, but back then I was very raw and naive.

Marsh has excellent contacts in the game. Among those he brought in to help was the former Test off-spinner Ashley Mallett, one of his colleagues in the great Australia side of the 1970s. Mallett talked to me about standing tall, using my height and following through with my action. He wanted me to put enough revolutions on the ball through the air so that it would dip as well as spin. Around this time Nasser Hussain talked about trying to find what he described as a mystery spinner for the England team. He meant a bowler who could make the ball go either way without an obvious change of action. I have never been able to master the 'doosra', which in my case would spin in to the right-hander off the pitch. Because I have a classical action it is very difficult to bowl, although I do go back to it from time to time. It would be a great asset for any finger-spinner, but the fact that so few are able to use it just confirms how hard it is to deliver consistently.

At the start of the winter – or summer, as we were in Australia – we all had a one-to-one meeting with Marsh to consider what we hoped to be able to take back to England. As well as bowling, he said that I would have plenty of opportunities to work on my batting and fielding, which were obviously not so strong. I knew that my fielding in particular was not up to scratch and didn't see any point pretending otherwise. Basically, my anticipation was

Hitu Naik and I at Wardown Park in Luton, where I first saw my idol Sachin Tendulkar bat.

With Mum and Dad, Gursharan and Paramjit – I was a very chubby toddler!

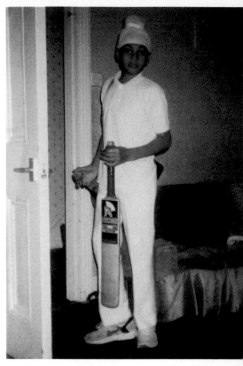

Aged ten with my first bat, a present from Hitu Naik who brought it back from India.

Happy at home with my brother Isher and sister Charanjit – I'm on the right.

Proud brothers with our prizes from Luton Indians. Isher won a batting trophy while I took a bowling award.

Studying in the library at Bedford Modern School, where I was a serious sixth former.

Aged 13 with Bedfordshire County CC – I'm far left on the back row. By then I was hooked on the game.

Kelvin Locke (*centre*), Jamie Wade and me – three Bedford Modern students who all played Minor Counties cricket.

Bedfordshire Under-17s – I'm in the centre of the front row.

Above left and right: You can see why these pictures of Bishan Bedi were reproduced in the *MCC Masterclass* book.

Right: Bedi has become a big influence on me. Here we are relaxing during the India series in 2007.

Celebrating a wicket for England Under-19s against Sri Lanka in 2000 – in those days I bowled wearing glasses.

Nick Cook taught me so much as Northamptonshire's second XI coach.

Tim Boon was my coach with the England Under-19s.

Below: David Capel, who helped me from the start at Northamptonshire.

Bottom: Bob Carter was the Northants coach when I made my first-team debut in 2001.

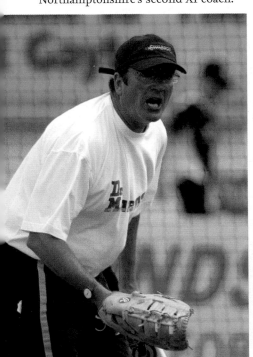

Doh, the strain! Playing for Northants second XI in 2001.

Deliberating where to land the ball in a one-day game in 2003.

Not sure what Matthew Hayden is telling me, but I don't seem very impressed.

I soon hit it off with Rod Marsh at the National Academy in 2002–03.

Kepler Wessels at Northamptonshire, before things started to go wrong.

Jason Brown and I are all smiles after taking ten wickets each against Yorkshire in 2005.

letting me down. Balls came my way when I wasn't really expecting them. I didn't put that down to concentration because I really focused on what the batsman was doing, but my agility wasn't very good, I could be slow and flat-footed and not very well coordinated. Because I didn't relax my hands, the ball would bounce off them. My team-mates nicknamed me Edward Scissorhands as a joke, but I suppose it hurt a little bit deep down. I read somewhere that Marsh described me as being slightly clumsy, like a baby giraffe. He was never cruel or nasty about it because he appreciated that I worked hard to improve and always did my best. As a bowler I always appreciate that nobody misfields or drops a catch on purpose.

I also spent enough time batting in the nets to feel I was getting better steadily. One day Ian Chappell, another of those rugged 1970s Australians, came to talk about ways to play short-pitched bowling. He played before my time but I knew he had been a brave player who did as well as most against the great West Indian fast bowlers. Marsh himself said something very positive about batting. He said that I would never be classed among the leading strokemakers but thought I had the makings of a sound defence and that every time I went into the nets I would have something to work on and improve. There would be intensity in every session. He said that I had the potential to play for England in a few years' time – which was why they had picked me – and he stressed that it was important to be able to do a job with the bat even if it meant no more than staying in while the guy at the other end scored all the runs. I could place that in the context of my own experiences because I know how frustrating it can be when a number nine, ten or eleven digs in when you don't expect him to last more than a few minutes.

As it turned out, we had a fair bit to do with the main England side. I remember the first ball that I bowled to Nasser Hussain in the nets at Adelaide. He nicked it and slip would have taken an easy catch had we been in a match situation. But I didn't know what I should do. He was the England captain and although I had no first-hand experience I knew he could be quite short-tempered and competitive. I wondered whether he might swear at me or throw the ball back hard. I tend to be quite exuberant when I get a net wicket – obviously not to the same extent as when I'm out there in the middle but I might clench my fist in joy or say 'yes' as a release. Fortunately there was no need to worry because he just said 'well bowled' and we got on with it. I didn't beat him again.

We played against an England side in a three-day match in Perth between the Third and Fourth Tests. By then the Ashes had gone and with the terrible injury to Simon Jones it had turned into an unhappy series. We lost the game by six wickets but it was great to bowl to the likes of John Crawley – another really good player of spin – and Mark Butcher. Being around those guys helped to give me an insight into the standard required. Australia is a very tough place for England teams to visit, as I was to discover myself four years later.

Gareth Batty and Ian Blackwell were the other spinners with the Academy and at various times we were joined by Ashley Giles and Richard Dawson, who were with the Test squad. I knew Kabir Ali and Ian Bell pretty well before we all flew out and Chris Read also became a good friend. Spinners get on well with wicket-keepers because they spend so much time in partnership on the field. I also got to like Rob Key. He had a very dry sense of humour and was always very quick with his little comments.

We were all quite competitive against each other, which I think Marsh was happy to encourage. Every one of us wanted to play for England. What would be the point of being there if we didn't?

At the same time we knew we were challenging each other to be next in line whenever an opening might come, but I never got the impression of anybody holding back information or ideas for themselves. I believe that if you push yourself against other people then it will raise the standard overall.

There are two parts to an Academy programme: the preparation, followed by a tour abroad. We came back for Christmas and new year before heading out to Sri Lanka in February for the second half. I had never been there before and found the climate quite a shock. I guessed that it might be like India, but almost as soon as we landed I could tell there was a significant difference in humidity. I hadn't known a steamy environment like it. When we played we needed drinks more than once an hour and when I was bowling I always had a bottle of water ready on the boundary for the end of the over. All those hours on the climbing frames made sense after all. You had to be super-fit to compete in the field for anything like a whole day, and overall I thought I stood up to the task pretty well.

Those games were a great challenge. I felt as though I was a little way behind the other spinners, but put that down to the difference in experience. Gareth Batty had been a really effective county bowler long before I had left school. Having said that, I thought I was better for the work I had done with Marsh. I was thinking about the game far more on the field and paid more attention to the way that individual batsmen were playing me instead of having a one-size-fits-all approach. At Northamptonshire I went with a traditional field to the right-handed batsman, with six men on the off side and three on the leg. That gave me a very solid foundation and is always a good basic starting point, but I realised there were times when it needed a tweak here and there.

Pitches generally were helpful. The senior Sri Lanka side are always very difficult to beat at home. In one-day cricket they have a lot of batsmen who can bowl a few overs of spin and do a good job. I remember sharing nine wickets with Batty in a game early on against their own Academy XI when we bowled together for a long spell. We lost 1–0 in the four-day series against Sri Lanka A, but won the one-dayers 2–1. I managed to take 5 for 20 in one of the final games in Colombo when things finally clicked together, but results were not the be-all and end-all of the trip. The important thing was to improve our games, return to England with a better idea of preparation and recognise the standard we needed to reach to be able to compete at international level.

In a peculiar way, what had gone wrong was just as important as the times when it all went right. You learn from your mistakes. I remember one game where I took three wickets quite early on and sensed it was going to be my day. But there was one batsman I just couldn't get out. His name isn't important; what mattered was the way that I fell back towards the old magic balls and became more and more frustrated when they refused to turn square for me. Afterwards, Marsh pointed out that my thinking was wrong. I should have varied things instead of repeating the same ball over and over again. We lost the advantage and I felt responsible. But I soon realised that Marsh was being helpful rather than critical. All I could do was remember the experience so that next time I was in a similar position I would have a Plan B.

It was only towards the end of the tour that I discovered that Marsh had been playing a little game with Nigel Laughton, the Academy manager. Whenever a batsman played me on the front foot, Marsh would get a point. If he went back, then the point would go to Laughton. After a while Marsh came to me and asked, 'When are you going to get me some points?' He wanted me to drag the batsman forward so that I could maybe take the edge or dip the ball enough to beat him with flight and bounce. I understood what he was telling me. Batsmen, though, can be very clever when it comes to disrupting length. They may go back to a fullish ball to make you think it is too short. You then over-compensate and end up feeding a juicy half-volley. A lot of them are good enough to do that, especially if they know the conditions and the pace of the surface better than you do.

By the time we returned home in March the 2003 season was not far away. Because I had taken a break from university I expected to be able to play a full part for Northamptonshire and was keen to put all my new-found knowledge to the test. Marsh had left me with some encouraging words in a frank assessment of where I stood. Basically, he told me that my bowling was good and that I shouldn't give up on everything else, even if I found it difficult at times. He has since left the Academy to spend more time with his family in Australia but we still speak when our paths cross. I look back on those few months very happily.

Back at Northampton I made sure that I met our new coach Kepler Wessels as soon as I could. Like Marsh, he had a reputation for being a strict man. He was heavily into boxing and the martial arts and that obviously helped him to find a discipline in his outlook to coaching and life in general. He is a strong character, in fact a strong personality – certainly not somebody you would want to get on the wrong side of the first time you met. I knew a few things about him. He captained South Africa during the 1992 World Cup, when they were readmitted into international cricket and were unlucky to be knocked out by England in a famous rain-affected game where they came back on needing 22 to win from one ball.

Whatever other people thought, I knew there was no reason to worry or be frightened by Wessels. He was on the same side as me, after all. It wouldn't be in his or anybody else's interests to go around terrifying players so they couldn't give their best or were afraid to ask for advice. So I wasn't surprised that we were able to develop a good relationship over time, just as I had with his predecessor Bob Carter.

Wessels had a certain way that he wanted to run the show, but he made sure he took a good look at us all before making any major decisions on the playing side. Basically, he just told us to play our cricket and said that he would take things from there. Things did feel different, but I think we all expected that. Carter had spent a lot of time at the club, while Wessels was an outsider coming in with fresh eyes. Nets were shorter and sharper and the training routines were altered to give more emphasis to fitness work. Once again, those hours sweating on the climbing frames had stood me in good stead. All the players began with positive attitudes and were keen to impress – just a typical first few weeks at work when a new boss moves in.

Although I played just five first-team games and took 11 wickets, I think of it as a season when I could have done more had I been given the opportunity. In between I bowled more overs in second-team cricket (341.2) and took more wickets (42) than any other bowler in the country. So I was getting through the workload I expected, even if I would have preferred to have bowled more of those overs for the first team. Obviously I wanted to build on my experiences at the Academy, but I could still put my new knowledge into practice whatever the standard. And, most important, I was still only 21. At the end of the season I went back to university for my second year feeling that my game was still going forward. Very rarely do figures alone give you the complete story. I certainly didn't think I was doing anything seriously wrong, and nobody told me otherwise.

Through July and August David Capel, who was with the second team, stressed that I had to make sure I was mentally ready to go into the first team because Graeme Swann or Jason Brown could break a finger or pick up another injury at any time. Often these things happen when you expect it least, sometimes in bizarre circumstances. I never had a problem approaching what may have seemed like a minor game with full concentration. It doesn't matter to me whether I am playing for England or Luton Indians: I just love playing cricket and want to be involved. That was motivation enough, and I believe that if you do your best for long enough and keep improving, then an opportunity will come in the end.

Sometimes players coming down from the first team can be affected by the smaller grounds away from headquarters, which are perhaps not as well maintained or do not get the same level of investment. The hotels, too, can be slightly lower in the ratings. Again, that has never bothered me one little bit. Luxury is nice, but it is not important in the grander scheme of life. I was young, and despite mixing with England players during the winter still felt wide-eyed about the opportunity to play with and against some famous names.

Under Wessels we were promoted in one-day and four-day cricket, with Brown and Swann both back to their best in harness. There was no point me banging on the door to demand more appearances. Wessels would just have pointed at the league tables. In situations like that it can be a disadvantage being a spin bowler because there are fewer of you in the side. With three, four or five spots for seamers that means more places up for grabs. Also, there is a temptation to rest and rotate the quicker bowlers, whereas the slow bowlers tend to be fixtures in the starting XI. When I wasn't playing for the second team I watched Swann and

Brown bowl together and admired the different approaches I talked about earlier.

Our batting was solid and Mike Hussey enjoyed another prolific season while Phil Jaques joined as an ECB-qualified player because of his English parents. Later he decided to try his luck in Australia and has since made his Test debut. Our other addition, Andre Nel, was a real character. He is one of the most vocal bowlers in the world and one of the most aggressive to batsmen out in the middle. Although he is South African rather than Australian, he reminds me of Merv Hughes with his attitude. Sometimes I could hear what he said to batsmen even when I was fielding on the boundary, but he was a great player to have because he would always support his team-mates. Like Hughes, he gave everything when he ran in to bowl. I remember him bowling to Vikram Solanki and stopping to say something after almost every ball. Sometimes a few of us would smile to each other in the field, as if to say 'he's at it again'. He was also like that in the nets. I copped a few words from time to time but I enjoyed batting against him for that reason – I knew he would be competitive and try his absolute hardest to get me out. Behind all the words and the stares he is a very clever bowler who can trouble the best batsmen in the world. I am not surprised that he has gone on to be such an effective player for South Africa.

The game I remember was our last of the season, against Worcestershire. One of us would be champions, but they were slightly ahead so we needed at least 17 points to overtake them. As it happened they declared with eight wickets down so we could not get the bonus points we needed. In the end it all became academic as we were docked eight points by the pitch inspector after the game, even though Worcestershire managed to score 311 in their second innings. The fact that we played three spinners suggests that we thought it would turn – and it did. I remember bowling Solanki behind his legs with a ball that pitched way outside leg stump, and he is one of the better players of spin in county cricket. It didn't feel like my dismissal at all because the pitch helped so much, not that I was complaining too loudly.

I would not go so far as to say that Northamptonshire get picked on for our pitches, but it does annoy me that places such as Worcester and Headingley offer just as much help for the seamers early in the season and get away with it. Although the totals can be similar, there seems to be something worse about a pitch that turns than one that seams. I think there should be more consistency here. In July and August, spinners are supposed to come into their own, so what is wrong with surfaces offering some help? Doing more to make pitches turn would also improve the standard of batting because players would have to think more about footwork and soft hands. I explained earlier that there is an art to bowling in helpful conditions. And I might be biased here, but I believe cricket is at its most entertaining when a good spinner is bowling to a top batsman who is using his feet and going for his strokes.

At the end of the season I did wonder about my future. In the short term, I knew it meant going back to the textbooks for the middle of my three years. That would be my primary focus for the next nine months or so. But I did start to think I might be better at another county where there was a vacancy for a spinner in the first team. I was out of contract and heard there were some whispers of interest from Middlesex and Warwickshire. I decided to devote all of my time from September to December to the university term and see if any concrete offers came my way. But the mailbox remained empty, so I signed the two-year deal that Northamptonshire had offered. It was no hardship, because they had been good to me. And deep down I probably wanted to stay all along. I hadn't been proactive in writing to any of the other 17 counties or employing an agent to sniff around on my behalf. I guess a move just wasn't meant to be and, looking at where I am these days, the decision to stay at Northampton cannot have been a bad one after all.

As well as the double promotion, things were lively off the field as one of the employees was prosecuted for defrauding the club of quite a lot of money. The case took everybody by surprise and Steve Coverdale, our long-serving chief executive, also decided to leave. There had been quite a change of senior personnel in little more than 12 months, but I had not been around for all of that time and was as baffled as anybody. I just think there is a lot of good about Northamptonshire. For example, the indoor cricket school opposite the pavilion on the site of the old Northampton Town football pitch is as good as any facility in the country, possibly with the exception of Loughborough. It is fair to say that some of the other parts of the ground may not be as modern, but you can only judge a place on your own experiences, and mine have always been very positive.

Having recommitted, I was really looking forward to the 2004 season. For the club, though, it was as disappointing as 2003 had been exciting. I didn't play a single game for the first team, while our record of one Championship win was our worst since 1939. As I wasn't around the main side, I am not in a position to suggest what went wrong. Perhaps it was simply a case of Division One being a higher standard; you would expect that to be the case, after all. The spinners were not quite as successful and opposition sides seemed to come better prepared. From what David Capel told me I think I came close to winning back my place on a few occasions, but the opportunity to play three spinners never arose. The club was changing, with a few Kolpak players joining the staff, but I didn't agree with some critics that it was losing its roots. I had more contact with these new boys than most of the Academy players managed, and it was always local kids getting that grounding. I expect some of them will come through in the years ahead and the balance may change again.

I do not think of it as a 'lost' year – rather a test of patience and perseverance. I did not arrive until the university season had finished and I think Kepler Wessels took the view that the experienced players were more likely to get the side out of trouble. My attitude was that I needed to work harder, but if ultimately I wasn't good enough then at least I was building a future on the education front. I certainly never thought of second-team cricket as being too low a standard to be able to improve. I made a point of trying to keep up the good habits, bowl the same way, really concentrate and, most important of all, keep enjoying the game. Rob White and Mark Powell had also had a taste of first-team success but were struggling to make the breakthrough. Sometimes apprenticeship can be a lengthy business. I can understand why some players might start to become frustrated, but I think that patience has always been one of my strengths. You would be struggling without it as a spinner. One added benefit was that I could play more games for Luton Indians – so much so that I was named as our all-rounder of the year at the end-of-season awards!

Around this time I began to take taekwondo more seriously. Wessels suggested that it might help my overall coordination and it had to be worth a try. Remember, this had been one of the causes of my problems in the field. Whether it has led to an improvement or not, I can't honestly say. Other people are probably better qualified to judge. But my instinct is that my balance is better and I am more aware of my body. I am still only a red belt, which is not very high. I think of it as a hobby rather than anything more serious.

Rumours that Graeme Swann was thinking of leaving had persisted through the final weeks. He had a different personality from Wessels and maybe he thought it was time for a change. Having gone on an England tour in 1999–2000 I guess he felt he might have slipped down the queue and an offer from Nottinghamshire – with the advantage of being a Test match county – proved too good to resist. It is true that none of the Northamptonshire players had been picked for a Test by England for a long time – Paul Taylor was the last before me – but I don't know if that is coincidence or something more. You do see selectors at county games, so I wouldn't have thought there can be any secrets. I was sad to see Swann leave because I enjoyed his company and thought we would miss his extrovert personality in the dressing room. At the same time, I would be lying if I didn't see his departure as the opportunity I wanted finally to secure a regular place.

5

ENGLAND CALLING

I guess that 2005 will go down as my breakthrough season, or breakthrough half-season to be more accurate. Statistically it was my best by a long way, with 46 first-team wickets at an average of 21.54. On the back of those figures I travelled to India with England and made my Test debut. The lesson is that fortunes can change quicker than you dare imagine. When I came down to Northampton in June, having finally completed my degree, I had only one target for the months ahead: to do well enough to earn another contract for 2006. And that wasn't a case of aiming too low. The fact is that I had not appeared in the Championship since September 2003. In fact, when I played against Essex in July – some 22 months later – I felt as though I was making my debut all over again.

I wanted to carry a positive vibe from the end of my studies into my cricket. Having followed the county's results from April onwards, I knew that we were struggling and thought there was a fair chance I would be given early opportunities, especially with Jason Brown, who had made a little alteration to his action over the winter, now back to his best and looking for a new spin partner at the other end. Everything seemed to be set up in my favour when I left Loughborough. I told myself this was it – an ideal opportunity to exploit the pitches, which always give spinners more help in the second half of the season.

Before Essex we had not won any of our first seven games, but the dressing room I joined was not a negative place. For one thing we had signed Lance Klusener, the player of the 1999 World Cup and one of the hardest hitters of a cricket ball the game has ever seen. He was a strong man and an equally strong personality. Our overseas player, Martin Love, was to become a massive influence on my season because he was such a brilliant slip fielder, the best in that position I have known. I don't know how many he took off my bowling but I do know how many he dropped: none. That is remarkable considering how sharply they fly in that position, high and low, left and right. He was just a natural, with soft hands and incredible reflexes. He was also a gifted batsman who played so freely that he made it all look easy. You could watch Love bat all day and still want more.

Even though I probably expected it, I still felt really excited when Kepler Wessels told me I had been chosen to go to Essex. We knew that the pitch at Chelmsford was likely to turn because they had picked two spinners in Danish Kaneria, the Pakistan leggie, and the all-rounder James Middlebrook. That was good for me, and not just because it would improve my prospects of taking wickets. I also knew that as long as I managed to keep things tight I would be given long spells, enabling me to get into rhythm for the weeks ahead. Unfortunately it was another bad game for us. We lost by ten wickets, having been made to follow on, and Essex only needed two balls in their second innings to knock off the runs. From a personal point of view, though, I knew that I had made an impression.

My analysis in the first innings read 56.3–15–181–7, and although I was a bit more expensive than I would have wished, I did get something from the surface. They are still my best first-class figures as I write. The unusual thing is that I dismissed both of the Flower brothers reverse-sweeping. The ball that got Grant was perhaps a bit too full for the shot, and to get Andy in particular was a big boost because, as I said earlier, he is renowned for the way he can work spin around. This time he top-edged one straight up into the air, but he succeeds many, many more times than he fails.

Some spin bowlers go crazy when a batsman reverses or even plays an orthodox sweep. The shot is still frowned upon in some quarters but batsmen have been playing it for long enough now that I don't see the problem. Personally, it doesn't concern me any more than other strokes and in some cases I am happy, because it can be quite risky compared, say, with an off drive when there is uneven bounce from the rough later in the game. Usually you can see the batsman shape to play the shot as you are about to release the ball. That can be quite off-putting. If you try to adjust the pace at the last moment, batsmen who have tremendous skill can adjust as well. The temptation is to bowl it a bit quicker, but that extra pace can make it easier for them to guide it to wherever they want. At the same time, if you change the line they can drag it for runs. The game is evolving quickly and players have their own little variations. I like to begin my run-up knowing exactly what I want to do and I've come to the conclusion that changing in delivery creates more problems than it solves.

The season was halfway through and we had yet to open our account, but that was about to change. And I remember the visit of Worcestershire for more reasons than simply the 82-run win. It was also the first time I had the pleasure of facing Shoaib Akhtar. Watching the great Pakistan bowler push off from a few yards short of the sightscreen must be an unnerving sight for a seasoned opener let alone a rookie lower-order player like me. My defence is usually not too bad, but having to see the ball, get into line and bring the bat up and down all in a split second with adrenalin coursing through the body is a challenge that is hard to describe. Shoaib is the quickest bowler I have faced either before or since, and I know a lot of players who feel the same way.

His first ball reminded me of the one from Steve Harmison I described earlier. It just took me completely by surprise. During that spell he alternated between bouncers and full-length balls that reversed towards my feet from around the wicket. The ball was hitting my bat and veering off to point or behind square or third man, and Shoaib was getting angrier and angrier because he wasn't getting the wicket he thought was there for the taking. When we lost our ninth wicket, Jason Brown joined me at the crease. That is where the real fun started.

Somehow, through all the hostile short-pitched stuff, we managed to put on 62. At one point Brown backed away to square leg and Shoaib followed him. It is not often that I pass on batting tips but this time I told Brown that he couldn't do that other- wise it would fire up Shoaib even more. My attitude has always been that by getting into line with the ball you give yourself the best chance of surviving. Besides, Shoaib could not stay on for ever. At one point, as he went redder and redder in the face, umpire Peter Willey had to have a quiet word to tell him to stop bowling so many bouncers. He had previously taken five wickets in less than an hour and his final figures were 6 for 47. Bizarre as it sounds, though, he helped me because I was able to turn the ball out of the rough created by his footmarks towards the end of the game. I managed to take 6 for 77 in the second innings and with 16 wickets in two matches since my recall I had never felt happier with my cricket.

I found Kepler Wessels a very helpful coach. He was not one

of those who says 'well played, great stuff' in a false way to try to make a player confident. When he says something, he means it. If I had taken two or three wickets in a session and came back quite excited, he would always say that the job wasn't complete. He would take me to one side and say that I was doing well, but had only got us so far and couldn't afford to relax. It comes down to his innate discipline. He stressed the importance of bowling in the same way in the same areas because he believed that consistency – if you were good enough – would win the day in the end. I liked the way that he pushed me. He had a natural presence but he was still somebody I could talk to and he never said 'you must do it my way or not at all'. I questioned him, but I never questioned his authority.

A couple of weeks later, I met Shoaib again when we went to Worcester for the return fixture. My batting must have made an impression on Wessels because I was up to number nine. Unfortunately Shoaib bowled me in the second innings, but I returned the compliment and we ran out winners by 137 runs to complete the double. It is amazing what a win can do for the confidence because we played really well in this game. Our captain, David Sales, who could easily have played for England if he had managed to avoid serious injury early in his career, scored 190.

The winning streak continued against Derbyshire in a game that looks very odd on the scorecard. Both teams did better in the second innings than the first – and this at Northampton. The ball seamed initially but that helped the spinners later on because we could turn the ball out of the little indentations in the surface. Between us, Jason Brown and I had combined figures of 88–37–143–9 in the second innings. When we are bowling well, neither of us gives a batsman much room to hit and this was one of those occasions when we really tied things down. We couldn't quite finish it off on the third day and had to come back for a fourth – when we took the final wicket with the second ball.

By this time the Ashes series had gripped the nation, which was starting to go cricket crazy. Northampton is not exactly a hotbed of the game but crowds definitely seemed to be larger in August and September as a knock-on effect of those fantastic Test matches. It did untold good for the game overall and the fact that England eventually won made it all the better. When we weren't playing I would be at home watching on TV, and when we were it would be on in the dressing room. If we were out fielding we would know when England had taken a wicket because of the cheers from the crowd. Most of them seemed to keep in touch through their little radios, but their loyalty to Northants meant they couldn't bear to be away from Wantage Road to watch on television. It could feel very strange when somebody cheered as I ran in to bowl, until I remembered what was going on. When Kevin Pietersen was playing that incredible innings at The Oval on the final day of the final Test, none of us wanted to leave the dressing room. I had never bowled to Pietersen in the flesh but he just looked an awesome player that day with incredible confidence.

As players we would talk among ourselves, and with the opposition, about what was happening, at the end of a day's play. I really felt a change in English cricket that summer. Until then England had never beaten Australia in the years since I started taking an interest in the game. Now, it seemed that the order was changing, that England under Michael Vaughan were finally standing up to them and slowly, steadily turning things around. I think we felt proud to be English cricketers that summer, even though we were not actually playing for England.

We did, though, take on Australia. They came to Northampton for a two-day game between the Old Trafford and Trent Bridge

Tests. It is a shame that the touring teams do not play as many county sides these days, because it is a great privilege for members and players. Unfortunately there are so many international matches that the space is just not there in the calendar. We were lucky to be able to play them and I was really looking forward to the chance to find out where I stood as a spinner against the very best in the world. The answer, as it happened, was still some way away from international standard.

Matthew Hayden and Michael Clarke both scored hundreds and both looked in fantastic touch. Hayden had been a great player for Northamptonshire and received a very good ovation when he came out to bat. I remember as I was about to come on to bowl that he turned to me from the non-striker's end and said, 'Good luck, mate.' I thought that was a nice touch from such a brilliant player. I didn't know whether he would remember me because I was only in the second team when he was at Northampton. But this wasn't the first time he had been generous to me. When I was at the Academy in Adelaide he saw me and called me over for a chat, just to say he was pleased I was making progress. Northampton had been good for him, because he left us to score mountains of runs for Australia in India. Maybe playing spin on our pitches had helped him along the way; he certainly didn't have any problems on this occasion. I don't think I was overawed, but he did get after me a little bit and I remember him sweeping me for six.

I had a bit more luck against another Australian when we resumed Championship duties against Lancashire. Andrew Symonds, one of their overseas players, drove one back firmly only to see it hit my foot and bounce up to give me an easy and unexpected wicket caught and bowled. Jason Brown took ten wickets in the game as we won by 285 runs and although our next

game against Somerset was rained off on the final day in an
intriguing situation, we were gradually making progress up the
table to the point where some people were suggesting we might
be genuine promotion candidates, not just dark horses.

As it turned out, we simply didn't have time to claw back the
gap, but we still ended the season in style against Yorkshire as
Jason Brown and I created a little bit of history by sharing 20
wickets in the game: he took 10 for 160 from 84.5 overs while I
finished with 10 for 128 from 73.5. Looking at the maths now some
two years on, it means that we must have bowled for the equivalent of almost five sessions of the game between us, a lot of that
time in tandem. Somebody pointed out later that it was the first
time that two bowlers had taken ten wickets for the same team
in a match since 1996–97.

The funny thing is that I took the first five wickets in the
second innings and then Brown the last five. I think we lost track
and it was only in the dressing room afterwards that we realised
we both had ten in the game. By the final day the ball was turning
a lot. I was bowling at a good pace so it bounced as well as spun,
and that was from middle and off, not the rough. However, the
pitch inspector found nothing wrong and Yorkshire managed to
score 278, so it was far from being a minefield. The two of us
worked hard for those wickets and Yorkshire, as you would expect
from a county with such strong tradition, put up some pretty
resolute defence. Even though they were already assured of promotion, they had a big incentive because they were trying to go
through the entire season unbeaten for the first time since 1928.

The wicket I remember best is that of Ian Harvey. As he came
in to bat some of our guys heard Craig White, the not-out batsman,
tell him the ball was turning quite sharply. So they suggested I
fire in an arm ball quite early – it would go straight on when he

was expecting something to spin away from his bat. I gave him a couple of normal balls just to let him know that White was right and then Riki Wessels, our wicketkeeper, gave me a hint that the time had come. The plan worked to perfection. He put his bat outside the line, the ball went straight on to hit his pad and we had a clear shout for leg-before. These things are fantastic when they come off – if only they happened like that every time!

One of the England selectors, Geoff Miller, was present at part of the game. He was due to give a speech at a dinner – which, incidentally, was hilarious – but I thought I might as well take the opportunity to approach him to ask what it would take to play for England. It must have sounded very cheeky from a young lad who hadn't even played a full season of county cricket, but I was asking for information rather than putting myself in the frame. Miller was very straight. He told me that as long as I kept taking wickets, then people such as David Graveney and himself – both former spinners, as it happens – would certainly take notice. He also reminded me to keep working on all aspects of my game and to make sure I learned as I went along. If I managed to find a specific weakness in a batsman, then log it for next time.

The fact is that after winning the Ashes, England were not looking to make too many changes. And as I had not been named even on the shortlist for the Academy it was coming towards the time when I needed to find something to do for the winter. We finished in fourth place in the Championship and I think everybody in the dressing room was optimistic about 2006. On a personal level I was delighted to take as many wickets as I did and a two-year contract gave me the security I wanted. As I played more games I felt more comfortable in the side and didn't worry so much when the team sheet was pinned up or read out for the next game.

Kepler Wessels was more disappointed than I was when I failed to be chosen for the Academy. He thought I ought to have been selected, but instead we decided between us that I should go to Australia from October until just before Christmas to work specifically on batting and fielding. The 2006 season would be my first without any studies as a regular member of the team and he said I should come back from Australia, get geared up at Northampton three nights a week in the new year and really hit preseason training in March ahead of the first game. He thought I had a good career ahead of me, with England prospects, if I continued to bowl as I had done over the previous couple of months.

Thus it was that I boarded the plane for Adelaide with my team-mate Bilal Shafayat, a really talented young batsman who has since moved to Nottinghamshire. We were both posted with clubs in the Glenelg region of Adelaide. Darren Lehmann, the Yorkshire and Australia player, had a lot of contacts in the region and helped to arrange for me to work with some of the South Australia coaches. We devised a programme for Monday to Friday, which included yoga classes, for better mobility, and fitness work, along with fielding drills and time in the nets against a bowling machine. At the weekend I would play grade cricket for Glenelg, and I lodged with the club president and his wife, Bob and Jenny Snewin.

Bob was a really lovely guy who did so much for his club. He enjoyed his cricket and arranged all sorts of fund-raising events. During the 1960s he had been in a rock band and he still had his own drum kit in one of the rooms. Having played the drums briefly in my teens, I lapped up his stories about those days, about the concerts and tours. He was always the life and soul of any bunch of people he was around and he let me have the run of his house. Glenelg itself is a wonderful place by the seaside, although with such a heavy workload I don't think I spent more than a few hours chilling out on the beach.

Over the ten weeks I really felt an improvement, especially in my fielding. I think when the Glenelg players first saw me they were a bit shocked. They expected me to be a bit more reliable, but I was honest with them and said straight away that I wasn't the best. That was why I had come to the other side of the world to improve. I asked them to be patient, and the banter and friendly jokes soon started to fly. Some of them said they were not all that hot either, so I was in good company. But even in those few weeks I became more confident at attacking the ball and relaxing my hands. I must have done hours of catching practice, just making sure that I didn't go too hard at the ball.

I usually batted at number seven for the club. The big thing was to be more aware of playing balls on their merit rather than premeditating. As I have said before, my defence was quite sound. What tended to let me down was my judgement of length. After a couple of half-volleys I would fall into the trap of trying to hit a good-length ball the same way. Professional bowlers are quick to work out things like that. The remedy was simple: a guy would overpitch a couple and then throw in a few normal balls and keep mixing them up so I had to adjust. Another problem was the way that my weight tended to go down, so I would miss the ball and get hit in front of middle stump too often.

Grade cricket was very impressive. In fact everything about the set-up seemed to be spot on. When I arrived at my first training evening, everybody from the first to the fourth team was very energetic and practising at full intensity. Even the guys in the lowest grade would warm up properly and throw themselves into proper fielding sessions. I could sense that everybody wanted to move forward into the next team up, and all the games were very competitive. I knew a few people from being in Adelaide with the Academy three years earlier, so it wasn't as though I had to prove myself as the English professional in the side. I bowled pretty well and never thought I needed to do anything spectacular to win anybody's respect. A good percentage of English players go to Australia at some point in their careers and I can't think of one who has come back with a negative experience. Most have returned with new friends for life, and I am no different.

Australians have a bad reputation for sledging, but I did not find it as bad as I expected. I think a lot of stories are exaggerated for effect. If they make people laugh at a dinner or in a book, then is there any harm in a bit of poetic licence? From my experience, some of the comments were funny rather than nasty. I remember one from Dean Waugh, the brother of Mark and Steve. Our captain Ben Hookes happens to be a fireman. During the game, Waugh cut one of our bowlers for six and the ball lodged on the pavilion roof. Quick as a flash, he turned to Hookes and said, 'Why don't you get your fire truck to fetch it back.'

Over in Pakistan, meanwhile, England were beginning to struggle. They lost the Test series 2–0 and although I wasn't able to follow events as closely as I would have liked, I did know that Ashley Giles had been forced to return home because of what was to prove a serious hip injury. They had not named a squad for India in the new year but with three spinners out there in Pakistan – Shaun Udal and Alex Loudon as well as Giles – they appeared to have pretty good cover. It did not cross my mind that I was anywhere near contention because I had not even been named on the Academy shortlist let alone chosen in the eventual squad based at Loughborough. In recent years England had started to go big on the idea of continuity in selection, which made a lot of sense but meant that those on the outside had to perform really well over time to find a way in.

Suddenly, from nowhere, things started to happen. I had only just arrived home from Australia and was still feeling seriously jetlagged when my mobile phone started beeping overtime with text messages. It turned out that none other than David Graveney, the chairman of selectors, had tipped me as a future England player in his predictions for the new year. I was sitting with a few mates, just catching up on the gossip from while I had been away, when somebody hit upon the bright idea of looking on Teletext to see what Graveney had actually said. I had a sneaking suspicion that I was being welcomed back with an elaborate wind-up. But no, there it was: Panesar to play for England.

By this stage I had learned to look beyond the headline to the actual quotes. It really came out of the blue and although it was great to read I assumed he meant that I had a chance for the 2006 summer – as long as I bowled well and took wickets for Northamptonshire. Even then I didn't imagine he meant in India in a couple of months' time. My mates were getting quite excited but I tried to explain where I thought I stood, which was certainly not in the Test set-up.

A few days later things got even stranger. I was called down to Loughborough with Ian Blackwell and Alex Loudon amid reports that they needed to fill the final place on the tour. Round about this time Kepler Wessels gave me a call to say that a few sources had told him that I was in with a chance of making the squad and that I should be ready for the good news. He also did something with a newspaper saying that in his opinion I was ready after the way I had bowled for Northamptonshire the previous summer.

The trouble was that nobody at Loughborough really explained the situation to me. I thought to start with that they wanted to check my fielding and batting for some reason, perhaps with a view to the Academy tour. Even though they never described it as a trial it began to feel that way. It seemed like a case of whoever could hit the handkerchief the most times would win the prize. I followed the normal Academy programme for three days with the drills and fitness work that I remembered from those years earlier – though thankfully without the same emphasis on the climbing frames. Nigel Laughton, the manager, and Peter Moores, who had replaced Rod Marsh, both told me to relax and think that nothing special was happening. I did begin to wonder, though. Would they pick a spin bowler to go to India, against the best players of spin in the world on their own pitches, based on eight games in two years crammed into half a season? Surely not. But in that case, what was I doing there?

Although the atmosphere was very relaxed, by the second night, curiosity was starting to get the better of me. I quietly sidled up to Peter Moores and asked if he could shed any light on what was going on. Was I really in with a chance of going to India? And if not, how long was I going to stay at the Academy? Moores told me that I was in the running, but had to be patient because something would be decided over the next couple of days or so. That didn't make the situation much clearer, but in fairness there was not much more he could say because he wasn't the guy who had a decision to make. It did seem that things were starting to happen quickly, and none of them were under my control.

Fortunately, I didn't have to wait much longer. The following morning I was playing touch rugby as part of the routine warm-up when Moores called me across. 'David Graveney is on the phone,' he said, 'and he'd like to have a word.' With that he handed over his mobile. Somehow I managed to stop my hands shaking for long enough to keep it against my ear as Graveney uttered the words I will never forget: 'Congratulations, Monty, you're going to India as sixteenth man.' I just didn't know what to say. In fact I think I was silent for the best part of five seconds before I asked him if he could repeat himself. 'That's right, Monty,' he said, 'you're our sixteenth man for India.' This time I managed to say 'thank you' and I must admit the rest of the conversation – which continued to be very one-sided – passed me by in a blur. I do remember him saying that I could tell my family and friends, but to try to be as discreet as I could.

I gave the phone back to Moores, but I don't know whether he had briefed the rest of the Academy boys or whether my shocked expression gave the game away because the touch rugby quickly stopped and everybody came over to shake my hand. I then had to see Laughton to go over some admin. He wanted to know where I wanted to be for the press conference when the squad was formally announced the following day. Press conference? This was new territory straight away. It had not crossed my mind that people might want to talk to me about being selected. There didn't seem much I could say. If the journalists were surprised, then that would be nothing compared with the way I was feeling. In the end we decided that I should go to Lord's so that we could control the interviews and get them all out of the way in one go.

The news had not really sunk in and as I prepared to leave and then drive myself back home to Luton my head was spinning with all sorts of thoughts. Not least how I was going to introduce myself to Andrew Flintoff, and how on earth I was going to bowl to my hero Sachin Tendulkar. When I told my family I think they were in greater shock than I was. Hitu Naik, too, was very proud. His ambition of nurturing somebody who went on to play for England was closer to being realised than he could ever have imagined. I hadn't even been the most naturally talented of his bunch.

Until the press conference I had never been to the ECB head-quarters at Lord's. I had certainly never seen so many cameras and journalists asking questions and writing down or recording what little I could think of to say. At the time I was probably a bit cagey about making sure I said the right thing, although I felt slightly better when I saw a face I knew in the crowd, Angus Fraser, who now writes for the *Independent*. He put me slightly at ease by saying 'well done' and I knew that at least one of the assembled press men and women would have an idea of what I was going through.

When it was all done I walked back to the car park, breathed a sigh of relief and gulped down some of the beautiful, fresh winter air. Then, as I was getting into my own car, a Mercedes pulled over and the driver wound down his window. It turned out to be Mark Ramprakash, the player whose highs and lows I had followed so intently during that 1991 series. What a place to meet for the first time! He shook my hand and said, 'Good luck, mate. Hope you do well in India.' All I could say was, 'Thanks.' But what I thought was, 'Tendulkar, Dravid, Sehwag – I'm really going to need it.'

6

BACK TO MY ROOTS

A N England tour begins before departure date. Players have to go through a series of fitness and health checks in advance as well as work through bits of administration to make sure that everything rests in good order. Being a new boy, what might sound like something dull and mundane was all part of the great adventure. And so it was that once again I found myself at Loughborough, this time among more illustrious company. I sneaked quietly into one of the dressing rooms, mumbled 'hello' to a few of the guys I vaguely knew, and scanned the area to take a proper look at my new team-mates. It really was a who's who of English cricket. Every way I turned I could see a face that would have been recognisable to everybody in the country. Welcome to Team England.

Basically, these were the people who had won the Ashes, paraded through Trafalgar Square, met the Prime Minister and collected MBEs at Buckingham Palace. It still seemed unreal that I could take my place among them. Everyone seemed to be mingling and talking, exchanging the banter that comes from spending close time together. I think Andrew Flintoff noticed I was feeling a bit left out, because he came over and introduced himself. I had never seen him before at close quarters, let alone met to shake hands, and I could immediately see what people meant when they described him as the heartbeat of the side. He was a huge presence.

In fact I found it quite an effort not to stare at him. I kept having to force myself to turn away in case he thought there was something not quite right about me.

I remember he was wearing a light blue Manchester City shirt. He made me feel as relaxed as I could have been, given that I was completely in awe. Even from the start, I realised he was a very down-to-earth guy. 'Hello, mate,' he said. 'It's good to meet you – are you all right?' Those were his first words. I was immediately taken by the idea of being a 'mate' of the great Freddie Flintoff. He had an incredible aura about him because of what he'd achieved against Australia. On the back of the Ashes series he had been named BBC Sports Personality of the Year, collecting his trophy in the early hours of the morning in Pakistan before Christmas.

For the fitness tests I paired up with Andrew Strauss, another guy I didn't really know. We had to do a little challenge, and I know I took him by surprise because he wrote about it in one of his columns for the *Sunday Telegraph*. I think I finished third out of the 16 players overall; I remember Flintoff came first. Nigel Stockhill, the England fitness trainer, supervised everything. These days every country has a strong back-up department so that no stone is left unturned in preparation. There is advice on every little facet and if you add together all the little one- or half-percenters, they can start to make a very significant difference.

We went paintballing as a team-bonding exercise. This was great fun, although the part I remember came well before we were given our ammunition. When I arrived I could see the big Volkswagens belonging to the rest of the side all lined up impressively. I'd arrived in my little lilac Hyundai 1.3, the car I'd used as a student, which I'd bought second-hand (at least) in 2001. It was very handy for driving around the campus and for small journeys in and out of university. I love it to bits but not even I would call it flash. The other guys were rolling around as I had to lock and unlock the doors one by one to remove equipment because I didn't have central locking. When I tried to explain how good it was for nipping around the site, the laughter just grew and grew. I wondered then if I should have let the train take the strain and kept the Hyundai out of view. Having said that, the car is still going strong and passed its MOT as recently as 2007 – not bad for an M-reg. Although I also have a Volkswagen Touareg nowadays as part of an England sponsorship, I am still happy with my little Hyundai.

The most important part of the preparations was to be passed fit and well and make sure that my passport and jabs were in order. Around this time I received another reality bite as my first-ever set of England kit was delivered to home. Signing for it at the door was another proud moment. Everything comes in one box – the shirts, tops, caps and other bits supplied by the team sponsors. It felt so special to me that I wanted to hug it like a teddy bear. I tried everything on, looked in the mirror and felt the goose pimples on my arm. Who was to say whether in a few weeks' time I might be wearing these same clothes in a real Test match for England?

That was the question I asked myself on a daily basis as the leaving day started to loom. My expectations were probably not all that high. Although I knew it would be a great experience, I also saw those few weeks as preparation for the 2006 season with Northamptonshire. I counted myself lucky to be able to have such a head start when I came back into county cricket. Even if I did not play in any of the warm-up games I could only benefit from the experience of mixing with so many great players and new coaches with different ideas. I was determined to learn something from every practice session and watch the different players to see how they went about their games.

Don't get me wrong. I wasn't unambitious. If I started the tour as the third spin bowler behind Shaun Udal and Ian Blackwell, then I was going to do my best to move up the pecking order. I knew that my experience with the England Under-19s in India would stand me in good stead, even if I had spent more time watching the ball disappear to the boundary than I would have wished. It was also true that England would probably want to play two spinners, so if Udal or Blackwell picked up an injury I would be next in line. But I didn't want to put myself under the pressure of thinking that I had to play, that this would be my one and only chance to play for England. Before Christmas, they had taken Alex Loudon to Pakistan for experience in different conditions as the last pick. I felt as though I was in the same boat this time. In short, nothing was going to prevent me from enjoying the tour and the series.

It had also emerged that I stood to become the first Sikh to play cricket for England – in fact, the first Sikh to play for any country other than India. I had not expected this to become such a talking point and attract so much interest. When I was younger my ambition had simply been to play for England, not to become the first Sikh to do so. I am a proud, practising Sikh and a proud cricketer, but these have always been separate parts of my life. One of them is my faith, which is very important and personal to me. The other is my passion and my livelihood. The fact that I would be the first Sikh to represent England did not seem to be anything more than coincidence. As time went on, I appreciated that my success might tempt other young Sikhs to give cricket a go. But, if anything, I saw myself more as part of an ever-growing line of players of Indian extraction to represent England. These

Fitness training at Loughborough before the India tour in 2006.

A taste of things to come – attracting a lot of media interest with Matthew Hoggard and Ian Bell after landing in Mumbai.

Three proud debutants – Andrew Flintoff hands England caps to Ian Blackwell, me and Alastair Cook before the First Test in Nagpur.

One of my first, nervous deliveries for England.

Above left: Got him! Sachin Tendulkar becomes my first Test wicket.

Above right: Must have pleased skipper Freddie Flintoff in Nagpur.

Right: A priceless memento – the ball that did for Sachin, signed by the great man.

Left: I like to see the sights while on tour, such as the famous rock garden in Chandigarh.

Below: Mohali is one of the smaller, more modern grounds in India.

Freddie Flintoff led by example in India, but Mahendra Singh Dhoni is alert for a chance here.

No doubt I'm about to be battered as Flintoff makes his way to the nets in Mumbai.

My training partner Andrew Strauss cracked a fine hundred in Mumbai.

Second time lucky – after missing Mahendra Singh Dhoni I couldn't afford to drop this one three balls later.

A picture tells a thousand words. Bowler Shaun Udal and the fielders were aghast after I bungled 'that' chance from Dhoni in Mumbai.

See, I can do it! Diving for a catch at a sponsor's event at Upminster CC.

I've really enjoyed being part of the npower Urban Cricket initiative. Here, I'm working with kids at the Purley Centre in Luton.

Left: Marcus Trescothick celebrates his hundred against Sri Lanka at Lord's in 2006.

Above: Saying 'well done' to Sajid Mahmood on his Test debut at Lord's.

Below: You can't catch me! Celebrating the wicket of Kumar Sangakkara.

went all the way back to the nineteenth century when Ranjitsinhji played in Test matches. More recently, Nasser Hussain, who was born in Chennai, had set a great example as captain. An England player represents the whole country, not just part of it.

Having been the subject of a lot of interest on the Under-19 tour, I had an idea of what to expect when we landed in India in the middle of February. It helped that we had a full-time media manager with the squad to handle all the requests for interviews. As before, I didn't feel it was being a Sikh that created the interest, more that my family's roots were in India. And it wasn't too long before reporters began to try to track down relatives of my mother and father in the north of the country, some of whom I didn't really know all that well myself.

The hectic schedule of international cricket means that modern tours are short, sharp affairs with the minimum of warm-up games to prepare. For fringe players in the squad such as myself it means that any opportunity has to be seized, because it might be the first and last. The three Test matches were going to be played back to back with only a pair of friendlies – if that is the right word – beforehand. The first was at the famous Brabourne Stadium in Mumbai, home of the Cricket Club of India. The fact that all of our squad were allowed to feature at some point against the Club President's XI meant that I would have a chance over the three days and although I took only one wicket I managed to shake off the cobwebs and enjoy a reasonably long bowl.

Unfortunately, in the hours after the game I started to feel distinctly under the weather. Somewhere, somehow, I had picked up a bug and the journey from Mumbai to Baroda proved to be a test of willpower. I was in agony with stomach cramps as the famous Delhi belly took hold and it was as much as I could do to sit still and keep everything crossed. I was also really upset because Duncan Fletcher had given a strong hint that the team to play in the second game, against an Indian Board President's XI, would more than likely line up in the First Test. If the captain and coach did not think I was up to the job, then fine. I could come to terms with that. But the last thing I wanted was to rule myself out because of a silly illness.

So when the doctor arrived in my hotel room, I asked for the strongest pills he had in his medicine bag. I told him I desperately needed to play, and I soon realised that he sympathised with my situation. He gave me two of the biggest antibiotics I have ever seen and hope never to see again. No exaggeration, they were the size of small biscuits. I think there were a few painkillers there as well, and I drank water as though it were going out of fashion to help swill whatever it was out of the system. After another difficult night I reported downstairs looking as fresh and sprightly as I could manage. When the medical team asked whether I was all right I said 'yes, fine' in a tone suggesting puzzlement at the fact that they'd asked. The truth? I'd say I was probably 50–50. But no way was I going to admit it.

One way and another a few of us were in the wars early in the tour. To start with, Marcus Trescothick had to leave for personal reasons. He went very suddenly and I don't think that any of us really knew the full extent of the situation. Marcus is a very popular guy within the England set-up. There is no side to him and he also happens to be a world-class opening batsman. I had found that out very early in the nets when he kept sweeping me, a bit like Matthew Hayden, another strong left-hander, all those years before. When I asked him why he did it, he just laughed and suggested I try varying the flight a bit more. But he was also very encouraging. He had taken on all the best spinners in the world and usually succeeded, so he told me not to worry. If he found it all quite easy, at least he didn't jolt my confidence by saying so.

As if that wasn't bad enough, four days later our captain Michael Vaughan and Simon Jones, another of the Ashes heroes, were also on the plane home with knee injuries. At the time we were not sure whether they would come back. As it transpired, the problems were far more serious than first feared. I had never known a run of bad luck like it at Northampton, and it made for a strange introduction to the international game. The team that had conquered Australia was being depleted on a daily basis, and as Andrew Flintoff took over the captaincy it seemed hard to keep up with all the comings and goings.

In the circumstances it wasn't surprising that we lost in Baroda. Their side included a number of good and promising players, including an old foe from my Under-19 days, Gautam Gambhir. He scored another century and Suresh Raina, who was to star in the later one-day series, was developing a lovely touch on his first appearance against us. I actually took his wicket and thought I kept a fair degree of control, but we were 104 behind on first innings and could set them only 55 to win in their second. They knocked off the runs in 17 overs and at that point I don't think too many neutrals were giving us a lot of hope for the Test series.

By this time I had started to work with Duncan Fletcher. I did not know much about him before the tour, and I think he liked to have that mystery about him. When you saw him on television his face never gave anything away. You couldn't tell from his expression whether England were in a fantastic position or deep in the mire. He is the kind of coach who watches a lot, sees everything and doesn't open his mouth for the sake of it. But if he thinks he can help, then he will. Early in the tour I remember doing a fielding drill on my own. I wasn't even aware that he was watching. He came across and suggested a different way of working that he thought would improve my peripheral vision. The important word there is 'suggested'. Fletcher had his own opinions about what was best and came up with new ideas all the time, but he never tried to impose something on me if I was unsure that it felt natural.

Right at the start I became aware that he wanted cricketers to be three-dimensional – a theme that was to develop over the next year. After those weeks in Adelaide before Christmas I had continued to work on batting and fielding. Fletcher reminded me that the pitches would be slow and low so encouraged me to work on the sweep shot as an option to get a few runs and rotate the strike. He is a cricket man through and through and our conversations about the game always finished with me being wiser on some point or other. Like all the best advice, a lot of what he says sounds obvious once you hear it. In a short space of time, he helped me to take that final and biggest step into the England team.

I didn't know that I would be making my debut until the team meeting the night before the First Test in Nagpur. Flintoff read out the names in batting order. Although I felt I had made a reasonable impression, I still thought I was behind Shaun Udal, who had so much more experience. If Ian Blackwell was going to play as an all-rounder, then Udal would offer variety as an off-spinner. Flintoff rattled through the names quickly – with no pausing for dramatic effect – until I heard him say 'Panesar' and stop. There were actually three of us due to make our debuts, Blackwell and Alastair Cook, a replacement for Trescothick, being the other two. By coincidence Cook, too, had gone to school in Bedford, though we had never played against each other because I am a few years older.

So that was it. I was in at number 11 for England. The other guys shook my hand and Flintoff, who must have read my mind, said, 'Don't worry, mate, you'll do well.' The rest of the meeting passed in a blur. I tried to concentrate on what was being said, but I just couldn't get rid of this image of bowling to Sachin Tendulkar and Rahul Dravid. When I left the room I still felt quite numb at the idea that my childhood ambition was about to come true. I headed straight for my room, lay back on the bed and closed my eyes. I kept telling myself I was playing for England, whispering those words to myself over and over again. Eventually, it dawned that I ought to ring home to pass on the incredible news. Fortunately my mum and dad overcame their excitement quicker than I had managed. It would have been an expensive phone call otherwise.

The next task was to come up with some plans. I found a few sheets of paper and a pen in the room and began to mark down some crosses to represent the fielding positions I had in mind for the various batsmen. When I knocked on Flintoff's door and handed over the results he seemed a bit bemused.

'This is what I'm thinking of doing,' I said.

'Ah, okay,' he replied, sounding as puzzled as he looked. 'No worries at all, mate. I'll take it on board and you have a good night's sleep.'

I decided I ought to leave quickly because I wasn't sure whether he wanted me in his room. It was only later that I found out I was the first person who had given him that kind of detail in advance and that he was impressed with my preparation. As it happened, I did not sleep well at all. Usually I don't get nervous the night before a match. This time, whenever I shut my eyes I saw images of a cricket match with grinning Indian batsmen driving and pulling balls between my carefully located fielders.

Perhaps this is a good time to knock down a story I've seen written a few times since Nagpur. Apparently, I had a premonition that evening of bagging Tendulkar as my first wicket. It would be a great tale if it were true. Unfortunately, that is not the case. I can only think that in an interview somewhere I said that I dreamed of getting him out – meaning in the way that other people might dream of winning the Champions League for Arsenal or flying a rocket to the moon. Somewhere there must have been a misunderstanding.

We were huge underdogs for the series. You couldn't really blame anybody on the outside for predicting a 2–0 or 3–0 scoreline. Even the great sides such as Australia at the turn of the decade had lost to India in India. And we were a long way from being at full strength. In time-honoured fashion, of course, that meant we had nothing to lose. We had a lot of young, inexperienced players in the side and I think we all felt that we were starting on a big adventure. There was a real hunger about the side in the dressing room that first morning.

The big advantage – in every sense – was Flintoff. At that stage I think I had played fewer than 30 first-class matches, so I had not served under many captains. Mike Hussey was a very busy leader, David Sales very quiet but always thinking, always in control. Flintoff was completely different: positive, upfront, an action man who wants to be in the game at all times. He reminded me of a Roman gladiator in the way he was always there at the front. It was as if nothing could harm us because Freddie Flintoff, the man who won the Ashes, was there at our side. I remember him saying to me, 'If anything happens on this field, Monty, just come to me and I'll sort it out.' There is more to him than just an aura, because he is also astute on tactics and I don't think a lot of people realise just how intelligent he is. Having said that,

I believe his biggest asset as captain is the way he leads by the strength of his own example.

Until that first morning at Nagpur I had never been to a Test match in the flesh. As a boy I had spent too much time playing to be able to go to other games. It was also my first experience of a sell-out crowd, numbering as many as 35,000, and even before play began the wall of noise left me astounded. In a sense I was a bit like the supporters as I spent the whole of the day watching the action unfold, admittedly from the privileged position of a place in the dressing room. We won the toss, batted and ground out runs against an accurate attack. I was especially interested to see Anil Kumble – a former Northamptonshire bowler – and Harbhajan Singh in action, but more pleased that Alastair Cook had made a good start to his international career with a patient 60. If one debutant could do so well, then what was there to stop another?

Like Cook, my first contribution proved to be with the bat. We were 327 for 9 when I walked out, with Paul Collingwood unbeaten on 79. In the final Test in Pakistan before Christmas he had been dismissed for 96 and then 80, so a maiden hundred was proving elusive. Although I had forgotten how frustratingly close he had come on that occasion, I desperately wanted to stay out there long enough to make sure he had another chance to reach three figures. The instructions from the dressing room were clear and straightforward: concentrate on every ball and try to give him as much of the strike as I could.

I don't know how much Collingwood knew about my batting, but he put me at ease straight away, giving the impression that he had every confidence in my prowess. I kept talking to him between overs, asking what he thought I should do and whether my shape looked solid enough. When he finally reached the landmark I felt so happy because I had helped him along to one of the great moments of his career and a little piece of history. It was something he would never forget. Nor, probably, will I. In all we batted together for more than an hour in adding 66 – of which my own contribution was a modest 9. However, the total of 393 meant we were more than in the game and I think it was better than a few people expected.

Matthew Hoggard soon had Virender Sehwag caught but Wasim Jaffer and Rahul Dravid steadied the innings. Watching most of the action from just inside the boundary, I tried to savour the atmosphere. The Barmy Army had brought out a strong contingent, so there was noise from both sets of supporters. Very often it is impossible to detect what anybody is actually saying and it was also hard to make out faces because the perimeters in India are some way from the stands, which are behind wire fencing. Flintoff has said that he thought I took some energy from all that bustling activity in the field when I came on to bowl. There was certainly no chance of dozing off. No amount of time at the Academy or in county cricket can fully prepare a player for a Test match in India.

As each over ticked by I realised I was getting closer and closer to my first bowl for England and I pledged to myself that I was not going to let the team and the captain down. By the time Flintoff called me over, both Jaffer and Dravid were very well set. If Dravid was not the top-ranked batsman in the ICC rankings at that time then he must have been very, very close. I had been impressed by one particular shot he played against Ian Blackwell when he went onto the back foot to punch a ball turning away from off stump between mid-on and midwicket. It looked so wristy and elegant and I knew that I was in the company of an extremely classy player.

I remember Flintoff asking whether I wanted a man at bat-pad and telling him I would rather have the extra fielder on the drive. Better to have the extra insurance, I thought. As luck would have it, I had bowled to Jaffer in one of the warm-up games, so I knew a bit about him. As I marked out my run I hoped that I wouldn't start with a full toss or a ball bouncing twice. I told myself that I had a reliable, repeatable action and had used it thousands of times before. All I needed to do was pitch that first ball on a length, and I would be up and running.

So it proved. After a couple of dot balls Flintoff brought the man in to bat-pad after all – he made the decision for me. Wicketkeepers are always noisy and Geraint Jones offered plenty of encouragement, but the shouts of 'well done, well done' came from all around the team. When I completed the maiden, I think every one of them ran across to pat me on the back. Once that first over was complete I felt I could relax a bit and get on with the job without having to worry. Unfortunately we could not take a second wicket that night, but Hoggard was at his very best the next morning when he swung the ball enough to get Dravid, Jaffer and V. V. S. Laxman in the space of 11 balls to turn the game on its head. In such circumstances a home crowd would normally have been quiet, but the collapse had brought Tendulkar to the wicket, whipping the support into a frenzy with his mere presence.

He could not afford to take any risks in that situation, but nor could we make another breakthrough as Mohammad Kaif batted with equal assurance at the other end. The time had come for me to try my luck again, but the presence of Tendulkar suddenly brought back the nerves I thought I had left behind the previous afternoon. For the second time I had to tell myself I was up to the task. I kept drawing him forward, but he seemed to be driving everything without any problems. At least with the field we had in place these were dot balls, in line with part of our plan to try to frustrate batsmen into making mistakes. Maybe the pressure started to tell. From nowhere, it seemed, Tendulkar went half-forward to one that straightened just enough to miss the bat and hit his pad.

The next seconds were just a blur. As soon as I saw Aleem Dar start to raise his finger I just ran and ran and ran. I could have made it all the way back to Luton if my team-mates hadn't converged and stopped me. Even then I was dancing, jumping and slapping high fives in the way that I suppose has become a signature since. I can assure everyone that it wasn't premeditated. I might have worked diligently frame by frame on my action in front of the mirror all those years before, but this was the spontaneous act of somebody losing all control of his emotions. Previously my celebrations had been quite restrained. True, I wasn't like those bowlers you see in highlights from the days of black and white television, who would take a wicket and shake a few hands with their expression unchanged, but I don't remember anything more exuberant than a clench of the fist, a grin and a cry of 'yeeeessss'.

Looking back, I think my reaction was a tribute to the greatness of Tendulkar. Had he been any normal batsman, I am sure I would not have been so excited. My response – somebody wrote that I skipped around as happy as Bambi – showed the effect that he can have on other people. And I did not think any less of him for the rest of the series, even though you could say I had brought him down to my level. Every time he hit the ball I wanted to chase after it to be part of his show. I was determined to take something from every single ball I bowled to him. I have never been one for predictions and I have no idea how long my career will last or where it will take me. But I would hazard a very strong guess that I have already enjoyed my happiest moment in cricket.

That little bit of philosophy came later. For now, there was a game to play. At 176 for 5, India were more than 200 runs adrift and we wanted to wrap up the innings to secure a positive lead. That proved easier said than done as Kaif and Anil Kumble frustrated us for almost 60 overs as they put on 128 for the eighth wicket. Kumble is a very proud man and a fierce competitor who underlined the importance of a lower-order player being able to hang around. I was starting to feel a little tired after burning so much nervous energy in the heat, but when Flintoff decided to keep me on for the last over I knew I could put everything I had left into those final six balls. Reward came from the last, one of the best I have ever delivered. It drew Kaif forward before dipping and turning past his defensive shot to hit off stump. I don't know if it hit a little pebble to turn so much, but for the second time I leapt around in excitement. It had been a long day and to end on such a positive note by removing a very stubborn player so close to his hundred represented a major bonus. With two days left we were still ahead and only one wicket away from wrapping up their first innings.

We did not have to wait long the following morning and knew that if we could bat for the rest of the fourth day we would be able to set a really challenging target and give ourselves time to bowl out India for a second time. The underdogs were beginning to surprise a few people, and things continued to go according to plan with Cook scoring a hundred on debut and Kevin Pietersen hammering a brisk 87 from 110 balls. For the second time in the match I could take my lead from Cook's performance. The fact that a newcomer had acquitted himself so well created a very positive atmosphere by the close. To bat for 364 minutes against some of the best spin bowlers in the world, having been in the West Indies with the A team a week or so before, was an incredible effort and, surely, the start of a great career.

Although this was new to me, I tried to think of the situation as the final day of a Championship game. India needed 368 to win and as long as we bowled well we knew that the possibility of losing should not really arise. The question was whether we could bowl them out and go one better than the draw. As it turned out, however, the game had a late and thrilling twist.

With Wasim Jaffer again looking solid and Rahul Dravid living up to his nickname of 'The Wall', wickets proved difficult to capture. They did not appear to be making any attempt to chase the target, making our task that bit harder. As a spinner I was a little disappointed that the pitch had not deteriorated as much as I hoped. This was certainly not like Northampton. Dravid actually took 168 balls to get to his fifty but suddenly he switched from first to fourth gear and India's plan became clear: with wickets in hand they were ready to turn the tables by putting us under pressure with a late charge.

Dravid showed the other dimension to his game, but fortunately I managed to turn one out of the rough on leg stump to hit off and I set off on another celebration. To get yet another great player in my first match seemed unreal, especially with what looked like one of those magic balls. It takes a lot to beat Dravid's bat, let alone hit the stumps as well, and this still ranks high among my favourite dismissals. But any thoughts that India might revert back to Plan A could be dismissed when Irfan Pathan walked out, followed at the fall of the next wicket by Mahendra Dhoni, to the excitement of the crowd. I think Flintoff thought I might be starting to go a little bit after I conceded a couple of boundaries and the captain proceeded to show his class by plugging the runs from one end.

Even then we had a brief sight of just what Tendulkar could achieve. Ian Blackwell was bowling and from looking at Tendulkar's eyes I thought I could guess where he would try to hit it. I anticipated the sweep, but not in front of square. Next ball I thought I would move a bit, only for Tendulkar to work it towards the area I had moved from. He turned in my direction and caught my gaze, as if to say 'you can't beat me, son'. That was a genius at work. Despite that, India had left themselves too much to do against the experience and forceful personality of Flintoff. Given the crowd and the importance of the game, I don't think I had known such a tense few hours on a cricket field.

Even though India had taken the initiative, we were happy with our performance over the five days. A draw was a good result and at no point were we ever out of the game. For long periods we actually had the better position, so there was plenty of room for encouragement. My own first-innings figures of 42–19–73–2 were good and drew a lot of positive comment. Duncan Fletcher said afterwards that he was surprised at my level of control, while Ashley Giles back in England said that I would be a challenge for his position when he recovered from injury.

It is always nice to hear comments like that from a senior player, but I knew that I was still a stand-in. I felt relieved to have got the game out of the way without being taken apart and the whole experience made me appreciate the high standards required of an England player in terms of concentration. My analysis looked nice in the scorebook, but it had not been an easy experience at all.

One of the best parts was getting back to the hotel at the end of a day's play to see the faxes and text messages from home. My parents had not come out yet, because they wanted to see whether I would be playing and thought the best time to visit would be the Second Test in Mohali, which is less than two hours from their families in the Punjab. I was not aware of the interest in me back home. At Nagpur the crowd had shouted 'Monty, Monty' a few times, but I did not read too much into that because spectators in India are always very energetic and shouting something.

Having made my debut, my parents confirmed that they would come over for the second game. It turned into quite a gathering as more and more relatives and friends decided they wanted to come along. My grandparents in Ludhiana and my close Uncle Kaka had never even been to a cricket match before, so this was a chance to watch their grandson as well as soak up the atmosphere. Phil Neale sorts out our complimentary tickets before every game and I really tested his ingenuity this time. When he asked how many I wanted, his face dropped as I said, 'Please could I have a hundred.' Fortunately, few of the other players and management had friends or relatives on the tour, so by putting them all together and calling in a few favours from sponsors he managed to come up with just over 70. I could see the group all sitting together from the middle. The players joked that they should rename that structure the Monty Panesar Stand. Unfortunately, timings meant that I could not meet everybody at the same time after a day's play. It would have made a wonderful photograph.

Earlier in the tour a few reporters had contacted my grandfather and asked how he felt about me playing for England rather than India. He told them he simply wanted me to play well and make a name for myself, which I thought was very kind. Reading some of those articles, I think he began to thrive on the novelty of being interviewed because he started talking about my childhood and said that I had cherished an ambition of being a pilot. I must admit that was a new one to me.

Playing for England in the Punjab region was a source of great personal pride. One of many reasons I was so happy with my debut was the fact that I felt sure I would retain my place for this game. I sensed enormous goodwill from people in general in both Mohali and Chandigarh, where we stayed. There are strong historical ties between the countries and it felt as though they were pleased at being represented in the England side by a Sikh with the same roots as themselves. I never heard anybody say that I was in the wrong side.

The ground is unlike most in India, which tend to be bowl-shaped with big, sweeping stands. Mohali is modern, with a beautiful, pristine pavilion that feels like the lounge of somebody well-to-do. Although I had been to the Punjab on a number of occasions, this was the first time I had been to the ground itself. Like most Indian people, my family were interested in cricket, but not so fanatical they would travel to watch the Tests or one-day games.

As Indians with an English interest they could not lose this time. I could, though, and the nine-wicket defeat came as a big disappointment after Nagpur. The pitch here was quicker and bouncier and Munaf Patel, a tall fast bowler we had met in Baroda, made a brilliant debut with seven wickets. But if I had to put my finger on one player who made the difference it can only be Anil Kumble.

People have said he has the mentality of a nasty fast bowler locked in the body of a spinner. I know what they mean. When I walked out to bat in the first innings he had dismissed Geraint Jones and Steve Harmison with successive deliveries, leaving me to face the hat-trick ball. And as if that was not enough to whip the crowd into a frenzy, Harmison had been his 500th Test wicket. Arriving at the crease, I heard Harbhajan Singh say, 'Come on, let's get Monty as well.' Virender Sehwag and Rahul Dravid seemed to be within touching distance around the bat and when Kumble got to his mark he gave me a glare that could have turned a man to stone.

Teams tend to play him as a medium-pace inswing bowler because he is quick for a spinner and gets bounce as much as turn away from the right-hander. Having said that, he produced a really good leg-break that bowled Paul Collingwood earlier in the innings. Fortunately, I managed to deny him the hat-trick. Unfortunately, the reprieve proved temporary. The next ball was a googly – which turned away from me as a left-hander – and I turned to see Dravid take a brilliant catch diving to his right at slip.

From being 283 for 5, the all-out total of 300 was less than we expected, but it was still a reasonable score that kept us in the game. As in the first innings at Nagpur, we broke the back of the Indian top order, only to be frustrated by the lower order. Irfan Pathan swung his bat and Kumble and Harbhajan Singh both struck important thirties so that India took a lead of 38. My contribution was to have Wasim Jaffer caught on the drive by Flintoff. It was quite appropriate that he should take the catch, because he had decided to put himself in that position. Jaffer is not one of the heralded India batsmen but he had become as stubborn as any of them, with the possible exception of Dravid, whose 95 this time underpinned the innings.

Second time around we were blown away. Patel took four wickets when the ball reverse-swung late on but Kumble removed three of our batsmen as he really exploited the bounce. I cannot think of another bowler like him in world cricket and although he had been around for a long time our batting line-up did not have a lot of international experience. Andrew Strauss seemed like a veteran, having been in the team for two years. Sometimes you can lose a game in a mad half-hour, but at other times you have to take your hat off to the opposition. This one was definitely in the second category and although Flintoff played patiently for his second half-century in the match we knew that a lead of 143 was unlikely to be enough. It was still another heroic effort by the captain, who had also taken four wickets in India's first innings.

We suffered more bad luck in the second innings when Steve Harmison picked up a shin injury, which turned out to be serious enough to keep him out of the first part of the summer programme. India decided that the best way to chase was to go quickly, allowing Virender Sehwag to play his natural, free-scoring game. My figures of 11 overs for 48 look pretty ordinary alongside Kumble's earlier efforts, but I consoled myself with the fact that he was in his 105th Test while I was playing in my second. With a bit of luck, too, I could have had at least one wicket.

Strauss dropped Dravid at slip and I remember feeling a bit annoyed because Dravid is such a good player and I was close to getting him out for a second time in the series. No bowler is ever happy when a chance goes down but we all react in different ways. I feel it is important to put it to the back of my mind and concentrate on the next ball. Let's face it, as Mr Absolute Shocker myself in the field, I am not in a strong position to complain when somebody else puts one down. I feel well qualified to state that nobody drops the ball deliberately.

I was actually more angry a few balls later when I missed a chance off my own bowling. This time I could blame nobody but myself. Dravid top-edged a shot and I could see the ball going slowly, slowly over my head. It seemed to be in the air for long enough to turn round and grab it but I just didn't have the sharpness to twist and take it. My mind said 'go' but my body would not respond. After all that hard work in Adelaide before Christmas and on the tour, my big flat feet had let me down again. I could have made it with a bit more arch. Afterwards I tried to be positive and tell myself that I was creating chances and troubling one of the best batsmen in the world, but you have to take these opportunities when they come.

At the other end, Sehwag wanted to take me on, and I was not alone in coming in for punishment. People think that he gives you a chance with the way he plays. That is true, but on his day he can take you apart. Nobody can score a triple hundred in a Test match, as Sehwag has done, without a good technical grounding. This time you knew as an infielder that if the ball went past there was no point giving chase. He does have a fantastic eye for the ball; in a way he reminds me of my old Bedfordshire captain Wayne Larkins. This was simply his day, and if it had been India's first innings he could have gone on to score 200.

We felt very down in the dressing room afterwards because at different times we had been in good positions, but ultimately nine wickets is a big margin of defeat. India were bound to draw confidence and with a more experienced side and greater knowledge of the conditions they were now even stronger favourites to win the series. I was particularly disappointed because so many of my family had come to see me play and I thought that I could have done better. But I never felt that I had let them down because they knew how hard I tried. I hope there is another opportunity to play for England in Mohali in the future.

A couple of days later I was able to put cricket into its true perspective. In Mumbai a few of the players along with Phil Tufnell were invited to do some promotional work for the Sport Relief charity, which aims to help, in this case, the railway children of the sprawling city. It coincided with the traditional Hindu festival of Holi, which is also celebrated by Sikhs. On the first day people light bonfires, on the second they throw coloured powder at each other. Thus its alternative name as the Festival of Colour.

I don't think the kids knew exactly who we were, but between us we had a riot. I really got into the throwing and paid a heavy price as my T-shirt, trousers and black patka soon became covered with powder. I hadn't enjoyed myself so much since I was their age myself and it was such an uplifting experience to see children with so little in life being as happy and joyful as they were. I felt very touched by their positive attitudes and realised how lucky I had been in life, even before I played for England.

Although we were 1–0 down, we felt very relaxed going into the final Test. Flintoff stressed again that we should feel very proud of our performances so far. We could have stood back and allowed their great players to dominate, but we had shown some fight and stood up to them. Despite our inexperience we had really pushed India on their own soil. Apart from Australia, I can't think of another country with a better home record. As it happened, we had another new face in our side this time with Owais Shah coming in for a debut in place of Alastair Cook, who went down with a tummy upset on the morning of the game. Ian Bell moved up to open. At the start of the tour I don't think anybody would have guessed our line-up for Mumbai.

I remembered the Wankhede Stadium from the Under-19 tour and I think the same thoughts were going through Bell's mind during practice. He turned to me and said, 'Isn't this where you got hit for that massive six?' There was no denying it. I thanked him very much, we laughed, and as I stared up into the vast expanse of stand where the ball had disappeared those five years earlier I thought to myself, 'I really hope that doesn't happen again.'

This time the ground was packed to the rafters. Mumbai is an amazing, vibrant city with its mix of traditional Indian quarters and modern business developments. By now there was a strong following for the England team from back home and with the usual loud, enthusiastic support for the home side the atmosphere was incredible even in the warm-ups.

With all our injury troubles we were due a piece of luck, and it came about 30 minutes before the start from an unlikely source. Flintoff had lost the toss but Rahul Dravid decided to put us in to bat. To say that we were surprised is an understatement. I have heard that when Ricky Ponting made England bat first at Edgbaston in 2005, a cheer went through the dressing room. Although the response was not quite as ecstatic this time, we were certainly very pleased. It looked like a decent batting pitch, but we thought it would start to deteriorate and become very awkward by the fourth and fifth days. We did not really want to bat last against Anil Kumble and Harbhajan Singh. Dravid's decision concentrated our minds. From being underdogs with our scratch team, we realised we had been given a chance to level the series. All we needed was to set up the game with a big first innings.

The batsmen soon took advantage. Andrew Strauss looked very determined, having taken some time to get used to the different pace of the Indian pitches, and his 128 proved to be the highest score of the match. In fact, the totals got smaller and smaller, suggesting that our reading of the conditions had been more accurate than Dravid's. Shah also batted really well for his 88. I knew from county cricket that he had so much time to play his shots. He could look a top-class batsman on his day, and this was one of those days. As they built their partnership, the rest of us in the dressing room knew that we were moving into a potentially winning position as long as we kept our concentration and avoided doing anything rash.

Our total of 400 set up the game and Matthew Hoggard again bowled brilliantly with the new ball. Jimmy Anderson came in for Steve Harmison for his first Test for more than a year and kept control, as well as taking four wickets. I had a long bowl with Shaun Udal – who was 37 on the first day of the game – and kept things fairly tight. By this stage India must have realised that they had left themselves with a fight on their hands because even such an attacking player as Mahendra Dhoni scored at a relatively slower pace than usual. He is an unusual batsman who reminds me of a tennis player sometimes with the way he whips the ball from his backlift. Unfortunately, I missed him straight after a drinks break at mid-off. He whacked Anderson quite hard to my left and I thought I'd held it, only for the ball to bounce out. Those hard hands again!

This was an amazing game for dropped catches on both sides. At least 16 chances went down, so I wasn't alone in wondering what had gone wrong. We talked about it and could not come up with a good reason. On some grounds it can be hard to sight the ball at a certain height because of spectators bunched together in the background. Whether that was the case here, I'm not sure. India spilt more than we did – though admittedly they were in the field for longer – and if poor visibility was the problem then they should have been more used to it at their ground. The answer may well be nothing more scientific than coincidence.

With a lead of 121 we wanted to grind out every run we could second time around. Although our scoring rate was little more than two an over, the game was never dull because everybody could sense the hard work that was going into every moment. Between them, Kumble and Harbhajan bowled 53.4 overs for 89 runs. Flintoff put in a magnificent effort to control his attacking instincts and score 50 from 146 balls. It was his second half-century of the match and yet another example of the captain leading by example.

In the end we managed to set a target of 312. They would have to bat brilliantly to get the runs, but then they did have brilliant batsmen. We identified Dravid as the key man because he was in form and the guy they would look to bat around. Because they were 1–0 up, a draw was good enough for them to win the series. And as they blocked ball after ball it became clear that a 2–0 score-line seemed out of the question. Even Virender Sehwag faced 16 balls without scoring. Their approach meant that we could set attacking fields, but at the same time we knew not to expect any easy wickets. It would take something out of the ordinary to break them down. Step forward, Johnny Cash.

By this time, the singer had become a big favourite of most of us. 'Ring of Fire' was established as the tour song. I must admit that I hadn't heard of Cash before we left England, but Flintoff soon changed that. I soon grew to like his songs and picked up some of the words. After lunch, a couple of minutes before we were due to go back out into the heat, Flintoff suddenly put the track on the music box and led us in the singing, clapping and dancing. I don't know if he had been planning this or whether it came out spontaneously. But it was inspired, a piece of captaincy with roots in his own irrepressible character rather than any text-book. I'd never known anything like it before, and what the crowd must have thought as 11 cricketers emerged from the pavilion laughing and smiling as though it were a club game, I can only guess. But if they saw the funny side their emotions soon changed to anger as the last seven wickets tumbled inside the next 16 overs.

Although we were back in the middle for only slightly over an hour, something happened in that time that I later realised would have a significant effect on my popularity. Mahendra Dhoni, having reined in much of his attacking flair in the first innings, decided that attack was the best policy this time. He had already been dropped at slip when he tried to slog Shaun Udal over mid-off. Instead, the ball soared high and somewhere in my direction.

But where in my direction? That was the question. As soon as Dhoni hit the ball I thought, 'Yes, this is mine.' I ran forward, looked up and saw a bit of sky, a lot of sun but no red dot. Eventually I spotted the ball. 'I've seen it, I've seen it.' And then I lost it again. 'Where has it gone?' Time was running out. It felt as though minutes had passed. Probably it was no more than six or seven seconds. I put my hands where I thought the ball would come down, held them there and felt nothing. I've read that it landed between two feet and three metres to my right. The distance didn't really matter. Whoever coined that phrase about wanting the earth to open up and swallow you must have known what it was like to miss a catch like that.

Not even in practice, ever, had I made such a hash of a chance. My mind went into a stream of consciousness. Something like: 'It's Test cricket, millions of people are watching all over the world and every one of them will think I'm the worst fielder of all time, and it's going to be replayed for ever, and what about all that work I did in Australia before Christmas, and what will they think at Glenelg and Luton and Northampton?' I picked up the ball, threw it back and looked around at my team-mates. Some of them were trying not to crack up. Udal just looked agog, as if he couldn't believe what had happened.

I told myself to think about the next ball and forget what had happened. Anybody could have made the mistake, it just happened to be my day. It wouldn't happen again. Except, three balls later, Dhoni played exactly the same shot. And being exactly the same shot it went in exactly the same direction. As I ran towards it again, my thinking was crystal clear, 'Drop this, Monty, and you'll never play for England again.'

But this time I saw it all the way up, and all the way down. I judged where it would fall, and it plopped safely into my trembling hands. I have never been as relieved in my life. Perhaps I wasn't a complete and utter shambles after all. The rest of the guys ran towards me, and this time they didn't have to contain their laughter. Flintoff started rubbing my beard and somehow, in all the excitement, my patka came off. They started patting my heart and apparently the beat was racing as though I'd just finished the bleep test at Loughborough.

People have said since that I showed a lot of bottle to take that catch. The fact is that I had no other option except to go for it. I was the nearest fielder; it was my catch. Looking back, I was fortunate that Dhoni gave me a second chance so quickly after I missed the first. I suppose it is like getting back onto the horse as soon as you can after a fall. The pressure next time would have been even greater if that 'next time' had been weeks or months away, whenever I was chosen for England again. It also meant that the drop was not as costly as it might have been in altering the course of the match.

If Dhoni had gone on to win the game, then the reaction would have been far stronger than a smiling shake of the head. As it was, they could laugh in the knowledge that no harm had been done. I also think that people could understand what I was going through while that second ball was hanging in the air. Cricketers are not the only people who face these little tests in our lives. Maybe I gave other folk a bit of hope by coming through this one.

Dhoni himself took a lot of criticism for the shot. In India somebody always has to pay for defeat, and 212 runs was quite a loss. He obviously felt that his natural game was the best way to go. That is usually a good Plan A. Reflecting now, I believe this was a game won by England, not lost by India. The scorecard shows a great team effort. Some of the unsung guys, including Geraint Jones with six catches, three of them full-length dives, Jimmy Anderson and Shaun Udal, all made big contributions. But for all that, Flintoff was a towering figure in every way.

Over the weeks away I had got to know him a little bit better, but I still couldn't separate the bloke I knew, the life and soul of every group of people he is ever part of, from the legendary Freddie Flintoff who won the Ashes for England. On one occasion when we were out together I suddenly burst out laughing. He wanted to know what was happening and I said, 'I don't know, I just can't believe I'm really out here with you.' He gave me one of his playful pushes and said, 'Behave yourself.'

The celebrations in the dressing room at Mumbai were just crazy. Like the sing-song during the lunch break, I had never experienced anything like it. I remember Duncan Fletcher jumping onto Flintoff's back and the pair of them hugging. We were leaping around, singing our team song and autographing bits of equipment for each other to keep as souvenirs. I was the only teetotaller in the squad but I got enough of a buzz from the Diet Coke and the sheer thrill of winning a Test match. Experienced players say that they play the game for the immediate aftermath of victory, when the hours and hours of preparation and dedication eventually bring reward. In Mumbai that day, I knew what they meant.

So was playing for England as I expected? In a way, no. I imagined that everything would be serious and probably quite regimented, that there would be a correct way to do things established at the highest level over time. I thought it would be a constant diet of cricket, cricket, cricket and that every minute together would be spent on striving to improve. The atmosphere was not as intense as I imagined. Yes, the hard-work ethic was there, ingrained in the senior players and management. But there was also time to relax and enjoy ourselves away from the game. Since those first matches for England I have learned the importance of having other things in my life apart from cricket. Very often it is enough to be in a good rhythm and doing the basics well. A day spent away from a ground can be a day well spent.

To draw against India in India was surely an endorsement of Fletcher's methods as well as Flintoff's leadership. One newspaper called it the Miracle of Mumbai. The way we pulled together, a lot of inexperienced players stepping into the unknown, I think did us a lot of credit. Personally, I thought I made a good start. I had dismissed two of the greatest batsmen in the world in Sachin Tendulkar and Rahul Dravid. On the other hand, I knew that a return of five wickets in three matches overall was quite modest, even though I had created chances to take a few more. The need to have a good stock ball with the same trajectory was reinforced, along with the need to be patient. If something is working, then don't worry about variety for the sake of it. There were plenty of positives.

As the Test players headed home, leaving the one-day squad in India for another three weeks, Fletcher took me to one side for a few words about my game. He thought that I had bowled well and would definitely be around the squad in the future, even if I was not always in the side. But he stressed the importance of contributing in more ways than one. He explained how a dropped catch can completely change the tone of a game. World-class players are so strong mentally that a reprieve will give them new energy and get their concentration going. Perhaps not in Dhoni's case in Mumbai, but at other times it will be the wake-up call they need. And they may not give another chance for a long, long time. What you can sometimes get away with in county cricket does not apply in the international game.

7

MONTY MANIA

U NTIL I arrived back home I had no idea of the impression
I'd made while I was away in India. When Andrew Flintoff
told me that interest had started to build, I assumed he was joking
and just got on with the job in hand. I thought I would be able
to sit back and relax for a few days to catch up with friends before
heading to Northampton for what was left of preseason training.
I suppose I received a small taste of what was to come with the
reception at the airport when we landed. The win in Mumbai
appeared to have caught the public imagination, judging by the
turnout. Less than a month after my debut in Nagpur, I realised
there was more to being a Test cricketer than batting, bowling
and trying to hold the occasional catch.

There were more requests for media interviews than I could
manage and interest came from areas I hadn't begun to imagine.
I went on the *Soccer AM* programme on Sky Sports, even though
I was out of touch with what was happening at Kenilworth Road,
home of the mighty Luton Town. That was despite the club making
me their special guest for the game against Ipswich Town at the
end of March. I had followed them since I was 13 or 14 and I still
enjoy going to the rickety old ground with its special atmosphere.

One offer I snapped up straight away was to appear on *A
Question of Sport*. I used to watch it as a kid and found it interesting to be in the studio to see how they put it together. The

strange thing was that I didn't feel nervous at all. The emphasis was on having some fun rather than taking the questions too seriously. Dean Ashton (football), Matt Burke (rugby) and Mark Webber (Formula One) were the other guests, so it made for a good mix. I was on Ally McCoist's side and could hardly stop giggling because he was so funny. 'Remember I'm Scottish – you're on your own for the cricket questions,' he told me.

Although the result didn't matter a great deal, I didn't want to make myself look an idiot by getting the cricket questions wrong. When I was being introduced at the start they showed the Tendulkar wicket and the Dhoni drop. The studio audience laughed and I must admit it was funny to see my face when I realised the ball had landed so far from my hands. Once we got going, I recognised Andrew Strauss on the picture board – just as well with him being my training buddy – and correctly said that Stephen Harmison had been Anil Kumble's 500th Test wicket. Fortunately I didn't have to admit that I was number 501.

At the start of April, BBC1 broadcast a 30-minute programme called *Monty Panesar: Monty for England*. The religion unit had followed me around for a month or so before I went to India, picking up on the angle of a Sikh playing for England for the first time. It became a kind of fly-on-the-wall documentary as they filmed me at Northampton, then at home and then at the temple in Coventry. I wasn't sure at first whether I would enjoy the experience and didn't think that many people would really be interested. I have always seen my religion as private, but the emphasis was on me as a cricketer. I enjoyed the finished product and from what I gather the feedback was good.

There were a couple of other engagements to fit in between practice. I had to speak at some property awards with Stephen Fry, who turned out to be a big cricket fan. 'Lovely to meet you,' he said, in that very distinctive voice. He reminded me a bit of Andrew Flintoff with his presence. Wherever he stood, people congregated around him. I think I had more jitters before getting up to speak than when I came on to bowl for England. I am pretty reserved most of the time and dreaded falling flat or dropping something at a key moment. As always, it wasn't nearly as difficult as I expected and having come through I took the view that I would be better equipped for next time. Travelling back home that day, I had to remind myself again that I'd only played three Tests. What would life be like if I ever got to 23 or 33?

I was getting to the stage where I wanted to be back on a cricket field doing what I knew best and enjoyed most. At least the next commitment, for a project called NatWest Cricket Force, had me back outside with a ball in my hand. The scheme is designed to freshen up facilities at clubs around the country and generally promote the game at the lower levels to encourage participation. I went to Upminster with Alastair Cook to do some interviews and pose for a few pictures with the local kids. People were quick to pick up on my fielding. I don't know if it was somebody's idea of a joke, but I was set up for a diving catch, which could have been very embarrassing. Luckily, given the number of lenses pointing in my direction, I managed to hold on.

With so much more going on than simply playing cricket, I relied on a guy called Dave Parsooth to look after things behind the scenes. His son, Nitin, was a good mate when we were growing up and we played together for Luton Indians. Nitin actually had far more talent, but wasn't as committed. I don't think of Dave as an agent or manager, just somebody who looks after things behind the scenes. I am pretty well organised in most areas but didn't have a lot of experience in sorting out appointments or working out fees. I would hate to be double-booked because I've forgotten to write something in my diary. Dave's advice was to concentrate on cricket because if I lost that focus, the other activities would soon dry up. He has a very sharp mind and I couldn't trust anybody more.

Much as I enjoyed these new experiences, I was relieved when 14 April and the game between MCC and the champion county, Nottinghamshire, eventually dawned. I was not used to playing so early in the season because in previous years I had still been at university. Even though the crowd looked quite small – Lord's being the biggest ground in the country, there were plenty of gaps – a small group took up the cry of 'Monty, Monty' that I'd heard for the first time in India. Fielding on the boundary, I found it all very peculiar and wondered when it would start to die down and get back to what I thought of as normal.

The game itself didn't go too well. We lost by 142 runs and Mark Ealham struck what proved to be the fastest hundred of the season from 45 balls. My figures were all right until he started to take advantage of a small boundary. The weather was cold and the pitch, as you would expect, was more a seamer's green-top than a dry surface suited to spin. At least I had a few overs under my belt and after an uneventful draw between Northamptonshire and Essex I decided to play against Cambridge University at the end of the month. A few players prefer to sit out these games but our coach Kepler Wessels thought it would be a good idea to get the extra practice in the middle. In any case, I've never needed to find a reason to play in a cricket match.

I also thought that I needed a good performance to convince the selectors to pick me for the First Test against Sri Lanka. Although Ashley Giles was still unfit, I didn't know whether they would go with an all-seam attack so early in the season. Shaun Udal had ended the India series really well in Mumbai, while my own figures were pretty ordinary. My last chance before the side was named came against Somerset at Northampton, and things worked out as well as I had hoped. The weather was good and the pitch gave some help later on. With Somerset on the defensive I could probe away and find the right spot. By the end, with an innings win and personal figures of 5 for 32 from 26.3 overs, I knew I had done all I could to hang on to my England place.

Selection was duly confirmed and it felt a bit like meeting up with schoolfriends at the start of a new term when we got together at the hotel close to Lord's. As well as being the first Test of the summer, it was also my first at home. Unfortunately, it turned into a very frustrating game because we could not quite nail the Sri Lankans, having been in a position where it seemed that only a change in the weather could deny us. *Wisden* said they pulled off one of the finest escape acts since Clint Eastwood burst out of Alcatraz. I didn't play a huge part in proceedings over the five days, but the question in my own mind about how the crowd would treat me after India was soon answered noisily.

As in Nagpur, I spent the first day as a specator as we built a good first-innings total. Marcus Trescothick came back into the side and batted as though he had never been away. Kevin Pietersen became the second century-maker the next day, matching exactly his 158 against Australia at The Oval eight months earlier. As on that occasion, I watched from a dressing room, though the view from the England balcony was rather better than the small television we crowded around while Pietersen was securing the Ashes.

Our total of 551 for 6 left us in a strong position and the bowlers soon capitalised. Sajid Mahmood took three wickets in nine balls on his debut and although Sri Lanka recovered slightly on Saturday morning, Andrew Flintoff enforced the follow-on with a lead of 359. I had not been required to bowl in the first innings but that did not stop the crowd from getting right behind me. They cheered every time I switched from long leg to third man for the right- and left-handers. I didn't want to offend anyone but at the same time I was reluctant to wave all the time as I thought it might seem big-headed and lead to accusations that I wasn't concentrating. I asked some of the other guys for advice. They said there was no harm in acknowledging the support. When I did wave the cheer was incredible.

I remember doing a sliding stop on the boundary and thinking I had done really well to get the ball in quickly and maybe save a run or two. Bearing in mind what had happened in India, I wanted to make a good impression in the field to remove the idea that I was just hopeless. Unfortunately I didn't realise that my foot had gone over the rope as I shaped for the throw, letting Sri Lanka get the four after all. That felt like a real let-down, because I had done my best, but at least I thought the crowd appreciated the effort if not the end result. There were times when I wondered whether they were laughing at me rather than with me. I didn't know if they were waiting for the fumbles and taking the mickey as if it was some sort of sideshow, rather than wanting me to succeed.

Despite opening up a big advantage, we knew that Sri Lanka would knuckle down. The pitch was blameless and it would be a bonus if the ball swung quite as much again. With the best part of two and a half days left, Upul Tharanga and Kumar Sangakkara began to dig in. And at this point, roughly five minutes before tea on the third day, I was finally given my first Test bowl in England. A roar went up as Flintoff called me over. 'I think they like you here,' he said, and we both laughed. Marking out my run, I visualised where I wanted the ball to land. I did my best to keep the noise out of my mind and concentrate entirely on the job in hand.

I have always tried to keep things very simple, and all the cheering – which I soon grew used to – was just one more distraction to overcome. I am not big on technical things like a high front arm and a strong follow-through. I know that my action is sound and don't want it to be complicated with lots of theories and biomechanical terms that will only be confusing. As long as the ball goes in the right place, I have never been too concerned about how it gets there. Nor do I stay awake at night thinking of special tactics for certain players. My attitude towards the Sri Lankans was that they faced Muttiah Muralitharan every day in the nets so they weren't likely to fall into any trap of mine. It isn't as though I can bowl the doosra anyway, though I do try in practice from time to time. On most pitches my basic strategy is to bowl for dot balls and hope to create a bit of pressure.

That was enough this time. By close I had bowled 15 overs for 22 runs and, more important, removed both batsmen to catches behind. Tharanga got a little inside edge while Sangakkara I beat on the outside. At the end Matthew Hoggard, who had just taken his 200th Test wicket, made an observation about the crowd, saying that he wasn't sure whether they were backing me or putting me under a bit more pressure. I didn't mind at all because at least for most of the time I felt it was good-natured. They pay good money for their tickets and are entitled to get involved. As in India, I think I drew on the energy in the field, and when I was actually bowling I managed to blank it out.

Sri Lanka were three down at close, then six down on Sunday evening. It really was slow work and when bad light brought an end to the game just before six o'clock on Monday they still had one wicket left and a good lead. Somehow, we found a last pocket of energy to be able to shake hands for a draw. In all, their second innings lasted for a little over 14 hours, but because they had followed on we actually spent the equivalent of more than three days in the field. The innings seemed to go on and on and on. Sri Lanka deserved a bucket-load of credit – six of them scored half-centuries and Mahela Jayawardene made 119 – but we were annoyed at dropping nine chances in the match. When he was asked about the problem afterwards, Flintoff said, 'I don't know what it is, but I hope it isn't catching.'

I thought my fitness level was pretty high, but I felt shattered afterwards. I've played in Championship matches that have not lasted as long as we spent in the field, and Tests in any case are far more intense. Coming back from India, I had decided to work on my concentration in the field. I felt I needed to anticipate the ball coming towards me better, so that I pounced on it a bit quicker. When I was bowling I still had a tendency not so much to daydream while the action was at the other end, as to think about the previous over and what I might try to do in the next. I made a conscious effort to mark my spot in the field and make sure I went to exactly that mark when the bowler walked in. That way I had something to focus on, but it became tougher and tougher to stay alert as the minutes ticked by.

An experience like this – especially with it being so cold – provided a great test and I thought I did pretty well overall. I will never be a Jonty Rhodes, but I didn't make any howling mistakes. The fatigue was eased a little bit by the recovery sessions we have at the end of every day. We have to stand in an ice bath – it actually bears more resemblance to a wheelie bin – and then go back to the hotel for some exercises in the swimming pool. It is all designed to get the lactic acid out of the system to feel better for the next day. Our food tends to be based around protein and carbohydrates to restore energy levels.

Because we were creating opportunities, we all thought that we would win in the end, despite making life hard for ourselves. But the real killer blow was a ninth-wicket stand between Chaminda Vaas and Nuwan Kulasekara lasting 45 overs – or half a day. Flintoff was criticised afterwards for not bowling me more, but conditions were probably better for pace bowlers and I think he wanted to front the challenge himself. It is very unusual for spinners to bowl much so early in the season and the cold can make it difficult because you prefer to have supple fingers. Even Muralitharan went for more than three runs per over and took a wicket on average every 96 balls. That is way below his normal strike rate. I certainly could have bowled more and, given the choice, I would love to have had more of a go. But then I always would. The fact is that if we had held the catches, then it would not have been an issue. We enjoy success together and when things do not go so well we take responsibility as a group.

I knew that my role might be restricted to a couple of overs before lunch, maybe a spell before tea and whenever the seam bowlers needed a rest. You have to trust the captain and with my previous experience stretching all of three Tests there was no way I was going to run to Flintoff and tell him I was the answer to the problem. I always wait for the call from a captain and never make a big show of warming up to try to catch his eye. It isn't like club cricket where the captain might just leave you at long on and third man because he has forgotten you are on the field.

As an England player, I now found myself being rested between the Tests instead of going back to play for Northamptonshire. This was a completely new concept. I had always believed that the way to improve was to practise for as long as time allowed. If I wasn't playing, then what was I supposed to do?

Fortunately the ECB had appointed a specialist spin-bowling coach, David Parsons, in January. As far as my career is concerned the timing could not have been better. He gave me a lot of help in those early weeks and months in working out what I needed to do and when I needed to rest. He gave me a purpose to every-thing I did, so when I did practise I wouldn't just bowl as though I was in a match situation. One day I might work on slower balls, then the next day on arm balls and so on. The sessions were not always long. A couple of times we worked together for only 20 or 30 minutes before he said 'that's enough'. I remember thinking, 'I haven't done very much there.'

Most of the work was done at Northampton. I had taken a little flat very near to the ground so that I had a base for cricket training and didn't have to commute from our family home in Luton so often. Parsons was very professional in his approach. I found it strange that somebody who had never played first-class cricket could know so much about spin bowling, but he was very passionate about the job and when he talked about my action and alignment he put it in language I understood. I also did a lot of fielding work, as well as going through fitness sessions with the county. These days I understand that I have to compartmentalise between all areas of the game instead of just going into a net and bowling. That is what would have happened, I'm sure, if it had been left to me.

We all did a bit of thinking before the Second Test at Edgbaston, and the period between the games simply reinforced our initial view that we had let Sri Lanka off the hook. They had battled well to secure the draw, but we were determined to make sure that their efforts would not be enough this time. And, as it happened, once again we dismissed them cheaply in the first innings, but on this occasion we managed to back it up in the second. Instead of a draw we came away with a six-wicket win and a day off into the bargain.

This time at least I was required to bowl in the first innings, albeit for only two overs. Once again the pace bowlers did the damage. Liam Plunkett and Sajid Mahmood were quite new to Test cricket but were starting to make an impression and came away with ten wickets in the match. Matthew Hoggard has been Mr Reliable since well before I came into the side and, with those three on song, Flintoff did not have to bowl himself for such long spells. Actually, it isn't being rude to say that Sri Lanka established only one good partnership in the match when Michael Vandort and Tillakaratne Dilshan put on 125 – more than half the total – in the second innings.

This one probably won't go down among the most memorable Tests of all time, but anybody who saw it will still remember Kevin Pietersen's 142 and in particular a reverse-swept six against Muralitharan. The next best score in the innings was only 30, but he seemed to be playing a different game. In some ways he is, because I can't think of another player who goes for that flamingo shot where he lifts his left leg and whips the ball through the leg side. I don't know about the crowd but he certainly entertains us.

I had not seen him bat as confidently as that before. He played really well against Anil Kumble bowling into the rough at Mumbai, but this was a different type of innings. He really stamped his personality on the second day. I have never bowled to him in a match situation but he must be a serious problem once he gets set because of the way he strikes boundaries one after another. Of all the great batsmen in the world he is the one I would most expect to follow one four with another. He just gets in that zone where anything is possible.

As characters I guess we are fairly different. People might think that we don't have a lot in common, but I like him because he is such a positive, happy guy. He reminds me of Matthew Hayden with his incredible self-belief. They are both big, dominating batsmen who work really hard on their games behind the scenes. Pietersen has not become one of the best in the world by accident. And he is good fun in the dressing room. If we want to know about the latest cars or new films or flashest gadgets, then Pietersen is the man to ask. He can laugh at himself as well, joining in the mickey-taking but copping some of the flak at the same time. I remember once sitting with our physio Kirk Russell, joking that I was filling in a form for an American Express card to see how Pietersen would react to the idea that I was moving into his league. He just laughed.

Unfortunately, I suffered in the field at Edgbaston. At one point Flintoff put me at leg slip and I reacted slowly to a possible chance. But the worst one came from Lasith Malinga late in the first innings. I was fielding at mid-off to Plunkett and I knew as soon as the ball went down that it would look terrible on television. I felt sorry for Plunkett, an inexperienced player as I was, but most of all I realised that I had to start holding on to these catches. It isn't a nice experience when more than 15,000 people laugh at a mistake or cheer sarcastically at an error. But I was the only person who could do something about it. I wanted the crowds to like me – of course I did – but not as a figure of fun. I convinced myself that another chance would come along soon and when it did, as long as I was concentrating hard, I would be able to take it. In the end I did get Malinga leg-before in my first over, but really the wicket should have gone to Plunkett some time earlier.

By pure coincidence – I think – I also took a wicket as soon as I came on when Sri Lanka batted again. Kumar Sangakkara had tried to sweep me really hard first ball, and I had a feeling that he would keep trying to attack to make a point after I had got him out in the previous Test. When that happens I just try to keep bowling in the same place and hope that something happens, on the basis that my stock ball is usually my best. The plan worked because he came down the pitch and chipped it nicely to Paul Collingwood.

My other wicket, Thilan Samaraweera stumped, is still one of my favourites. Even though we were only on day three the ball turned a lot and Geraint Jones finished it very quickly as Samaraweera tried in vain to get back, having come down the track. Bishan Bedi once told me that a stumping is the best dismissal for a left-arm spinner because it means you have got the batsman out twice: once in the flight and once off the pitch. To me, even the flukiest wicket is worth celebrating – and I do – but at the same time I have to agree with the great man.

Spin bowlers get their wickets not off the pitch, but in the air. It comes down to the skill of deception, which is why you sometimes hear a slow bowler described as a magician or a conjuror. Our trick, when things go well, is to convince the batsman that the ball will land in one place when really it is going to pitch in another. The way to do that is in the flight. If you can tease him forward and make the ball land a little bit shorter than he expects, then it has the chance to turn past the bat. A stumping is the ultimate because the batsman is far enough short for the ball to have turned, usually, beyond the outside edge. It is not quite like a magic show, of course. A batsman, however gullible, usually takes more persuading to succumb than a passive member of the audience in the stalls. But that makes it all the better when you can finally produce the rabbit from the hat.

Personally, I am very much at the apprentice stage. Members of the real Magic Circle take a vow not to divulge their tricks, but the fact is that at present I do not have a lot to pass on. I have a pretty good instinct but, as I wrote earlier, I am not always sure why things happen. By bowling at a slightly faster pace than a lot of spinners, I can get good bounce on most pitches. If I do drag a batsman forward, it gives me that chance of getting an edge from high on the bat. Sometimes, as with Sangakkara at Edgbaston, I can get a clue about the way somebody is going to play. There are also little bits of body language that are helpful to notice. One obvious thing is to look at the practice shots a batsman might be playing between deliveries.

Unlike me, Muralitharan is a fully qualified wizard. It was a strange experience being his opposite number in this series. Any comparisons between us were made for that reason and that reason alone. I tried to ignore them because I knew he was in a different class, and I don't say that out of false modesty. The facts are there. He took ten of our 14 wickets at Edgbaston, for example. If he had not been in the Sri Lanka side, perhaps we would have won by an innings. He has helped to make Sri Lanka into one of the biggest forces in the game and he was to have an even bigger say in events at Trent Bridge a week later.

Murali has definitely been an asset to the game as a whole, not just to his own country. I love the way he runs in to bowl with those short, light steps and his big eyes bulging out from under his thick eyebrows. Then, afterwards, he gives you that toothy grin as if to say 'you're falling into my trap'. He is a very joyful person, although you could say that, with his wonderful record and gift of being able to spin the ball so far, he has a lot to be joyful about.

While I always try to learn from every spinner I meet, I found it very hard to take anything from Murali because his action is so unorthodox. He bowls from the wrist as much as the fingers. He is also right-handed. I have tried to imitate him in the nets, just quietly for a bit of fun and to see how far I get. It doesn't really work, but then I don't have the advantage of being double-jointed. I did study the way he works on a batsman, the way he probes away, the fields he sets and the body language. The word I would use to describe him is 'unique'. That and 'great'. With his variety of deliveries he has given cricket another dimension.

After Edgbaston, Duncan Fletcher told a press conference that he felt I was under pressure to improve my fielding. He was speaking, I think, in response to a question, not singling out the issue voluntarily. The fact that reporters asked about me showed that interest and, I suppose, concern was starting to grow. Actually, I didn't feel too much pressure at all. I already knew that I had to keep practising, and would have known even if Duncan had not told me himself in India. I was doing extra work with England to try to reach the standard expected. Although there may not have been much evidence, I quietly felt I was making progress. Duncan discussed my cricket as a whole. He said that he liked my attitude and could not fault the effort that I was putting in. As he saw the players during our preparation, he knew better than anybody. We all respected him not only for his knowledge but because he does not say anything in public that he wouldn't say face to face.

I did think back to my teenage days when I had spent so much time working on my bowling. I wished I had spent an extra hour on fielding instead of devoting everything to just one part of the game. There is a hill in Luton with little steps to the top. Hitu Naik suggested I ought to run up and down them once a day to make my feet work quicker and improve my coordination. I must have been 14 or 15 at the time and that was probably the one thing he asked me to do that I was reluctant about. And now here I was, an England cricketer, thinking 'if only . . .' But then, who knows? Maybe if I had spent that time on throwing and catching, then my bowling would have fallen short and Northamptonshire would not have been interested in the first place.

Fielding seemed to be more and more of a talking point with every game that passed. Around this time, the commentator Henry Blofeld called me Monty Python. It was a slip of the tongue, apparently. At the time I didn't know that Monty Python was an old comedy team. I thought it was the name of a circus. Sometimes my coordination is not great and I might look like a comedy act, but I am a serious cricketer doing a serious job and I wanted to change the subject and move on. I knew that it was down to me to show that I could field. At the same time, I was able to put the whole business in a wider context. Nobody was getting hurt. And there were times when I could smile, like the afternoon when I went home and my dad offered to take me out for some catching practice.

There are players who are reluctant to pick up the newspapers when things are not going right for them. I don't fall into that category. If a paper is lying around during a game, then I don't mind having a quick look to see what people think. It helps me when something I believe is reinforced by a cricket correspondent. For example, if a journalist writes that I have a good, repeatable action, it confirms that things are going pretty well. It is always interesting to see other people's opinions about field settings and you can also get an insight into the way other people play. I certainly don't have any complaints about what has been written about me.

I guess I must look pretty different to the writers and commentators. Some of their descriptions make me laugh. I have been compared to Bambi on ice and a baby giraffe because of the way I run. Rod Marsh called me Monty Panadol because he thought I could give batsmen a headache. I thought that was very funny.

At the end of the day, cricket faces a lot of competition from other sports and if we can fill some space in the papers and get interviewed by lifestyle magazines or appear on television, it has to be good for the overall profile of the game.

Edgbaston was a really good win for us. We were expected to beat Sri Lanka at home but they had a lot of experience and a genius of a bowler in Muralitharan, so we knew it would be easier said than done. In the two matches so far we had never looked like losing at any time. We should have been 2–0 up, admittedly, but even so there was every reason to feel full of confidence going into the final match at Trent Bridge. However, we didn't anticipate arriving in Nottingham to find a pitch that could have been prepared especially for Muralitharan.

On the first day of the game a story on the news pages of *The Times* came up with a novel reason for my fielding lapses. At the start of the season I had been fitted with special contact lenses, the kind that are designed to help sportsmen by keeping moisture in the eye. I have been short-sighted since my teens and wore glasses at school. It turned out that my left lens was the wrong prescription. This placed a greater strain on my dominant right eye and led to tiredness. Somehow, our physio at Northants, Barry Goudriaan, suspected what was wrong from watching me in practice, and a second visit to the optician before Edgbaston resolved the problem. However, the eye takes a fortnight to adjust to a new fitting. The article hinted that now those two weeks were up I would be a different man in the field.

It all sounded nice in theory, and I wish it was that simple. Unfortunately my fielding had been short of the mark for years rather than weeks. What really amazed me was the way the article found its way on to the news pages. Things really were moving forward if editors thought I was worth that sort of coverage. I had only just come to terms with seeing my name and picture in the sports sections. The other players had grown used to me asking them lots of questions but this time they wanted me to explain what was happening. Not being an expert on the human eye, I was as puzzled as they were.

Until the Test I had never played anything more than a second-team game at Trent Bridge. It is one of the prettiest grounds in the country if not the world, but the square had problems with broken roots, which meant the surface did not always hold together. We thought it looked dry and might bounce and turn later on. Obviously that meant the spinner would come into play, but I didn't feel concerned about possibly bowling in the fourth innings. I take a fairly simple approach and there always seems more pressure when the pitch doesn't turn because it is then harder to take wickets. I also had quite a bit of experience bowling on the turning surfaces at Northampton and had been successful enough to get into the England team in the first place. People can over-complicate things by spending too much time peering at the square. I remember a story about the Australia spinner Stuart MacGill when he was asked to comment on a pitch. He said, 'It's twenty-two yards long and that's all I care about.'

This one couldn't have been too bad for the pace bowlers either. For the third time I was barely needed in the first innings, sending down only five overs as we skittled out Sri Lanka for 231 after Mahela Jayawardene won the toss, removing any chance I might have had of bowling last. With Muralitharan clearly going to have a say, we knew the importance of getting a first-innings lead, but once again we let them off the hook from being 139 for 8. Their recovery underlined the importance Duncan Fletcher places on a lower order being able to contribute a few runs, or at least being able to hang in while a better player has a go at the other end.

Our own first innings never really got going. Sanath Jayasuriya had flown into the country and although he looked a bit rusty with the bat he gave Muralitharan good support as a second spinner. He does not turn the ball too much but he is very low and slow, and difficult to hit. That makes him a very effective one-day player and even in this match he went for little more than two runs an over, as well as taking three wickets, including a big one in Andrew Flintoff. By now we knew that Freddie was having problems with his left ankle. He needed to go off the field a few times when we bowled and towards the end it was possible to detect a slight limp. But as captain he always wanted to be in the thick of the action.

If I am being honest, I have mixed thoughts about their second innings. Unless Muralitharan turned an ankle we probably knew, even though we did not say so, that their total of 322 presented a massive challenge batting last. Being more selfish, I will remember it as my first five-wicket haul for England. Up to that point I thought I had bowled reasonably well on the whole, but usually in a supporting role. Now, in my sixth game, I felt I was able to show what I could do when conditions were more helpful and spin was the most attacking option.

There may be a tendency to think that all Asian batsmen play the same way, but I felt that the Sri Lankans in general were different from the Indians I had encountered over the winter. They have the same bat speed but their hands are very quick, allowing them to adjust and direct their shots that split second later. Beyond that I don't agree that players from a different country have a set way of playing. Their openers Upul Tharanga and Michael Vandort played just as differently as Wasim Jaffer and Virender Sehwag during the winter.

Tharanga is not quite in the Sehwag category, but he certainly likes to give the ball a hit. He soon forced me to the off-side boundary and then lifted a six, but three balls later I managed to take revenge when I got one to bounce a little more than he expected. An inside edge looped to Alastair Cook at short leg, and I was on my way. A lot of the credit should go to the captain for having the confidence to keep that close fielder in when Tharanga was looking for the opportunity to attack. By this stage the ball was turning off the pitch, not just out of the footmarks, and I knew that I had to keep hitting the right spot, give nothing away and wait for the chances to fall. I did not have to wait long in the case of Jayasuriya, who went down to try to sweep my first ball to him and was given out leg-before by Darrell Hair. This was becoming a mammoth spell and Farveez Maharoof became my third wicket when he left a ball that went straight on.

Had we been able to get the last three wickets quickly we would have been in with a chance. But Chaminda Vaas had been a real thorn in our side throughout the series, using his experience to just hang in and hang in at times when we thought we had broken through. The extra 48 runs he helped to add before the end of the third day were crucial because we went to bed knowing we would have to chase something in the region of 300 instead of 250 on a pitch that was not going to get easier.

Eventually we wrapped up the innings the following morning. I spun one enough to bowl Lasith Malinga around his legs and with four wickets I was starting to feel quite excited at the prospect of a fifth. Muralitharan was only going to play one way, so I knew I had a chance as long as I could keep spinning the ball, because he was bound to misfire sooner or later. Lo and behold, a big heave soared towards long off and even before Andrew Strauss completed the catch I could see Andrew Flintoff out of the corner of my eye running across to celebrate. He likes to give a playful neck-lock or arm-twist, but because he doesn't know his own strength it pays to anticipate what will happen. As Strauss held on, I took a big deep breath just before Freddie could hit me with one of his brick-wall hugs. Once he'd let go and I could breathe again he ushered me forward to lead the team back into the pavilion as the members stood up to clap.

At the press conference on the fourth evening I'd said that 350 would be gettable, but that was wishful thinking. It would have taken a tremendous effort to score even the 325 we eventually needed. If anything, Sri Lanka may have felt under pressure being in such a good situation. Our openers Marcus Trescothick and Andrew Strauss started really well to give us a little bit of hope. Muralitharan, though, is at his hardest when you first go in, which is why the loss of one wicket can lead to a second or third in quick time. Once Trescothick had misread a doosra, the writing was on the wall. Muralitharan proceeded to take 8 for 26 from 17.3 overs and was on course to become the third bowler to take all ten in a Test innings until Matthew Hoggard was run out.

Critics used words such as 'limp' and 'soft' to describe our batting but I prefer to think of a quote I saw later from Nasser Hussain. Apparently, he said on television that there is no shame in being bowled out by a genius. This is a guy who spins the ball so much that he can turn it into the side of the net as a trick. When we don't play well as a team we acknowledge it, but this was an occasion where we had to admire one of the all-time great bowlers. As a spinner myself, I would have enjoyed watching his display against any other side. His final figures of 8 for 70 were the best ever in a Test match at Trent Bridge, which puts his performance into context.

Preparations are very thorough and we all have access to footage of Muralitharan and the other bowlers on our computers. We can see how he bowls the doosra and how to tell it apart from his stock ball. From what I saw that afternoon, batsmen were no more nervous than usual when they went out. Before we go out we can knock a few balls around the dressing room just to get the feel for what might happen, we play a few practice shots to get the hands and feet going. But clearly the Sri Lankans were on a high, and no practice can ever replicate the situation of going out against a confident side who feel they are on the verge of a great win.

When the ninth wicket fell the scoreboard read 153. In other words, we were just under halfway there. Victory seemed unlikely. As I picked up my bat and started to walk towards the door the final encouraging words came from Flintoff. 'Enjoy yourself, mate,' he said, giving me one of his firm pats on the back. 'There's nothing to lose.'

Good advice, I thought. Back in the dressing room I'd decided that the best option was to try to sweep Muralitharan. I practised getting down into the right position for the shot. And there wasn't much point worrying about the doosra. I was pretty sure I wouldn't be able to spot it, so why let it complicate my thinking? As I emerged from the pavilion the cheers seemed to be louder than when I'd led the side in before lunch. I guess crowds like an underdog and I think, like Freddie, they were hoping to see a bit of fun after the flurry of wickets.

According to the scorecard on Cricinfo, I was out there for 27 minutes. It felt more like seven. Everything happened so quickly. It was like being on one of those rides at a theme park where the adrenalin starts rushing through your body. I hit Muralitharan down the ground and then struck him again. He decided to put a man back. I looked up to the balcony and could see people laughing and clapping. At the other end, Liam Plunkett was smiling as well. He couldn't believe it. For those few minutes the force seemed to be with me. Time to try out that sweep. I went down, swung, felt the ball hit the sweet spot of the bat and watched it go high over the boundary on the leg side for the first six of my England career.

If the crowd were amazed, then how do you think I felt? Or Muralitharan, for that matter. It seemed like carnival time at Trent Bridge as people began to shout and dance in the stands. The mood had suddenly changed. It was a case of 'don't look closely at the scoreboard, just enjoy the moment'. I was so excited I wanted to do my little jig, but that isn't easy when you're wearing pads and gloves. It is well known that the Sri Lankans can be a bit chirpy on the field. Kumar Sangakkara looked at me and said, 'You're enjoying yourself here, aren't you?' I couldn't deny it. I'd not had so much fun in years.

I've been asked since whether that shot was premeditated. The honest answer? All those shots were premeditated. And we all knew that it couldn't last. Plunkett, Sangakkara, Muralitharan, the crowd, the guys watching from the balcony – and me especially. Sri Lanka had so many runs in the bag that I could have hoisted Muralitharan a few more times and we would still have fallen short. I suppose the annoying thing was that after a shot like that I got out to Sanath Jayasuriya at the other end.

Here's a confession. I knew exactly the odds you could have got on me hitting a six in that game. Betting is a strict no-no for players, so before the ICC's Anti-Corruption Unit get on the case let me stress that I was aware of it only because of the display in a bookmaker's window in Nottingham, which caught my eye before the game. I am not a gambler, but I stopped out of interest when I saw my name. I was 33–1 to hit that six, and I think 40–1 to get a catch and 45–1 to get a run-out. With odds like that last one you can see why bookies win in the long run. The funny thing is that a few of my mates in Luton had seen something similar. They aren't bound by the same strict rules, so I pretended to be upset that they didn't have enough faith in me to put on a few pounds at 33 to one.

Once we'd stopped laughing in the dressing room the disappointment started to set in. There was not a lot we could do at Trent Bridge for the reason Nasser gave: we were beaten by a genius. At the same time, Muralitharan had so much going for him even before the luck of the toss. Would we have been given a green seamer for Steve Harmison in Colombo or Galle? I can't imagine the Sri Lankans hopping around on the back foot in the way that we were made to grope at Muralitharan. But for all that, we knew that the blame really rested with ourselves. We had plenty of opportunities to win at Lord's but let them pass by. Sri Lanka are too good a side to be let off the hook like that. The funny thing was that I'd now played in two 1–1 draws. The first in India felt like a victory, this one felt like defeat.

I managed to speak to Muralitharan for a few minutes afterwards. I wanted to know what he thought about my bowling. Without getting too technical, he said that my seam position was good and that he liked my action. He said that the Sri Lankans had talked about how to play me and had been impressed. That was a major compliment coming from a guy who will almost certainly put the record as leading Test wicket-taker into the stratosphere before he retires. Andrew Flintoff knew Muralitharan well from Lancashire and said that he was a nice, approachable guy. That proved to be true. He was happy to talk to me. Facing him is one of the strangest experiences of my career because he is so unusual. Trent Bridge was the first time we came face to face, at least with me at the batsman's end. I'd heard that you could actually hear the ball whistle as it came down because he spins it so much. I wouldn't say it was quite like that, but I did have a helmet on and there was a lot of background noise.

Like the Dhoni drop and catch, that short passage of play seemed to have an effect on my profile out of all proportion to what it actually meant in the context of the game. I think people liked the way that I had a go and that I managed to achieve something – hit a few runs in this case – beyond what they thought was my level. I said afterwards that I couldn't understand why I was getting so much attention when I'd played only six matches and not, if truth be told, really played much of a part in the two wins. Guys such as Andrew Flintoff and Kevin Pietersen deserved to be getting the headlines. They had achieved far more than I had.

I read somewhere that people were happy to see somebody from a different culture being able to integrate so quickly and be so happy in an England side. That was a bit heavy for me. All I ever wanted to do was play cricket for England. I've never felt distinct from any of the other guys in the side, even if I stand out with my beard and my patka. I am a cricketer like Flintoff, Pietersen and all the others. Nothing more, and nothing less. My attitude has always been that if my presence in the England side helps kids from an Indian background to start playing cricket and finding out what a wonderful pastime it is, then great. And if it encourages non-Indians, then that is great as well. Other people have the right to analyse but, as far as I am concerned, that is as profound as it gets.

When I went back to Northampton after the series there was a huge stack of mail to collect. People wanted autographs or signed photos. Some of them sent pictures they had taken themselves for me to sign, and in a couple of cases I wouldn't have minded keeping them for my own collection. Apart from being taken aback on a personal level, the mailbag made me realise the place that cricket has in the country after the 2005 Ashes. Had it not been for that success I don't think there would be the same level of interest in players such as Saj Mahmood, Alastair Cook and me, who have come in since. Young players for many years will owe a big debt to Michael Vaughan and his side.

8

ONWARDS AND UPWARDS

Not being part of England's one-day squad, I headed back to the Northamptonshire dressing room almost as soon as the Sri Lanka series had reached its disappointing end. The next few weeks proved a new and invigorating experience. Twenty20 has really captured the imagination of the public since the first games in 2003 but until then my commitments had been restricted to a spectating role. Some of the time I watched from inside the dressing room but on other occasions I sat in the stands and joined in with the singing and clapping that helps to create the vibrant atmosphere now associated with the format. When somebody hit a four or six I would wave my cardboard placard with the rest – although I did draw a line at leaping onto the bouncy castle. I wasn't sure whether I would be asked to put on the coloured clothing in 2006. I was a big hitter in my early days and the shot against Muttiah Muralitharan proved this, but I needed to be consistent, and my fielding needed to be polished. But coach Kepler Wessels thought it would be an ideal opportunity to work on these weaker areas of my game, and I needed no second invitation to give it a go.

It is easy to see why Twenty20 has been so successful, first in England and now in the rest of the cricket-playing world. Counties were very quick to market the game and bring in new fans. Runs arrive fast – in fact everything rushes along in top gear. As a player it is great to see the stands full. To watch those hundreds of people including women and children filing through the gates at Wantage Road is a really encouraging sight, given the small number who usually turn up for Championship matches. Every county needs its faithful members, the people who put in so much for their clubs, but the game has to attract additional supporters to survive and prosper. Already I think people are looking back on the tremendous success of Twenty20 and wondering why they didn't think of it earlier.

The fact that Kepler was so keen for me to take part shows that it also has a role to play in developing young players. I know from experience that there is a gulf between county and international cricket. One difference is in the size of the crowds. A bigger gate creates a buzz around a place that you always find at Test or one-day internationals, so anything that can help to bridge the gap is worthwhile. The pace of Twenty20 also adds to the pressure on players at all times. Northants had reached the quarter-finals in the previous two seasons and we were taking it seriously again this time. In the build-up we spent a lot of time against the bowling machine trying to hit balls into unusual areas that we thought might be unprotected. The reverse sweep was another shot to receive a lot of attention in practice. That was good for me, because it created opportunities to counter batsmen when they shaped to play that shot.

With so many people watching who are new to cricket I believe there is also a responsibility to innovate and entertain. When we go out there we can let our hair down – though not literally, in my own case. I did find I had to adjust my expectations. I remember guys coming over to pat me on the back at the end of an over and say 'great bowling, Monty' when I'd gone for more than a run a ball. I think my worst experience was against Somerset when Justin Langer hit 97 and my figures read 4–0–51–2. The best moment, without any question, came against Worcestershire at Worcester when I ran out Daryl Mitchell with a direct hit from backward square leg. If only Duncan Fletcher had been there to see it! That moment alone justified Kepler's decision to put me in the side.

Contrary to all the initial, doom-laden predictions, spinners have been very effective in Twenty20, with Nayan Doshi of Surrey and Leicestershire's cunning captain Jeremy Snape leading the way. Snape is highly qualified and even runs his own business in sports psychology. He worked with England during the 2007 World Cup. You don't need quite that level of intelligence to be able to succeed, but one thing I did discover was the importance of keeping an alert mind at all times. My role was to try to outguess the batsman, to work out whether he was going to come down the wicket or squeeze the ball away square. Any variety came from changes of pace rather than spin. In a game lasting a total of 40 overs the pitch will not really deteriorate and turn sharply, although we did have a surface for our home game against Somerset that raised interest from the ECB's pitch panel. Shame, because that one was a real thriller, ending as a last-ball tie.

Once again we managed to qualify for the last eight. Unfortunately I couldn't play in the quarter-final against Nottinghamshire, which we lost heavily. Unfortunately, too, when I rejoined Northants after the Pakistan series, Kepler had left the county in unhappy circumstances. Some of the players had complained to the PCA – effectively our union – because they found his regime too strict and even dictatorial. As soon as that happened a change became inevitable, and I actually discovered that he was going via a text message from Kepler himself. It all seemed very abrupt and on a personal level I found it sad that he was leaving. I did not have a problem on the disciplinary side and he always treated me fairly. He had the gift of keeping things simple. Yes, I suppose he was strict, and he liked everybody to do things his way, but I always knew exactly what he wanted and never doubted that he wanted to improve me as a cricketer. I think he succeeded.

Having appointed Kepler from outside to replace a club stalwart in Bob Carter, the county reverted to Plan A this time in promoting David Capel from his position of Academy director. All of us apart from perhaps the overseas players had worked with Capel before and knew of the service he had given to Northants for more than two decades. It would have been a popular appointment at any time and when I returned towards the end of August there were happier faces in the dressing room. He has an opportunity to show what a good coach he is and I think all of us as players have a responsibility to work hard to try to improve after the way that Kepler left.

There is so much international cricket around the world these days that Test series are compressed as tightly as possible, with back-to-back matches and often just a single game slotted in for the tourists at some point between those fixtures. It becomes difficult to keep track of what is happening at county level. For regular contracted players in the one-day and Test teams, England has become the equivalent of the county side because that is where they play most of their cricket. Those as young and talented as Alastair Cook and Ian Bell could easily finish their careers with more runs for England than for Essex or Warwickshire.

Continuity is a good thing, although it felt different when we gathered in July for the series against Pakistan. Andrew Flintoff was missing because of the problem with his left ankle that had deteriorated through the games against Sri Lanka. As things turned out, he was to miss the rest of the season, but initially we thought he would be available after the First Test at Lord's. Andrew Strauss declared himself a 'stand-in for a stand-in' because Michael Vaughan, the first choice, was also unfit. That made the captaincy a difficult job, but Strauss gradually imposed himself and didn't make the mistake of trying to be like Flintoff. As you hear the crowds singing up and down the country, there really is only one Freddie Flintoff. When he doesn't play we effectively have to replace two players with one – and that's even before you count his sheer presence as a character.

I think the biggest difference between Flintoff and Strauss was in their style. Flintoff led from the front, and while Strauss set an example with his batting at the top of the order he maybe thinks laterally a little bit more on the field. An example springs to mind easily, from the final Test at The Oval, when he decided to put in a leg slip for Mohammad Yousuf. As a left-arm bowler I turn the ball away from Yousuf, but there was a tennis-ball type of bounce in the pitch and Strauss figured that if a delivery held its line, he might glance one at catchable height just wide of the wicketkeeper. No captain had ever put in a man there to my bowling but I could see what Strauss was thinking, even if it didn't produce a wicket on that occasion. It gave Yousuf something new to consider, and now that the seed has been sown I'm sure I will try it again at some stage when the conditions are right. During the 2005 Ashes, Vaughan earned a lot of praise for his imaginative field placings and Strauss may have learned something from his team-mate.

From a personal point of view, I knew that the series would not be easy because Pakistan are such good players of spin. In fact their three, four, five of Younis Khan, Yousuf and Inzamam-ul-Haq is probably the best in the world, Australia included. I decided that the key was to hold my nerve. I knew they would go for their shots. There would be periods when I was being hit to all parts, but in those situations I could draw on my recent experience of Twenty20. My mind also went back the six months or so to India. Now as then, I would keep a simple mechanism and make sure the basics were sound. As long as my action remained strong, I knew I would be able to bowl ball after ball in roughly the same place, and small variations in the pitch as well as slight changes of angle and pace would create enough differences to keep the batsmen on their toes. There is nothing special about me. The key to my bowling is retaining control. If I lose that ability to bowl dot ball after dot ball, my days will be numbered.

Although we did not win at Lord's we felt we put in a really good team performance. Most of us contributed at some point. Had it not been for a brilliant double hundred by Yousuf, I am sure we would have taken a 1–0 lead. Strauss was criticised by some of the media for continuing to bat on the fifth morning instead of declaring overnight. We began the day with a lead of 331 and wanted to put the possibility of defeat completely out of the equation so early in the series. Pakistan had enough talent to be able to chase 332 in a full day, especially on a pitch that would not offer us a great deal of assistance. Without Flintoff we had been forced to go into the game with only four front-line bowlers. Matthew Hoggard removed Salman Butt with the first ball of the innings but, as it turned out, we could only take three more wickets. Clearly the extra half-hour in the morning when we could have bowled would not have made much difference. The contest petered out and the crowd were left simply to enjoy the sunshine.

If we missed Flintoff with the ball, Ian Bell more than filled in with the bat. His typically composed hundred was the first of three in successive Tests, and with Alastair Cook and Paul Collingwood also raising their bats in the first innings we were able to control the game from the first day. We never let that initiative slip. It would have been interesting to see who the selectors would have left out for the next match if Flintoff had recovered. One of the batsmen would have been very, very unlucky.

When I think back to that game now, the name of Mohammad Yousuf springs straight to mind. I had not bowled to him before Lord's. Like all the best batsmen he picked up the length very early, which allowed him to get into good positions to play his shots. Although he never dominated the bowling, he always had more runs on the board than we thought. Even his boundaries were gentle – a fine cut here and a stroked drive there with minimal follow-through. When he got to a hundred we thought he was nearer to fifty. At least we were not alone in suffering. In 2006, Yousuf hit an incredible 1,788 Test runs, breaking the record of Viv Richards for the highest aggregate in a calendar year. Three of his nine centuries came against us.

Given his form, I was delighted to take his wicket three times over the four matches, including the second innings at Lord's. He let one go pitching on middle expecting it to turn away. Instead the ball went straight on for a clear leg-before. I found it funny to read the accounts of the dismissal in the papers the following day. Whenever you take a wicket people think there must have been something special about the delivery. This one was written up as a clever arm ball that Yousuf failed to pick. It's nice to be thought of so highly, but the truth is much less glamorous: a routine ball for some reason didn't turn. Of course, it works the other way as well. Sometimes what you think of as a brilliant ball can easily go unrewarded because it turns too much. Just as a good striker celebrates every goal that comes his way even if the ball rebounds in off his backside, you will never hear a bowler complain about the way he accumulates his wickets.

After seven Tests I thought I had made a reasonable start to my England career. But I feared it might come crashing to an end when the squad was announced for the Second Test at Old Trafford. Jamie Dalrymple had been one of the best players in the one-day series against Sri Lanka and when he was named in the 13 it seemed clear to me that the selectors were thinking of a different approach. With Flintoff now finally ruled out for the rest of the season to undergo an operation on his ankle, Dalrymple could step in as the all-rounder. That would allow David Graveney and his colleagues to pick four specialist seam bowlers. I knew that Duncan Fletcher liked three-dimensional players and there was an opportunity to bat at number eight, which I would relish since my ideal scenario is to be an all-rounder batting at number seven or eight and doing my usual bowling stint.

Nevertheless I was pleasantly surprised when Dalrymple was released from the squad after practice the day before the game. But his original selection had given me a jolt, which perhaps I needed. Although I never assumed that a place was automatically mine – and never will – this reminded me that I had to work on my batting and fielding at every opportunity, so that I could bring more to the team than the overs of spin they needed. I was relieved to keep my place and thought that the time had come to do more than simply chip in, especially as we were coming towards the second half of the season when pitches generally give more help to the slow bowlers. I told myself that while I was still relatively inexperienced – a year before I had considered myself a student first and a cricketer second – I had been handed the responsibility and was taking up a place in the side because the selectors wanted me to do a job now, not to prepare me for the years ahead.

I don't know if it was coincidence, but Andrew Strauss said the same things in more general terms at the team meeting on the eve of the game. He pointed out that a few of us had made solid enough starts to our England careers, but needed to adopt the same mentality as the senior players instead of perhaps leaving it to Kevin Pietersen, Marcus Trescothick, Steve Harmison and Matthew Hoggard. It was the job of all of us to produce match-winning performances even though we were not considered world-class players. If we could all provide a little bit more, then the draws would soon turn into wins. It was a very effective address. Strauss, my old training buddy, probably thought that he could impose his own personality on the side a little more, knowing that Flintoff's absence gave him three successive games in charge. Nobody could argue with the tone of his message, and nobody did.

His words clearly had the desired effect. We won by an innings and 120 runs inside three days and Strauss said afterwards that we came close to playing the perfect game. It was also my best performance for England up to that point, with eight wickets including five of the first six to fall in the second innings. But Harmison was the real star. When he gets his rhythm right he is the best out-and-out fast bowler in the world and this time the force was really with him as he finished the game with figures of 11 for 76. Pakistan had anticipated the difficulties. In London, they purchased a marble-topped slab of granite, which they then used in the nets to generate sharp bounce, simulating the threat they expected. There was nothing wrong with the idea, which showed the foresight you would associate with their coach, Bob Woolmer. But Harmison proved that nothing could entirely reproduce the real thing.

I'm not a great one for reading pitches, but even I could see there was a bit of pace in this one when I took a peek the day before the game. And I think it gave us all a real lift in the field when Harmison ran in for his first over, fizzing the ball through with real pace and hostility. Imran Farhat went almost straight away and as we gathered in the middle I said to Harmison, 'You know you're on for six wickets here.' He gave me a playful slap on the head and just said, 'I hope you're right.' But the innings was over before tea and as he led us off with the remarkable analysis of 13–7–19–6, I remember telling him, 'You should listen to me, mate.' He bowled really intelligently because most of his wickets came with balls pitched up. It would have been easy to get carried away with the bounce and overdo the short stuff. Batsmen were reluctant to get onto the front foot because they knew that a very nasty bouncer could be directed at their heads at any moment. That threat created the opportunities. In the same way, you often hear it said that if a batsman thinks a pitch is spinning, then it doesn't matter whether it is or not. So much of the game is played in the mind.

People might think that I do not have much in common with Harmison, but I always enjoy the time we spend together. Although our backgrounds are a little bit different we are both down-to-earth in our own ways. One thing we discovered in India was a shared love of pool and darts. Away from home he usually has a room next to his best mate Andrew Flintoff, and they carried a dartboard around on that particular tour, pinning it to one of the walls wherever we stayed. Unfortunately I am not as accurate with the arrows as I am with the ball and that first 180 is proving difficult.

I did manage to play my own relatively small part in the first innings at Old Trafford, supporting Harmison with three wickets, including the one to spark Pakistan's collapse. With the minutes ticking towards lunch, a ball to Yousuf kept a shade low. After that I expected him to be very watchful until the break, then come out and start afresh. Instead, he shaped to cut the next delivery and got a thin nick instead, which Geraint Jones snapped up with deceptive ease. Those little chances to a spinner are always harder than they look because there is so little time to react. But Pakistan were never as threatening again once Yousuf had gone. In all, their last eight wickets fell for only 29 as they crashed to 119 all out.

For me, it was especially pleasing to see the back of Shahid Afridi. Having suffered on my debut when he scored a blistering hundred for Leicestershire, I knew his potential only too well and I thought he might be in the mood for a repeat when he began to sledge me in Punjabi. 'I'm going to hit you now,' he said, backing up those brave words almost immediately with a big six. And as if to emphasise the point he turned to me with a menacing smile, and added, 'Do you believe me now? I wasn't joking.'

This was the kind of assault I anticipated when I planned for the series. At least I had my own pre-series plan upon which I could fall back. Now, more than ever, I needed to hold my nerve and not get drawn into the private battle by either saying something back to Afridi or pushing the ball through too quickly. At the same time he clearly wasn't going to change his own approach, especially as Strauss decided against putting in a deep cover. The captain was almost daring him to hit over the top again. Two balls later, he went for another big hit but slightly misjudged the flight, sending a huge top edge towards Kevin Pietersen. As he left the crease, Afridi did not say a word, in English, Punjabi or any other language.

Sledging is one of those areas that seems to fascinate spectators. I guess people like to know what is being said in the middle because they think that it spices up the game. It is a myth, however, to imagine that players come out with one witty comment after another. Most of the time things are said by a fielder to one of his colleagues, but loud enough to be heard by the batsman. During an innings in Australia the following winter I remember Shane Warne at slip saying to Adam Gilchrist, 'This is going to be a yorker.' Brett Lee promptly ran in and delivered a bouncer. You get used to taking everything with a pinch of salt. A lot of the time I am concentrating so much that I either don't hear what is being said or the words simply do not register. My way is just to keep quiet and play.

People react in different ways, and I will not criticise anybody who likes a bit of banter. I know that Pietersen is one who doesn't mind exchanging the odd word because it fires him up. For some reason he seems to attract comments in any case. I guess it comes down to personality. If I started behaving like Warne when I bowled, it would look silly and feel wrong because that is not in my character. There is every chance that my bowling would also suffer a loss of focus. Being relatively quiet does not make me any less aggressive. I think it is obvious how much I want to win when I celebrate a wicket.

Back to Old Trafford, and with Shoaib Akhtar still injured, Pakistan did not have anybody with the pace of Harmison to challenge our batsmen in the same way. Mohammad Asif might have been dangerous because of his height but he, too, was not playing. Alastair Cook hit another hundred and Ian Bell's 106 not out was one of the most attractive innings I have seen in my short time with England. Everything seemed to be going right for us. Even when Harmison pulled up with what appeared to be a side strain on the second evening – potentially a very nasty injury for a bowler because those are the muscles you stretch in the delivery stride – the early fears proved to be unfounded.

With a first-innings lead of 342 and with a good attack for the pitch, we knew that victory was within sight. Surely Pakistan could not do to us what Sri Lanka had managed at Lord's. 'Let's make sure we nail it this time,' Strauss said before we went out on the third morning, perhaps thinking back to those frustrations earlier in the season. Once again I spent a long time bowling in tandem with Harmison and the combination continued to work well: I could draw the batsmen forward while he pegged them back. And the pitch was helping both of us. I'm not sure I have turned the ball as far consistently in a Test in England – certainly not as early as the third day.

Our catching was also top class and Geraint Jones took a really sharp stumping to account for Yousuf with his toe on the line as he overbalanced slightly stretching forward. The only shame was that Duncan Fletcher could not be credited on the scorecard for his part in the dismissal. In the build-up I had been working a lot with the coach on my body alignment. I wanted to make sure that my feet were in the right position on delivery. If they get too far apart in that stride, everything else can be thrown out of sync. The body is like a machine and one small alteration can ruin the whole operation. During the lunch break, Fletcher took me to one side in his usual, quiet way. He wanted me to lower the pace and give the ball a bit more air to try to confuse the batsmen about its flight and give it more chance to bite off the surface. That is exactly how Yousuf fell first ball after the break. When I turned to look at the dressing room after the handshakes and high fives were over, I gave a signal to Fletcher as if to say, 'Spot on, boss.'

With Pakistan's key player gone it was just a case of taking the chances when they came along. If the Yousuf wicket was down to sharp observation and planning, then Inzamam's dismissal contained an element of fortune as he jabbed the ball onto his boot and watched it balloon up for an easy catch. I managed to get Younis Khan with an arm ball and completed my second five-for in Tests when Faisal Iqbal edged to slip. Harmison finished it off so that, between us, we took 19 of the 20 wickets over both innings. If we could carry that form into the Third Test a week later we had every chance of winning our first series since the Ashes.

Headingley has become known over the past four or five years for the stag parties and other groups who turn up wearing fancy dress. This is especially popular now on Fridays and Saturdays. And, for the first time, I became aware of people wearing cardboard 'Monty masks', many of them supplemented by false beards and a bandana or pretend patka. One particular bunch of five or six also wore Superman costumes. Now that really did give me something to live up to. It just so happened that they were in the seats close to the boundary. I couldn't help laughing every time I walked towards them at the end of an over. It was very weird, when I heard a guy shout, 'You've got them on the rack, Monty,' to look up and see my own spitting image. 'Concentrate, concentrate,' I had to keep saying to myself. It was funny to think of people being in fancy dress when I looked like that in real life. I suppose that is one of the consequences of looking a bit different from the rest of the England team.

In the months since Headingley, I've grown used to posing for photographs with impersonators. Towards the end of 2006, Dave Parsooth, who looks after my working arrangements, received a nice letter from a man called Richard Horswell, along with a copy of a picture taken at a county game against Derbyshire. There were three Montys in it – me in the middle sandwiched between his son and a friend. I mentioned this in my column in the *Daily*

Mail, and Mr Horswell wrote: 'Monty said some very nice things to the two boys and gave each of them one of his personal patkas. He was already a legend in their eyes and he has moved beyond that.' Words like that are always very nice.

Unfortunately, a very small section of the Headingley crowd let themselves down and gave the game the sort of publicity it can do without. Sajid Mahmood was on the receiving end of some unpleasant comments from a group of Pakistan supporters, who were basically questioning his right to play for England. Although I don't think any of the media picked it up, I must admit that I was also subjected to a nasty word or two. I am not going to repeat any of them here. Fortunately, you do not hear that sort of thing very often. Let's just say that as my mate Saj was born in Bolton while I come from Luton, these people – and I can't stress how few we are talking about – had clearly not done much research.

My response was to laugh off the bad comments. Most of the crowd were on my side and on England's side. I received so much cheering and encouragement over the five days, there was no way I was going to allow the negatives to ruin the occasion and draw attention to people who did not deserve the publicity. By not responding or even being seen to be angry, the situation passed. But Saj did get upset. I think a few of the words were just too close to the bone. Maybe he was the target for more abuse because of the rivalry between Yorkshire and his own Lancashire. His roots are also in Pakistan, whereas mine are in India. A week or so earlier, Saj had said that he supported Pakistan as a young child. Perhaps some people took offence at that. At one point, after he had taken a wicket, I told him not to worry about the crowd. 'Ignore them, man,' I said. 'Just focus on your bowling and your areas and you'll be fine.' I think the experience served to fire him up, because he discovered a really good pace and rhythm to finish with figures of 4 for 22 in the second innings. That was the most emphatic answer of all.

Saj was a big factor in our second successive win – an incredible effort given that Pakistan scored 538 in their first innings, including 363 in a third-wicket stand between Younis Khan and Mohammad Yousuf. In the old days a victory would have been unthinkable after conceding so many runs, because the Pakistan innings would have spanned at least two days. Given that we had already posted 515, the contest would have petered out into a dull draw. Times have changed. Batsmen are so much more aggressive now that a run rate of four per over almost goes without comment. The running between the wickets is sharper and I think the advent of Twenty20 has encouraged batsmen to play their shots. Australia showed what was possible under Steve Waugh, with Adam Gilchrist leading the way. The rest of the world has watched and decided to follow their lead. For example, that stand between Younis and Yousuf lasted 84 overs – in other words, six overs less than the equivalent of a full day.

At 447 for 3 the sky must have seemed the limit for those two. But, as if to underline how quickly a game can change, we took three wickets in ten balls, a spell that ended with the comical dismissal of Inzamam. This really was one that couldn't have been planned, and the weirdest wicket I have taken at any level. The problem began when he lost his balance trying to sweep and saw the ball falling towards the stumps via his midriff. His momentum caused him to keep toppling and as he hit the ground he lost all control and somehow managed to remove the bails. Poor Inzy could hardly come to terms with what had happened and if my celebrations were relatively muted, I think I was in a state of disbelief as well. You don't like to laugh at another player's bad luck, but it did look funny on the big screen.

Pitches don't tend to turn much at Headingley, so every wicket a spinner manages to take deserves to be cherished. I managed to get a couple more in orthodox fashion, and when I slumped into one of the comfy dressing-room chairs after bowling close to 50 overs I was looking forward to watching our own batsmen post a stiff fourth-innings target. A century from Andrew Strauss pointed us in the right direction but it was a plucky innings by Chris Read, on his recall after more than a year, that I think inflicted the real damage on Pakistan. Our eventual lead of 322 looked defendable, but without Read's half-century I am sure it would have been within the range of Pakistan.

Not being a member of the 2005 side, I can only imagine how it must have felt for the players to drive to Old Trafford on the last day of that Australia game with thousands of people hanging around outside the ground, desperate to get in. The final day here at Headingley is the closest I have known. Tickets cannot usually be bought in advance for day five so it is a case of spectators having to turn up and pay at the gates. When we arrived a couple of hours or so before the start, the queues were already stretching back for what seemed like hundreds of metres. 'I hope we don't let these people down,' I said nervously to Saj Mahmood before we went out for our warm-ups. 'No, we'll be fine,' he replied, obviously a lot more laid-back than I was.

In the end he was right. The key moment came when Paul Collingwood ran out Mohammad Yousuf with a direct hit from backward point, the position he has made his own in one-day cricket. By going for such a sharp run to a brilliant fielder, Pakistan suggested they were trying to win rather than playing for a draw. But every wicket brought the crowd to life and I felt a huge wave of support behind me whenever I came on to bowl. Saj was in the middle of a really determined spell and although I couldn't match his effort I did manage to produce what I still think of as my best single ball for England to bowl Younis Khan. The fact that he was in such brilliant form – which was good enough to earn him the man-of-the-match award – and is such a wonderful player of spin in any case made my managing to breach his defence incredibly satisfying.

Wicketkeepers usually have a better idea of these things than the bowler because they are watching from directly behind the wicket in a steadier position. In the huddle after the high fives, Chris Read told me, 'I knew he would struggle to keep that one out from the moment it left your hand.' I must admit that everything felt right. It came out at precisely the right moment and landed where I wanted almost to the millimetre, pitching on middle and leg stump, drawing him forward and turning the perfect distance – enough to beat the bat but not so far that it missed the stumps. As it clipped the top of off I just thought to myself, 'Wow!' I must admit that I watch a replay of it from time to time and always break into a smile when the ball hits the surface and starts to deviate. For a spin bowler it doesn't get much better than that. After the game Younis came to me to say 'well bowled', which I thought was a kind gesture from such a good batsman.

Read finished off the innings with a good stumping when Inzamam came down the wicket in an attempt to strike me over the top. With another 168 runs needed and the last pair at the crease, he did not have much option except to go down fighting. That gave me six for the match, but in the circumstances I would happily have given that last wicket to Saj Mahmood to complete what would have been his first five in an innings for England. He was bowling at the other end and the way the ball was coming out I'd have backed him to end the match within the first few deliveries of his next over.

The important thing was that we ended our post-Ashes duck

and Andrew Strauss had won his first series in charge. I thought we were good value because we had been on top at Lord's even before the convincing wins at Old Trafford and Headingley. Strauss's words before the first of those victories clearly had a very positive effect. Newer players as well as the established guys had made a big impact. It was going a bit far to suggest that the Ashes side had broken up, because Michael Vaughan, Simon Jones and Ashley Giles were all likely to return when they recovered from injury. But at least people could see some strength in depth among the squad and in English cricket generally.

I guess it was natural to think ahead to the coming Australia tour. In my case I still didn't feel assured of a place despite all the good publicity in the newspapers. I was still relatively new to Test cricket and knew that Giles was making good progress after surgery on his hip. He would be first choice because of his experience in 2005. The word was that Duncan Fletcher wanted to use that side as a strong core for the rematch. With Giles certain to go, I wondered if Jamie Dalrymple would take the second spot because he could play as an all-rounder if the coach ever felt the need to go with two spinners, at Sydney for example. I had to make the most of every opportunity to bowl for England and keep working on my batting and fielding to reach the standard required.

In other words, when I arrived at The Oval I had no thoughts at all beyond two days of preparation and five days of hard cricket. I came away a week later with my head spinning, still trying to come to terms with one of the strangest endings in the history of Test cricket. Although we won the game to finish 3–0 winners in the series, we felt there was little to celebrate in the manner of the latest success. A few months later I heard Michael Vaughan describe the affair as silly. That is a very simple word, but I can't think of anything more appropriate.

The first three and a half days can be summarised quickly. With Mohammad Asif recovered from an elbow injury, Pakistan bowled us out for 173 before another hundred by Mohammad Yousuf helped them to a lead of 331. Then, on the Sunday of our second innings, fourth umpire Trevor Jesty ran out with a box of balls, allowing Kevin Pietersen to choose a replacement. Normally, that task falls to the fielding side. And then, to add to the drama, Darrell Hair tapped his left shoulder with his right hand and our total went up by five runs. I had never seen the signal before and had to ask somebody in the dressing room what was going on. We turned up the sound on the television to listen to the commentators speculating. It turned out that Hair had penalised Pakistan for tampering with the ball, setting a remarkable and unwanted story in motion.

The real drama came a couple of hours later following a break for tea and bad light. Pakistan refused to come out, in protest at Hair's decision. They must have felt really strongly, because although we were batting better in our second innings we were still behind and had already lost four wickets. Apparently, Nasser Hussain on television had suggested that they might take some sort of action, but we were taken completely by surprise when the umpires were back out in the middle with no sign of the fielders emerging from their dressing room. Paul Collingwood and Ian Bell were both padded up and ready to resume the innings. Ten minutes later the umpires went back out and this time the batsmen joined them on the field. I remember watching to see whether Pakistan would join them. Obviously there was a lot of speculation in our dressing room, but personally I didn't have a clue how the stalemate would end. In fact I remember asking Andrew Strauss what was going on. 'I'm not sure,' he said, 'but make sure you don't go far.'

Even when Darrell Hair took off the bails to signify the end of the game, I didn't really think it would be over. By now we had thumbed through a copy of *Wisden* to check the laws and had worked out between us – with a bit of help from the commentators – that Pakistan appeared to have handed us victory on a forfeit. But there was none of the usual hand-shaking or breaking open of drinks. It just seemed impossible to think the series had ended in such a fashion. We gathered together for a debriefing and Phil Neale, the team operations manager, told us we were going back to the hotel but to make sure our mobile phones were on through the evening.

I decided the best thing to do was to stay in my room, get something to eat and flick through the TV channels. There was no point trying to watch something because my mind was just playing through what had gone on and what might happen next. I may have sent the odd message to Saj Mahmood or Ian Bell to find out if they had heard anything. Phil is good at keeping in touch and we received regular messages over the next couple of hours until the final word came through at just after nine o'clock. I don't know who had been involved in the negotiations, but the game really was over. We were declared 3–0 series winners.

It shows how much we expected to return that we kept all our kit in the dressing room. Bell was going for a fourth successive hundred and I said to him, 'You've been cut off in your prime, mate.' He was actually 9 not out. But on Monday morning we headed back to The Oval, a bit later than planned and without having to weave through spectators on the way. We had to go into the ground through a different entrance for security reasons. Perhaps it was just a way of avoiding the dozens of reporters and camera crew who had turned up to try to make sense of it all. By the time we arrived I think Pakistan had been and gone, but the journalists were still milling around. I slipped away quietly, wishing we had celebrated the series win after Headingley. We had decided to wait until after the final game, but somehow it just didn't feel right. So we went our separate ways, and for those like me who were not part of the one-day set-up, the international season had finished in a very low-key fashion.

A day later I went back to Northampton for a four-day game against Leicestershire. As soon as I walked into the dressing room, Chris Rogers, our Australian batsman, said, 'Ah, here's a man who knows what's happened.' I had to disappoint him, but the aftermath of The Oval was the only topic of interest. 'Sorry, I'm still trying to work it out myself,' I said. By this stage it was plastered all through the newspapers – front and back pages in some cases. To be honest, it was a relief when we lost the toss and had to bowl first, so I could get back onto a pitch and play some cricket. Not that I found complete respite, as over the next two days Leicestershire smashed 151 runs off my bowling, including two sixes in an over from Paul Nixon.

I had just about managed to put the issue to the back of my mind by the Friday, when news broke that Darrell Hair had offered to hand in his resignation to the ICC for a one-off payment of $500,000. By now the story seemed like something from a work of fiction. Had somebody reported that Hair had been abducted by aliens, I'm not sure I would have dismissed it completely out of hand. We really did seem to be in the realms of fantasy, with Pakistan threatening to pull out of the one-day matches in protest. Fortunately, those games went ahead, with the return of Shoaib Akhtar adding a bit more spice to the contest.

Looking back now, more than a year on, I'm still not sure who I blame for what happened. I didn't really know much about Darrell Hair except that he was a good umpire, very experienced and a stickler for the laws. Although he had also umpired at Headingley, we had not had an opportunity to talk properly. Other players in the side who know him better said that he was very straight and would not shy away from making difficult decisions. I am not one for cricket politics, or any politics come to that. I do think that somehow the game should have been able to resume on the Monday without loss of face on either side. Technically we had been awarded the game, but I do not think there would have been any complaints from our camp if that decision had been overturned.

The whole episode made for a difficult experience, but overall I could still reflect on a good series personally. I felt I had bowled well at Old Trafford and Headingley in particular and was gradually becoming more confident with being in an England dressing room. I will never be the life and soul in that sort of environment, but I was happy to give and take with the banter that flies around. Perhaps the biggest regret was that I never managed to sit down for a good chat with Bob Woolmer. In an article in *The Times* he compared me to Bishan Bedi and I wish I could have asked him what it was like to face the great Indian spinner. The article ran next to photos of the two of us side by side and for all the similarities there was still a perfect smoothness about Bedi that is missing in my own action. I would love to have asked Bob what he thought I needed to do to get there.

9

HIGHS AND LOWS IN AUSTRALIA

W ITH its history and rivalry there is nothing in sport to compare with an Ashes series. And here I was, preparing to fly out with most of the guys who had made themselves heroes little more than a year earlier by ending the long wait to beat Australia. The interest was phenomenal and I lost count of the number of times that strangers would stop me in the streets to say 'Good luck, Monty'. In Luton, Northampton and everywhere else it felt as though people were genuinely optimistic about our chances of repeating the 2005 success. As the days ticked down I sensed more and more that I was about to set off on the adventure of a lifetime.

I have kept a few of the letters and cards that were sent before the tour. One of them came from Ross Edwards, who played for Australia in the 1970s and now lives in England. He wrote: 'I doubt you will get as much turn out there as you do here, perhaps with the exception of Sydney where it turns later in the match. If Tony Lock can take over 300 Sheffield Shield wickets for Western Australia when at least half his matches were on the WACA, which in those days was much faster than it is now, I am sure you will be successful.' Lock, like me, was a left-arm spinner and bowled alongside the great Jim Laker for Surrey and England. I knew all about Laker, having recently been to a big dinner in London to celebrate the 50th anniversary of his 19 wickets in the Old Trafford Test against Australia.

Another letter made a very big impression, written by Peter Hall who lives in the Wirral. He told me he was born in Hong Kong of Eurasian parents and emigrated to Sydney after the Pacific War. Mr Hall wrote: 'I am sure as a newcomer to Test cricket and a British Sikh you will definitely be targeted by the Australian crowds and by the Aussie team in a different way. Try to remember this: Australians like a person when they call him names. If you are not liked, you are ignored. If and when you get barracked, respond in a positive way and you will win their hearts.'

Then there was a note from a different angle. It was from a seven-year-old boy at a school in Oxfordshire whose class had been told to give a little talk about somebody famous. He decided to take me as his subject and sent a copy of his speech. Not only that, he had dressed up in his cricket kit and worn a false beard to deliver it. With the serious business ahead, that really made me laugh.

We knew that Australia would try to put pressure on us at every opportunity. I felt an example of that first-hand a few weeks before we left. Steve Bull, the England team psychologist, had done a session with the whole squad about dealing with the tough moments we were bound to face and offering suggestions about how to cope. For some reason, one of the newspapers wrote this up incorrectly as Monty Panesar going for a one-to-one to learn how to deal with the hostility of crowds. My attitude was to expect the worst. That way I wouldn't be surprised or intimidated by anything. And if things weren't so bad, then I hoped I would be able to thrive on the positive energy, as I had done in India and England.

But the world is a very small place these days, and it wasn't long before Glenn McGrath picked up on the story and passed comment. This must have been like a half-volley to him. The trip, he said, was a sign that I was soft and would struggle once I touched down in Australia. Inevitably, the press invited me to respond. It literally was something out of nothing, given that I had not specifically met Bull in the first place, and it seemed best not to keep the story going. I didn't want to get involved in any kind of banter with a bowler who had taken more than 500 Test wickets when I'd been playing for a matter of months. If I had, I might have pointed out that a number of Australia players had been to sports psychologists in the past and said how useful they found the exercise. It was an eye-opener that McGrath thought it worth trying to unsettle a guy who had been a part-time cricketer struggling over a dissertation at university only a year before. At least he knew who I was now.

Things had certainly changed. Bizarrely, it seemed that I was in the running for the BBC Sports Personality of the Year award. Zara Phillips eventually won; she was a far more deserving candidate. At another level I was being held up as a role model for young Sikhs in England. My attitude there had not changed at all. If, by playing for England, I am encouraging kids of any background to believe they can do the same, then great. I am lucky to have close friends and family who treat me in exactly the same way as they did before I played Test cricket. If anything, they now use the ammunition in the newspapers to take the mickey more than ever, saying things like: 'Have you got your right contact lenses in today?' Or: 'Are you off to see the shrink again?' If my brother and sister and friends ever treat me as though I'm special, I might start to believe my own publicity and will become a worse person as a result.

Most of the time before departure date, I stayed well away from the public eye. Most days were spent at Northampton, working with David Capel and David Ripley on my bowling and general fitness. I didn't keep more than half an eye on the Champions Trophy in India, although I couldn't help noticing that Australia appeared to be in a determined mood. I would be lying if I said that I didn't think about the Ashes at some point every day. And one of the biggest questions I asked myself was this: would I be playing in Brisbane on 23 November?

The truth is that I thought I had a chance. Ashley Giles had not played Test cricket for a year. Although he is a useful batsman, he is not an all-rounder like Jamie Dalrymple. I had drawn a lot of confidence from the recent Pakistan series because I took the wickets of good batsmen. So I was going into the tour with form behind me. I thought that Duncan Fletcher and Michael Vaughan might give me a chance in the First Test, because if things did not work out, there would still be four Tests to go with the chance to recover. In that sense, there would be less pressure going straight into the side at Brisbane rather than for one of the later games when we might have to win to stay in the series. They could test the water and pull me out if they decided it was too hot.

I had one more thing to do before we left. With interest building in my own career, a friend of mine came up with the idea of setting up my own website, www.monty-panesar.com. The idea was to put out information and incorporate a question-and-answer section so I had an interface with fans. I couldn't have wished for more enthusiastic support in my first few months with England – or since, for that matter – and this seemed to be the best way of making myself available. If people were going to the trouble of dressing up and wearing masks, even cheering when the ball came to me in the field, then this seemed to be the least I could

Howzat! A passionate appeal for leg before.

All concentration in the Second Test against Sri Lanka at Edgbaston.

My favourite wicket of the Sri Lanka series as Geraint Jones stumps Thilan Samaraweera.

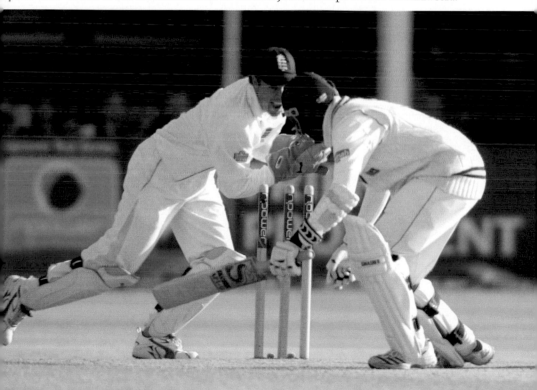

Trying to give the ball a real rip from my big fingers.

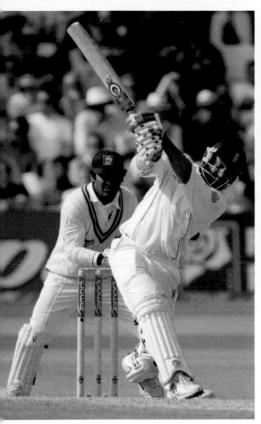

I'm glad this was captured on film otherwise nobody would believe it – striking Muttiah Muralitharan for six at Trent Bridge.

Walking off with Liam Plunkett after losing in Nottingham. At least we went down fighting.

Leading off the side after my first 'five-fer' in Test cricket at Trent Bridge.

Above left: I knew from our first day as England Under 19 team-mates that Ian Bell would be a brilliant player.

Above right: Steve Harmison – bowling here to Imran Farhat – was unstoppable against Pakistan at Old Trafford.

Left: Bowling to Younis Khan at Old Trafford. Umpire Simon Taufel is a model of concentration.

Poor guy – Imran Farhat in agony after being struck in the groin region by Steve Harmison.

A deadly combination – leaving the Old Trafford field with Harmison after victory against Pakistan. He took 11 wickets; I got eight.

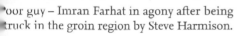

The ball of my life – beating Younis Khan's forward defensive shot at Headingley.

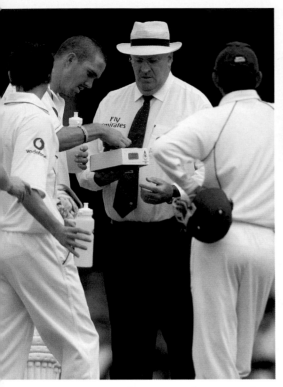

Kevin Pietersen chooses a replacement after Darrell Hair penalises Pakistan for ball-tampering at The Oval.

The late Bob Woolmer talks to Pakistan bowling coach Waqar Younis at The Oval.

No pain, no gain! Working on core fitness in Sydney during the Ashes series.

I had been desperate to play in the Third Ashes Test at Perth and could not contain myself after removing Justin Langer.

I learnt so much during a chat with Shane Warne at the end of the Ashes series in Sydney.

Delighted with the wicket of my old Northants buddy Matthew Hayden – and it was great to have Michael Vaughan back for the one-day series in Australia.

Paul Collingwood batted brilliantly in the first one-day final at Melbourne.

We deserved to celebrate after winning the Commonwealth Bank Series in Australia. I didn't drink the beer, but I was happy to hand out the bottles.

do. Unfortunately, I did not really have time to get involved with the groundwork myself. I would like to have put my knowledge of computers to good use. But the website was up and running by midway through the Ashes series and the response has been positive.

After our preparation we knew what to expect when we landed in Australia. We were not disappointed. 'Good luck, Monty – you'll need it, mate,' said one of the customs men as I passed through. 'Hayden's been waiting months to get after you,' he added. Yes, the message was getting through. Sport is massive in Australia. When their side does well at cricket, or an individual wins a medal in swimming or athletics, the whole country seems to get a lift. Nobody could fail to realise how much it meant to them to win back the Ashes. With our back-up team and security men, we had roughly 30 people in our party. It was going to feel like our 30 against Australia's entire 18 million population.

We all had a laugh in that first hour on their soil. But almost immediately, in a funny way, I sensed that the Australians wanted us to do well. Not win the series, obviously, but to make sure the Tests were as hard-fought as the incredible contests in 2005. A lot of the comments were genuinely nice. People would say 'good luck, Monty' without the obligatory follow-up 'you'll need it'. I felt they were looking forward to seeing me bowl. Perhaps they thought I was different because of my appearance. I know that I don't look like your average England cricketer. With that, and the fact that I'd made a reasonable start, there was some interest in the Australian media and people seemed to want to make up their own minds.

Newspapers there were like those in England, with saturation coverage of the event. Almost every day one batsman or another would describe how positively he would play against our bowlers, me included. In fact they'd been saying it since at least midway through our own season. As with the McGrath comments, I thought I could take confidence from the fact that they thought I was going to play. They were only answering questions and I guessed there was not much else they could say. If somebody asked Ricky Ponting whether he was going to be positive against me, he could hardly say 'no'. Besides, going into Brisbane, Ponting, Matthew Hayden and Justin Langer, their top three, had scored 78 Test hundreds between them. No wonder they were positive.

Even with Andrew Flintoff captaining the side instead of Michael Vaughan, we could draw a lot from 2005. I made sure that I learned whatever I could from Ashley Giles. He was a big part of that success, even if his figures did not reflect his importance to the side. I talked to him to try to break down his bowling and watched to see how he went about things in the nets. This was a great chance to learn. He is a different kind of left-arm spinner in some ways – he prefers bowling over the wicket whereas I like to go round and attack middle or middle and off to try to get the edge. Ashley was criticised for being negative in 2005, but part of his role was to frustrate batsmen who like to score quickly by removing that opportunity. He deserved respect because he had played in a team that beat Australia.

One of the early tasks was to get used to a different type of ball. This may sound like a minor detail – it is red, round and weighs the same, after all – but they can feel different in your hand. In England we use the Duke ball, which has quite a pronounced seam. In Australia – and other parts of the world – they use the Kookaburra, which has a seam that is flatter but broader. The seam is important because it affects the way the ball moves off the pitch. All things being equal, the bigger the seam, the more chance of getting the ball to dart off the straight. By the time I got a Kookaburra ball, the seam was usually flat.

The point of our warm-up games was simply to adjust to different conditions. We began badly against the Prime Minister's XI in Canberra as they scored 347 for 5 from 50 overs and then bowled us out for 181. Arriving in Sydney the next day, I couldn't help but notice the headline in the *Morning Herald* newspaper: 'How on earth did we lose the Ashes to this lot?' Well, there were several reasons – one of them being that England were not jetlagged during the Test matches. My body was still on a slightly different timetable and we all expected to improve over the two three-day matches ahead of Brisbane.

I was in the news in the first of them, against New South Wales, because of some comments from the crowd. With so many predictions of abuse in the weeks ahead it was obvious that the media would keep their ears open for anything that was said. In this case a reporter from an Australian newspaper heard somebody describe me as 'a stupid Indian' while I was on the fine-leg boundary. There was nothing said that I could not cope with and, as at Headingley a few months earlier, my attitude was to laugh it off. If people really think like that, it is their problem, not mine.

I did not take a bagful of wickets at Sydney or in the final warm-up, against South Australia at Adelaide, but I did feel well enough prepared to go into a Test match, which was the point of the exercise. At the end of the Tests, the schedule was criticised for not including enough preparation time. There is so much international cricket these days that tours tend to be kept as short as possible. And with the Champions Trophy running into November, it would have been difficult to slot in many more games. I did not play in the First Test, so I don't know how I would have bowled. All I can say is that I felt good. With previous experience of playing in Australia, I had a good idea about the pitches and was satisfied that any slight tweaks to my normal length were in place. As a rule, the surfaces in Australia are a little bouncier than in England. There is not a lot of turn, but I still wanted to encourage batsmen to drive, and aimed to deceive them in the flight. The danger of trying to rip the ball is that a batsman can use the pace to steer it away if the disciplines are slightly awry.

The bad news arrived the day before the Test in our team room at the hotel. Andrew Flintoff read out the names: 'Seven, Geraint Jones . . . eight, Ashley Giles.' Oh well, I thought, maybe we would go with two spinners. But the blow was delivered as the list went on: 'Nine, Matthew Hoggard . . . ten, Steve Harmison . . . and eleven, Jimmy Anderson.'

During the next few seconds I felt like a balloon slowly deflating – not a big prick but with the air being gradually taken away. All my energy had gone, so that I felt no emotion at all, not even disappointment. I didn't know what to do and when I looked up I saw everyone going over to congratulate Ashley. I followed and said to him, 'Good luck, mate. I really hope you do well.' Those words were so difficult to say. But once I'd said them I realised how deeply they were meant. This was England against Australia and I was supporting England in everything we did, in every decision we made. In fact, what I thought was even stronger. I wanted to tell Ashley that he deserved it for the courage he had shown in coming back from his terrible injuries. He could rely on getting any support from me that he needed.

But it wasn't long before disappointment took over again. As the buzz of celebration cooled and players started to leave the room, Duncan Fletcher called me into a corner and said, 'Monty, I'd just like a word.' I was unable to lift my head when he started talking. I told myself to get my chin up and meet him eye to eye, but my body wouldn't respond. I had gone into that meeting hopeful that by the end I would be looking forward to sharing the same pitch as Shane Warne, the great Shane Warne. I cannot describe how much I wanted that. You get energy from being around players of his calibre. I had felt it when I bowled to Sachin Tendulkar. Now it seemed that something had been taken away. I hope this doesn't sound selfish because I know I have no divine right to play for England. But I am a human being, and this is the truth about the way I felt at that particular time.

Fortunately my body clicked into gear. When I finally managed to look up, I said to Fletcher, 'Sorry, can you repeat that, please.' He explained for a second time, telling me that he was worried about Australia bowling first and taking early wickets. He wanted the insurance of some extra batting lower in the order. I understood what he was saying and knew that Ashley offered more in that department. Given the balance of the side they wanted, he was the better pick. And Fletcher had made so many good calls on selection down the years as coach that I was in no position to argue.

I spent the rest of the evening in my room. For the first 45 minutes I lay on my bed just looking at a spot on the ceiling, trying to think but getting nowhere. It struck me that having so much passion for cricket carries one big downside: devastation when the cricket is taken way. Looking back, I think the fact that Marcus Trescothick had gone home because of his illness had a bearing on the decision. His departure took a senior player out of the side as well as a good catcher behind the wicket. Leaving out Ashley would have deprived the team of more experience and another sound fielder. I'm sure that all of these things were considered before Fletcher and Andrew Flintoff took the decision.

By the morning, with a good night's sleep behind me, I realised that things were not so bad after all. This was the most eagerly anticipated series in history and here I was in the England squad getting a privileged insider's view. There was no reason to feel sorry for myself. I was going to enjoy the game, get involved as much as I could and make the experience something to remember.

There were a few nervous guys on the ten-minute bus drive to the Gabba, but once we got to the ground, sorted out our kit and went out to prepare, everybody seemed to be very vibrant and positive. The grounds in Australia are bigger than in England. Lining up for the national anthems with the rest of the squad and the management team, I looked around the packed stands, listened to the singing for both countries and felt a few goose pimples on my arms. Even though I wasn't playing in the game, that is a memory I will always cherish.

I was sitting on the dressing-room balcony next to Chris Read when the months of hype finally ended and the cricket got under way. What happened next has been described by the finest sports writers in the world and been replayed over and over again on television. I cannot compete with those accounts, so I will just restate that Steve Harmison's first ball veered away from wicket-keeper Geraint Jones like a car out of control to Flintoff at second slip. It has come to crystallise what happened over the weeks ahead, as if we were beaten from the first ball. But I don't believe anybody would have thought '5-0' on the basis of that single delivery. Personally, I took it for what it was – a nervous loosener. It certainly wasn't a big thing in the dressing room. I seriously think that Australia were so focused on the first morning that a ball like that was more likely to bring a loss of concentration than boost their confidence.

By the end of the first day, Australia stood on 346 for 3. It had clearly been a tough time for England, with Ricky Ponting hitting yet another hundred and Justin Langer and my old friend Mike Hussey moving close. I was tired out just watching, so I daren't imagine how much energy was spent in the middle. This wasn't just a normal day's cricket for me, because I wanted to remember every ball. By trying to do that, I can't actually recall very many. But I can picture Ponting at the crease. This was my first sight of him in action. You can't appreciate how strong he really is from his appearance as he looks quite wiry. I've never seen anybody put away bad balls so ruthlessly. His footwork is as nimble as any of the Indian batsmen. I wonder if Duncan Fletcher thought back to the first day of the 2002–03 series there when Australia had again taken control.

After that, the week was actually quite busy for me, even though I wasn't playing. Nigel Stockhill, our fitness trainer, put the five of us not involved through drills to keep up our strength. I also spent time in the nets with Fletcher, just going over one or two things with my bowling. As in the summer, he wanted me to try to get a little bit more loop on the ball. He stressed that I could be called upon at any time, although as it happened the closest I came to the action at Brisbane was when taking out a couple of drinks.

We never really recovered after that first day. Australia passed 600 before bowling us out for 157. There had been a lot of talk in the press about whether Glenn McGrath would be ready because he had not played a Test match for ten months. When he walked off with figures of 6 for 50 he pretended to hobble, making a point to his critics. I've mentioned the importance of keeping things simple a few times in this book, and McGrath's career underlines the point. If, as a bowler, you can put the ball where you want it to go, then you really don't need a lot of tricks.

Despite losing heavily, we showed a lot of character in the second innings. Kevin Pietersen and Paul Collingwood counter-attacked really well until we lost our last five wickets on the final day. That effort gave us some heart for the rest of the series. It was also clear that we would be brilliantly supported by the Barmy Army, who were able to congregate together for the first time on that last morning and did everything they could to encourage us. The result could have been worse, and far more dispiriting.

Meanwhile, the Australian papers were picking up on every little thing to make life more awkward. One evening in Brisbane I went to a restaurant called 'Gandhi'. A day or two later a reporter wrote a short piece saying that I was disloyal to India because Indira Gandhi had been assassinated by a Sikh. I hadn't expected anything like that and really did not know what to make of it. I like to give politics a wide berth, but I will say that one of my heroes is Mahatma Gandhi – no relation to the late Prime Minister – because of the way he advanced the cause of independence without ever firing a bullet.

I had been looking forward to the Second Test in Adelaide because it meant a chance to catch up with friends from the Glenelg club. A lot had happened in the year since they chris-tened me the Turbanator after India's Harbhajan Singh. The Adelaide Oval is one of the prettiest grounds in the world, with the trees and cathedral forming a special backdrop. But on this occasion I was more interested in looking down towards the pitch than up at the lovely view. As soon as I saw the surface on our first day of practice I thought that we might go in with two spin-ners. Even if Fletcher and Flintoff decided on just one, I hoped they might go with me as an attacking option.

For a second time, I missed out. The disappointment was not as acute this time but I did admit in a diary column I was writing for the Cricinfo website that it was becoming a frustrating time. The problem with a tour as against a home series is that you don't have a county to go back to and play for to keep in some sort of rhythm. I was itching to bowl out there in the middle. You can work on bits and pieces in the nets but however hard you try the intensity is not the same. What I didn't appreciate at the time was the strength of feeling back home about my omission.

A mate emailed to tell me that callers were ringing Radio Five to complain and that other people were getting together a petition demanding that I play. Things seemed to be going crazy. There is an old saying that you become a great player when you are not in the side and it seemed that my ability was becoming exaggerated. Nobody spoke to me about how to deal with this kind of publicity, perhaps because it didn't affect me. I don't remember any mickey-taking in the dressing room either. It was great to have so many supporters, but at the same time the team always comes first and I was determined not to do or say anything that might encourage people to criticise the team selection.

The response of the Australian people shocked me more than anything. On the first morning when the teams had been announced I bumped into Rod Marsh, who had stepped down from the Academy to spend more time with his family back home. Rod had been a big influence and is still a man I respect. I didn't know what to say; I didn't want him to think I'd let him down by not making the side. He was always forthright, and this time he said, 'I can't believe it, mate; I just can't believe what's going on.' It's fair to say that I am a bit less forthright, and I think I mumbled something like, 'Well, you know . . . how are you anyway, Rod?'

That kind of thing was repeated during the game when I walked around the ground to the nets. Australians would shout 'Monty, Monty' even as I practised. I think the response confirmed my initial thoughts on arrival, that they wanted to see me in action for themselves. Before play one morning, Matthew Hayden came over for a brief conversation to find out how I was getting on. 'Don't worry, I know you'll get a chance before the end of the series,' he said. Then there was the time when I ran on with some drinks for our batsmen and passed Brett Lee on the way. 'Still not playing then, mate,' Lee said. 'Don't worry, we'll get you by the end of the series.' He had a twinkle in his eye, so I joined in by saying, 'That's what I'm worried about.'

The game itself was just incredible. If I have to pinpoint where we lost the series it would be the final day at Adelaide. That might sound obvious because it left us 2–0 behind with three to play. But the impact went beyond the result because the defeat seemed to come from nowhere. For the first four days we were heading for a draw at the very least. In fact, with 551 in our first innings and Australia 65 for 3, we had every chance of our first win. They would have been 78 for four if Ashley Giles had held a chance from Ponting on 35. Ponting went on to score 142, and with Michael Clarke also scoring a hundred our overall lead was pegged back to 38.

You cannot allow for brilliance and Shane Warne won the game on the final morning with a lesson in spin. It isn't just that he turns the ball a mile, although that is a pretty good start. He can put the ball where he wants and still make it turn more than anybody else I have seen. Afterwards, he said that his final spell was the best he had bowled in Test cricket, which puts it into context. We were a bit unlucky to lose Andrew Strauss to a close catch, but once Warne thought he had the edge he made the very best of his advantage. I think this match will pass into Australian legend, in the way that Headingley 1981 lives on in England. Warne's figures of 32–12–49–4 will become as familiar as Ian Botham's 149 not out.

At the time I could not appreciate the masterclass for what it was. I could see the impact it was having on my team-mates – my mates – in the dressing room. Even after being bowled out for 129, we briefly threatened the Australia batsmen before Mike Hussey led them home, but the effort of our bowlers did not lift a terrible mood of sadness. I never want to be in a dressing room like that again. I felt like crying just to see so many unhappy faces, and I had not even been playing. Nobody wanted to look anybody else in the eye. There was Paul Collingwood, who had scored a double hundred, and Matthew Hoggard, who bowled brilliantly to take seven wickets in their first innings. Kevin Pietersen had made 158. These were great performances, and what did they have to show for them now? I tried to think of something I could say to lift the mood. Nothing came to mind. To make matters worse, the dressing rooms at Adelaide are quite close together, so we could hear the Australians celebrating. They were entitled to. It was a great win for them.

Time heals, to a certain degree, and it was good to get away from the cauldron of Test cricket for a week when we went to Perth. I had been looking forward to this since the Adelaide team was announced without my name in it, because I knew I would get a chance. We had two games. The first was a festival match at Lilac Hill against an ECB Chairman's XI. Alec Stewart captained our side and scored 69. I am convinced he is fit enough to play at county level even now. That was also the first time I saw a guy called Luke Ronchi. He could be a wicketkeeper-batsman to look out for in the future because his approach is straight from the Adam Gilchrist textbook.

The more serious game was against Western Australia at the WACA the next day. I knew that I really did have a chance now to get back into the Test side. I wanted to put the matter beyond doubt, to make the selectors pick me in a positive way rather than drop Ashley first and call me in because I was the only other spinner. As it happened, I took just one wicket, but with 25 overs in the Western Australia innings I enjoyed my longest bowl of the tour and went for less than three runs an over. At one point I think my passion got the better of me as I snatched my jumper from the umpire at the end of an over when he turned down an appeal for a catch. Overall, I felt pleased rather than ecstatic with my performance. But with plenty of bounce in the surface, I knew I could make an impression on the Test match due to begin at the same venue four days later.

While we were in Perth a lot of the squad went to see Elton John in concert. An amazing show was just what we needed after Adelaide. And then, the following evening, Andrew Flintoff read out the Test team. 'Nine, Matthew Hoggard . . . ten, Steve Harmison . . . eleven, Monty Panesar.' So there was the confirmation I wanted. This time, back in my room, I went through the Australian batsmen in my mind the same way I had gone through the Indians earlier in the year. It would be a daunting proposition, but what did I have to fear? We needed to win two of the last three games to retain the Ashes and I was ready to give it everything I had. The sad thing was that Ashley had decided quite rightly to go home to care for his wife who was due to undergo surgery in England.

Next morning I had breakfast as usual – cereal, toast and some juice and fruit – and with the WACA ground being very close to the hotel we were in the dressing room five minutes after stepping onto the coach. I felt nervous and excited, but not apprehensive at all. Dave Parsons, the spin-bowling coach, was a great help in that last hour before play. 'I've never seen you look so energetic and enthusiastic,' he said. 'You're looking better than ever.' A few words like that at the right time can be worth any number of dry, technical comments in the nets. Since the summer I had developed the same kind of relationship with Parsons that I had with my tutor at university. He is not one of the best-known people within the ECB – perhaps because he didn't play for a first-class county – but he has given me a good understanding of how to prepare as an international player.

As it happened, I did feel energetic and enthusiastic, but Parsons confirmed it and as we ran out to a packed house, with thousands of people cheering for England, it sank in that this was the highlight of my life. The volume of noise was incredible when I came on to bowl. As he went through the field with me, Andrew Flintoff grinned, and said, 'You know, this crowd is going to lynch me if I have to take you off.'

We had made an excellent start, removing Matthew Hayden and Ricky Ponting quite cheaply. Perhaps it helped me that I delivered my first Ashes over to Mike Hussey. All those hours in the nets at Northampton would pay off here on the other side of the world. The downside was his watertight defence. When he pushed forward I could not see a chink of light between his bat and pad. He was clearly going to take some shifting. In fact we didn't shift him, because he was still there at the end of the innings on 74 not out.

Fortunately we had more luck at the other end. I enjoyed a day I will never forget. Things went right from the first ball of my second over. It was the last before lunch and I think Justin Langer was playing for the end of the session. He is an incredibly determined batsman with big, staring eyes that almost bore into the ball through its flight. But this time he played inside the line, perhaps expecting it to turn in, and by the time it hit the stumps I had begun my whoops of delight. I think that was my biggest celebration since the Sachin wicket – my first ever in Tests and now my first in the Ashes.

As at Old Trafford in the summer, I thought I bowled well in tandem with Steve Harmison. Anybody who says that Brisbane destroyed him is forgetting his effort on this first afternoon at Perth. With the breeze behind him he troubled all their top batsmen. In the end we shared nine of the ten wickets, and the cricket statisticians discovered that my final figures of 5 for 92 were the best by an England spinner on the ground. But it took a great piece of captaincy by Andrew Flintoff after lunch to keep me on the road to success.

Andrew Symonds had been recalled by Australia, when Damien Martyn decided to retire after Adelaide, and he was determined to play his own way. He duly struck me for two straight sixes, and at the end of an expensive over I expected to be told to take a rest. Instead, Flintoff ran up to me and said, 'I'm keeping you on here, Monty. I think you're about to get him.' To be given that show of faith on my first day in front of a huge crowd after a battering from one of the biggest hitters in the world made me feel ten feet tall. I took the ball for my next over with fresh confidence. Symonds went to cut one that bounced a bit more than he expected and top-edged a catch to Geraint Jones. Sprinting over to Freddie, I think I just shouted 'yes, yes, yes, yes, yes' as we exchanged high fives.

Bowlers get credited with wickets, but wickets are very rarely down to just one man. Flintoff deserves more praise than I do for the Symonds dismissal, but doesn't get his name on the score-card. At least catchers get noted, and Ian Bell deserved every bit of applause for a brilliant effort running back from short leg to chase an inside edge via Adam Gilchrist's pad. He took it with his arms straight, a technique we had been practising in the build-up.

Shane Warne was the next man, and as he passed me on the way to the crease he winked and whispered, 'Well bowled, mate, that was a good ball.' By now I was on cloud nine. Warne gets a lot of stick for some of the things he says in the middle, but he is a really fair guy and an inspiration to other cricketers. There's an unwritten rule among players that what is said in the middle should stay there. But I have no problem repeating what he told me, because people deserve to know about the good side of his character. It underlines his love of the game and respect for other players.

Needless to say, it didn't stop him trying to get after my bowling, but after a few bold shots he was caught as he tried to cut one close to the stumps, and then Brett Lee became the fifth wicket on an lbw decision from Aleem Dar. As soon as the finger was raised, Freddie ran over and lifted me up as though we were in a lineout. His strength is incredible. Apparently, replays suggested that the Lee wicket was closer than I thought, but I did think I had had Mike Hussey out with a bat-pad catch that wasn't given. Umpires have such a hard job these days, with so many television gadgets to analyse every decision, I am amazed at how much they get right through the course of a six-hour day.

For most of the time I was fielding in front of Australian supporters. They started to play a little game when I walked in from the boundary as the bowler ran in. They must have noticed how my feet are a little flat, because they started a beat of 'yip, yip, yip' with every step. I played along by making small, quick steps as I went back, so they went 'yip-yip-yip-yip-yip' really smartly. Then I tried to fool them by keeping my foot in the air.

This time they went 'yiiiiiiiiiiip' as I finally put my foot down. I guess it was a sign of my growing confidence in Test cricket that I felt I could play along with a crowd. I wouldn't have dared do that in India or maybe even at the start of the summer in England. The fact is that if you can get the crowd on your side, fielding becomes much easier and more enjoyable.

All in all, it was a really good day for England. Australia's 244 turned out to be their lowest first-innings total of the series, but as I unwound in my room that evening I didn't think in terms of being vindicated. Emails from friends told me that the newspapers back home were full of articles wondering why I had not been picked earlier. But those first two Tests were in the past and my priority was to help England win this one. That was a far bigger incentive than trying to make a point.

Not for the first time – and not for the last – we could not manage to press home our advantage. The bounce undid our batsmen, and Australia's batsmen were a different proposition in the second innings. It was certainly another side of Ashes cricket for me as Gilchrist completed the second-fastest hundred in Test history from 57 balls. He smashed it everywhere, hitting me for three sixes and a four to finish in one over. I actually thought I was bowling quite well. In fact, with each of those sixes I turned round expecting to see a fielder underneath the ball. That really was wishful thinking because in every case they soared over the rope.

In the context of the match I'm not sure it was all that important. Australia were over 400 in front by that stage, well on their way to establishing an impossible target. With his onslaught, Gilchrist simply gave Ricky Ponting more time to bat on or bowl, depending how he saw the finish unfolding. I sounded out a few people after the innings, including Duncan Fletcher, to get an idea of how else I might have dealt with Gilchrist. Maybe I could have gone around the wicket or speared in a yorker – at least that way he would not have been able to get under the ball to lift it high to the leg side. In the end we decided that the best option might have been to get him off strike and slow down the innings that way. As a young spinner still learning the game, I find these chats fascinating. The bottom line was that however many wickets I took in the first innings, I still had plenty to learn.

The same was true of my batting, although I demonstrated progress by hanging around for 40 minutes in the first innings. Second time around, we showed a lot of fight in the face of a daunting 557 target. With the game lost in all but name I did not last as long, and when I missed a slog-sweep against Shane Warne, Australia were confirmed as Ashes winners with two games remaining. That was also Warne's 699th Test wicket and there was barely time to say 'well done' before they were off on their celebrations. Out in the middle it felt like being a stranger at somebody else's party.

Their fun had started while I was actually batting. I somehow managed to read a ball from Warne as it left his hand and instinctively shouted 'googly' as I got into position to let it pass. I don't usually do that, so what happened this time I don't know. I think it was just a subconscious way of reinforcing to myself that as it was going to turn away I ought not to play a shot. But the close-in fielders who heard me cry out milked the moment. Ricky Ponting shouted, 'You're finished, Warnie – Monty's sussed you out.' I was a bit annoyed at giving them ammunition and could imagine this running all the way through the rest of the series. Warne didn't say anything, but when he was at the top of his mark he let me see that he was spinning the ball in his hand as though he was about to deliver a googly again. Needless to say, it was a leg-break. Needless to say, too, I made a point of playing it with my mouth closed. 'Ooh,' Ponting said, 'he didn't pick that one. You've still got a future, Warnie.'

With eight wickets overall, the game had gone really well on a personal level, but that paled alongside the significance of the defeat. The dressing room was not as downbeat as it had been at Adelaide because Australia had been on top for longer this time. It did not feel as if victory had been snatched away. Andrew Flintoff told us to keep our heads high and said that he couldn't fault our effort and commitment. But for Freddie and the others who had worked so hard in 2005 the result must have been shattering. Australia had learned from England and now, I thought, we had to see what we could take from them to recover. The biggest thing was consistency over five days. We had some great sessions but some very bad ones as well. Once Australia got on top, they made sure that they stayed there.

With two games remaining we also had the opportunity to salvage something from the tour. Unfortunately the matches at Melbourne and Sydney resulted in heavier defeats. Both matches felt strange, like farewell events for some of the Australians as much as competitive cricket matches. Warne announced before Melbourne that he would be retiring at the end of the series, provoking an incredible media circus before his last appearance at his home ground, the MCG. The word was that he would have finished after 2005 if the result had gone the other way. That just shows the determination of the Australians to win the rematch.

Glenn McGrath and Justin Langer also said over the next few days that they would be stepping down. I felt lucky at managing to play against all three in the nick of time, especially Warne. Nobody who had followed his career would have betted against something special at the MCG and he lived up to local expectations by taking his 700th Test wicket – Andrew Strauss hitting around a leg-break – and going on for a 37th five-wicket haul. Both of those figures are incredible. From time to time I have tried to bowl a few wrist-spinners in the nets for fun. It is an incredibly difficult business that puts a lot of strain on the shoulder. When you stand close to Warne you can appreciate the upper-body strength that enabled him to bowl so well for so long.

Perth was special for me as the venue of my Ashes debut, but standing in the middle of the MCG at our first practice there made me realise that the Fourth Test would be another occasion to remember. It was rebuilt for the Commonwealth Games and was said to be more impressive than ever for its 100th Test. The capacity is roughly 95,000 and the early predictions were for a world-record attendance over the five days. It is bowl-shaped, with seats all the way around, but what shook me was the size of the stands. I played a little game, looking down at the pitch and moving my head up slowly to see how long it would take before my eyes reached the top row of seats. After six seconds, I was there.

In the end the crowd figure could not beat the 400,000 who turned up to watch India play Pakistan at Eden Gardens in 1999. The main reason was that the game finished in three days. But the weather was also a factor. On Christmas Day we had a big team meal with players, management and families, but once we got outside the restaurant it was freezing. I wouldn't have been surprised to find out that Christmas Day had been warmer in England. That chill, along with a blustery wind and scattered showers, continued on Boxing Day. At one point they put on the floodlights so we could play, and but for the presence of Warne

I think people would have left earlier. So here was yet another tribute: even in the cold, nobody wanted to take their eyes off him. When he came on to bowl for the first time, extra security men had to be posted inside the fence.

From our point of view, I think the less said about the game, the better. I bowled just 12 overs in the match and went wicket-less – although Australia did have to bat once only. Rain had spiced up the pitch and the seamers did most of our bowling. At least I could reflect on some progress, moving above Matthew Hoggard to number ten in the batting order for the first time. Defeat by an innings and 99 runs suggests that Australia won easily. They did, in the end. Yet again, though, we were in front at one point, our first-innings score of 159 looking respectable when we reduced Australia to 84 for 5. By the time we split the sixth-wicket stand between Matthew Hayden and Andrew Symonds, they had moved on to 363 and the lead was too big to pull back. Brett Lee and Stuart Clark – a ready-made replacement for Glenn McGrath – did the damage second time around.

A couple of days after the game I heard that I'd won a very strange award: Beard of the Year for 2006. The other contenders were Fidel Castro, Inzamam-ul-Haq and Bill Frindall. Is that stiff competition? I'm not sure. Once the announcement was made I told a reporter I was delighted that eight years of effort had finally paid off. I have never shaved in my life, so I will probably never win anything more easily.

Being a Test cricketer brings a number of privileges and one of them was being able to go out into Sydney Harbour to watch the traditional fireworks on New Year's Eve. Some of the guys stayed at an event in Darling Harbour, but I decided to take up an offer from Andrew Flintoff to see things from a boat he had hired for friends and team-mates. I hope I wasn't too antisocial, because I was like a kid watching the display with the stunning backdrop of the Harbour Bridge against the sound and colour of the fireworks.

The Fifth Test was really an extension of the Fourth. Attention continued to centre on the retiring Australians. We were really determined not to go down to a 5–0 defeat. We did not deserve that, but we were where we were and Australia would be going all out to complete the whitewash and make it a memorable farewell for Warne, Langer and McGrath. I wondered whether the emotion might be too much for them. At tea on the first day they were serenaded by an opera singer, and it was interesting that the usually reliable Langer dropped Andrew Strauss early on. That apart, they seemed to thrive on the occasion.

We batted quite well in parts and threatened to take a first-innings lead, but once we had let Australia off the hook there was no way back – a familiar story by now. McGrath took 6 for 105 from 50 overs in all, incredible figures these days, while Langer was there at the end as Australia sealed the ten-wicket win. And Warne was on course for his first Test hundred until Stuart Clark, the last man, arrived. At that point Warne tried to charge me and missed, giving Chris Read the stumping. I was the last person to take Shane Warne's wicket in a Test match.

I could sense the disappointment from the fans. Many of them would have expected a Warne century because his career had been like a Roy of the Rovers story. Stranger things have happened. Actually, though, he was fortunate to get as far as he did. Early in his innings he gloved one off me but was given not out. His face was bright red and I knew he'd hit it, but you just have to pick yourself up and get on with it. If he had not been such a brilliant bowler, I think he could have developed into a good all-rounder because he has such a good eye for the ball. His innings of 71 was the turning point of the game.

As in Melbourne I bowled to some fairly defensive settings. Looking back, they may have been too defensive, but we needed control when their batsmen were trying to attack. The idea was to frustrate them by stifling their scoring opportunities and hope they would make mistakes. I also think that spinners find it instinctively easier to toss the ball up knowing that fielders are protecting the boundary. I was one of our most expensive bowlers at Sydney, so it wasn't my best game by some way. Then again, I did not expect everything to go as well as that first innings at Perth.

Warne was the first person to come over and shake our hands afterwards. And when the presentations were over I had one of the best half-hours of my career as we sat together in their dressing room chatting about cricket. I say chat – it was more a case of me listening while he talked about spin bowling. Warne has always made himself available in situations like this and I'd hoped for weeks that a chance would arise. Even to go into the Australia dressing room was an amazing experience. By their changing pegs they all had their own sheets of paper with pictures and motivational slogans.

Warne was Australia's equivalent of Andrew Flintoff. Without making an effort, he was clearly the hub of activity. He has that same presence. In the corner of the dressing room he was surrounded by people. As I chatted to my old Northamptonshire mate Mike Hussey I kept looking over to see if there was a way into Warne's conversation. 'Do you think he'll talk to me?' I asked Hussey. 'Jeez, Monty,' came the reply. 'He'll talk all night about spin bowling.' I knew Terry Jenner, Warne's coach, who could see what was happening and eventually invited me over. Hussey was right. Warne has forgotten more about spin bowling than I will ever know, but he also expresses it in a clear way.

'The key is simplicity,' he said. I always believed that myself, but it was interesting to hear it from a guy with so many variations. He smiled at that and added, 'It's batsmen who worry about those variations, not me.' He talked about setting fields to different players and putting more men in attacking positions if a batsman is in a bad run or under pressure for his place. 'The more you play, the better you'll feel situations and trust your instinct,' he said.

The press were very critical of England. I guess it was hard not to be with a 5–0 scoreline. We could not hide from the fact that we had disappointed a lot of people who had come over in the hope that we could retain the Ashes. The Barmy Army were incredible, supporting us to the end instead of turning against the team. They were great to me in particular. In fact, Flintoff would sometimes send me down to field in front of them. 'They like you, Monty – get them singing again,' he would say.

I felt sorrier for Freddie than for anybody else. As captain he was the man who fronted up after every game and he never once had a go at us in public. He took a lot of the criticism on his shoulders and was beginning to feel his sore ankle by the end. If it had not been for Freddie, we would not have had the Ashes to defend in the first place. People should remember that. He was prepared to take on the responsibility of captaincy and he was always there for me when I needed a friendly word of advice.

When the series was over, both Freddie and Duncan Fletcher stood up in the dressing room and said again that we had done our best. It took 10 or 15 minutes for the mood to lighten and the banter to start again. In years to come I think people will appreciate how good Australia were. There was an incredible deter-mination, which we have to match in 2009, but with so many really good young players coming through and Australia in a rebuilding phase at the moment, I really think we have a good chance of repeating what happened in 2005.

10

THE WORLD CUP
BECKONS

O NE morning towards the end of the Ashes series, I took one of the most unexpected calls of my life. 'Hello, Monty,' came a familiar voice. 'It's David Graveney here. How are you?' The chairman of selectors was back in England, where it must have been quite late at night, and when the small talk was over he told me that I was going to be included in the one-day squad for the Commonwealth Bank Series against Australia and New Zealand, straight after the Fifth Test. I had barely played limited-overs cricket for Northants, let alone thought about wearing the blue of England. In fact, it was quite an effort to stop myself asking Graveney why I'd been chosen. I didn't think that would go down too well. So I simply said 'thank you' a few times and reflected on another long-term ambition about to be fulfilled much earlier than expected.

I had been looking forward to getting home in time for a big Sikh festival to celebrate the birth of Gobind Singh, our tenth Guru. It wasn't that I wanted to leave or was fed up with playing cricket. But I had a certain date fixed in my mind for arriving back in England and had started to make plans around it. It just didn't cross my mind that I might be staying on for another five weeks. In fact, the implications ran far deeper. With the World Cup due to get under way in March, these would be the final matches before the big event. A few good performances here would put me in pole position for a place.

The one-day series gave us a chance to draw a line under the Ashes and start afresh. We had a new captain, Michael Vaughan, who imposed himself straight away. Although he was involved in the two-day friendly in Perth, this was the first time I had actually played under him as leader. It wasn't long before I grew to understand what other players said about his calming influence. He has instant authority through winning the 2005 Ashes. But he also makes a big issue of players going out there to play their game and have some fun.

Almost immediately, Vaughan had us in for one-to-one meetings. He explained how he saw my role over the weeks ahead. He said that he liked what he had seen over the past year and wanted me in the side as an attacking spin bowler rather than somebody who would just keep the runs down. Without promising that I would play in every game, he said that some pitches would help the spinners and that he expected me to take wickets. In one-day cricket, situations change quickly, so I had to be warmed up and ready to come on to bowl at short notice any time. 'Does that sound all right?' he asked. 'Yeah, yeah, yeah, fine,' I said quickly, hardly able to conceal my excitement.

Before then we had a Twenty20 international against Australia in Sydney, and I was thankful again that Kepler Wessels had given me those opportunities for Northants the previous season. Everybody has their own song and I walked out to the soundtrack to *The Full Monty*. I wasn't convinced that it was exactly right to be linked with a film best remembered for a group of men taking off their clothes. Not really my style at all. But everybody else thought it was a good idea. More to the point, I could not think of anything else.

The match itself was a fantastic experience under lights at one of the most historic grounds in the world. Unfortunately, Australia won comfortably, so that any hopes of a strong beginning to phase two of the tour were dismissed straight away. There is a strong element of fun about Twenty20 at the moment and I hope it doesn't become too serious once a World Championship is an established part of the scene. Australia played with nicknames on their shirts, which was a nice touch, but they were also as ruthless as they had been in the Tests. Their batting line-up was full of power hitters. I went for 40 from four overs but had Mike Hussey stumped, a dismissal I will be able to remind him about for the rest of our careers.

The proudest man on the pitch was Paul Nixon, our wicket-keeper, who was making his first appearance for England at the age of 36. I had come across Nixon as an opponent and knew how he could get under the skin of opponents with his persistent jabbering behind the stumps. I also knew that his unorthodox batting was just right for the one-day game. He is the only batsman I can remember who has reverse-swept me for six. His strokes never really got going in Australia, but when things clicked at the World Cup later on he was awesome.

They say that wicketkeepers are crazy – I've never met a quiet one, not on the field at any rate – but even for a keeper, Nixon is something else. He is one of those guys who is always on hand for advice. He was brought into the side for his personality as well as his skills and he was not going to allow inexperience at this level to hold him back. We were a good pair – he loved talking about cricket, telling his old stories about the characters he'd come across in 15 years on the county circuit, while I would listen all day. We needed that new source of energy after the Ashes.

At the end of every over he would come up to me with a few

words about where the batsman was aiming to score his runs or where his technique might be slightly vulnerable. He tries to distract and irritate batsmen, so if somebody is going well he will say to nobody in particular, 'He's under pressure now, lads; he can't afford to get out here.' One of his tricks is to pretend that he's seen something, so he might say to the batsman, 'Jeez, make sure you don't look up there – third row back from the sightscreen.' Of course there is nothing really there to see, but it might confuse the player and upset his concentration.

The tour was to have an incredible ending for us as we won the last four matches to take the series, winning our last three against Australia, including both of the finals. At long last we showed that we could play winning cricket. Before that, though, we gave probably our worst two performances of the trip in a terrible week at Adelaide. We were bowled out for 120 by New Zealand and then 110 by Australia on Australia Day. If people on the outside were mystified about how a team could fluctuate so wildly, we were just as puzzled ourselves. The most bizarre fact was that we eventually won without our best batsman, Kevin Pietersen, captain Michael Vaughan or the new-ball attack of Jimmy Anderson and Jon Lewis. Who would have predicted that?

Maybe there came a point when subconsciously we were just ready to go home. We knew that it could take one individual effort to turn things around, but deep down we must have questioned whether it would really happen. Australia were still proving so strong, but we also lost a couple of games to New Zealand after winning a scrappy match in Hobart. I thought my best perform-ance in the series was at Perth when the pitch was turning. After my eight wickets there in the Test match I was looking forward to going back, and when I did I took 2 for 35 from ten overs. New Zealand still managed to score 318 overall and we lost by 58 runs.

But looking back at the end of the series, I could see that we turned things around in the last few overs of this game, when Nixon and Liam Plunkett managed to deny New Zealand a bonus point with some really imaginative hitting.

That gave us the lift we desperately needed and we had a lucky break in the next game against Australia at Sydney when Shaun Tait dropped Ed Joyce on six. Joyce went on to score 107, and Plunkett then gave us a great start in the field with a brilliant inswinging yorker to bowl Adam Gilchrist first ball. It was all very well to say that if Tait had held that catch then Australia would have won that game and sent us home. Maybe, but these things happen. If Ashley Giles had held Ricky Ponting in the Adelaide Test, then the chances are we would have levelled the series 1–1 with three to play.

Somebody worked out that our first win against Australia came 89 days after we left England. It wasn't one of my own better games, as I went for more than a run a ball, but I was enjoying the challenge of bowling under pressure at different points in the innings. In some games I came on during the power-plays, with only two men on the boundary and batsmen going well. I have always managed to stay calm, I think because I don't confuse myself with anything complicated.

We then beat New Zealand in a really tight game at Brisbane before Paul Collingwood produced what must be the best ever one-day performance by an England player in the first final against Australia at Melbourne. It started with a great catch to get rid of Ponting off my bowling, continued with two run-outs with direct hits and ended with an unbeaten hundred, including a straight six off Glenn McGrath, to lead us home with three balls to spare. That win prompted our best celebration of the tour. We have a team song and we bellowed it out in the dressing room with

Nixon, Plunkett and me on the floor pretending to row an imaginary boat – three of us to celebrate the sequence of three wins. I may not have been able to drink any of the beer, but that did not stop me from handing out the bottles.

By the last match in Sydney we were full of confidence. The game was badly hit by rain and showers and we won on the Duckworth/Lewis system. It was a bit of an anticlimax because the presentation ceremony had to take place indoors in a small room along the corridor from the changing rooms, which also served as a spot for lunch and tea and press conferences. By this stage Michael Vaughan had gone home because of a hamstring injury. After all that had happened, I thought it was fitting that Andrew Flintoff should be the one to receive the trophy. I gave him a big hug when he came back into the dressing room and just said, 'Thanks, Freddie.'

There was still a good contingent of Barmy Army people supporting us out there and we didn't mind the weather as we ran over to pay our respects. Not that I went as far as Nixon, who threw himself into the crowd, having first lobbed his equipment in their direction. But I think I was starting to feel more confident around the dressing room. I could make the others laugh by getting up to dance to some bhangra music, which is a sort of Punjabi hip-hop. It's great. I always explain that the dance is easy – just imagine you are screwing in a light bulb overhead with one hand and patting a dog with the other. A lot of the guys have had a go at some point, though I could never quite convince Duncan Fletcher that he would be a natural.

So my first trip to Australia ended on a happy note. My one-day form had been a bit up and down, but I had done enough to make the World Cup squad. Suddenly the bookmakers made us second favourites behind Australia, and when their side (without

Ricky Ponting and several others) lost 3–0 in New Zealand it seemed that the competition would be wide open. We may have lost the Ashes 5–0 but, perhaps, with the squad back to full strength, we were peaking at the right time.

That, at least, was the hope as we regathered at Gatwick Airport for the final chapter of the winter adventure less than three weeks after arriving back from Australia via Heathrow. It felt as though I had only just managed to catch up on the local gossip with family and mates when I was off again. I don't think cricket is like any other sport for spending so much time away – perhaps with the exception of sailing, when you can be out at sea for months at a time. That is why you need bubbly characters in the dressing room, such as Nixon and Flintoff, to keep everybody upbeat day in, day out.

There had been some scare stories ahead of the World Cup about the strain on the airlines and problems at new and redeveloped grounds. In the end it seemed they were exaggerated. I was a bit concerned when I saw a rat scurrying across my room in the hotel in Antigua, but a quick switch solved that problem – at least as far as I was concerned. Some of the practice facilities were not quite as good as we would have liked ideally, but what struck me all the way through was the pride of the West Indian people in staging the event. Even when the criticism was at its strongest – some of it from people who were not even out there – the volunteers kept on smiling and doing their best.

We certainly couldn't have any complaints about the location for our warm-ups in St Lucia, the hotel backing on to a beautiful white sand beach. Three-quarters of a mile away at sea was a small rocky island and some of the guys immediately took up the challenge to swim there and back. Paul Collingwood and Andrew Strauss made it, but I decided to chill halfway and turned back.

Strauss made a joke in his weekly newspaper column that I'd been rescued. Somehow, a rumour began to spread that I'd been gasping for air, barely able to breathe, and had narrowly escaped drowning. I was very lucky that the tall tale didn't make the newspapers, otherwise my friends back home would have had more ammunition for their mickey-taking.

After a very happy week we made our way to Jamaica for the opening ceremony. This was yet another fantastic experience with all 16 teams staying in the same hotel. You could walk down to the lobby and see all the biggest names in the sport wandering around, filling in time by drinking juice or coffee or looking through the souvenir shops. The ceremony itself at the new Trelawny Stadium was a tribute to the effort of the people. It lasted three hours, but I was never bored listening to the singing or watching the immaculate dance routines. The players came on in a parade and once again I had to pinch myself to think that 12 months earlier I was barely an England cricketer. I turned to Mike Hussey in the Australia line-up and grinned. 'You look like you're enjoying yourself here, Monty,' he said. That was an understatement.

The format of the competition was for the top two sides in four groups to go through to the Super Eights, but points from the meeting of those two would be carried into the next stage. Our group also included New Zealand, Kenya and Canada, and barring any catastrophe it was pretty clear that our game against New Zealand would be the one, if you like, to count double. The fact that it was also our first of the event meant we had an immediate focus. In our four recent games in Australia the score had been 2–2. We knew everything there was to know about them.

Before that we did our bit for Comic Relief. The rest of the team lined up wearing red noses while I looked even more

The World Cup opening ceremony in Jamaica was full of colour and I was enthralled from first to last.

Bob Woolmer's death cast a pall over the competition. Jimmy Anderson, Duncan Fletcher, Phil Neale and I observe the minute's silence in St Lucia.

I was so nervous before meeting the Queen during the Lord's Test against West Indies in 2007. Her hand seemed tiny next to mine.

Floating on air after taking the wicket of Denesh Ramdin in the Third Test at Old Trafford.

You can see the intensity on my face after removing Dwayne Bravo at Old Trafford, a happy hunting ground for me.

A sight you don't see every day. Here I am in the slip cordon against West Indies at Chester-le-Street.

On the rostrum with Michael Vaughan after being named Man of the Series against West Indies.

At the premiere of *Die Hard 4.0* in Leicester Square. Bruce Willis is one of my favourite actors.

Our new coach Peter Moores – pictured here at Loughborough – is one of the most enthusiastic people I have met in cricket.

Not sure what I've done to upset Indian bowler Shantha Sreesanth in the First Test at Lord's.

My big hands – measured at around 11 inches from wrist to fingertip – help me to impart good spin on the ball.

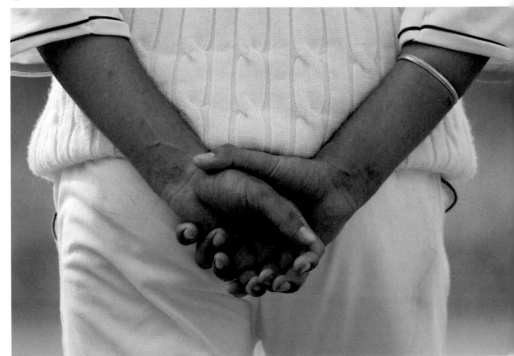

Left: Michael Vaughan and Simon Taufel inspect the Trent Bridge pitch before the Second Test against India.

Above: Watching thoughtfully from the Trent Bridge pavilion.

Left: Reflective and thankful after taking the wicket of R.P. Singh during the Second Test.

Below: The game at Trent Bridge was keenly fought. Rahul Dravid (*right*) rushes towards Zaheer Khan as he has a word with Michael Vaughan.

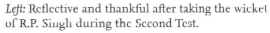

Massage therapist Mark Saxby helps to loosen me up before the Third Test against India at The Oval.

A pair of great England batsmen, Kevin Pietersen and Michael Vaughan.

Shaking hands with Anil Kumble after his maiden Test century – in his 118th game – at The Oval.

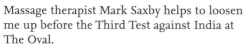

conspicuous in a red patka. Npower, who sponsor Test cricket in England, had offered to donate a pound for every run we scored through the competition. But when I did an interview for the ECB website, I got the figure wrong and said they were making it a thousand pounds each time. I couldn't understand why the interviewer's face suddenly dropped. Fortunately we were not going out live, so I could do a retake. The sponsors wanted me to wear the red patka instead of my normal black one against New Zealand, again to raise money. That would not have been a problem for me, but I guess the management thought it would be a distraction.

The game itself ended disappointingly. We really battled to get up to 209 for 7 and then whipped out their top three with the new ball. But New Zealand made their experience tell with Craig McMillan, Scott Styris and Jacob Oram getting them through. Styris went on to have a great World Cup with the bat and Oram batted really sensibly in support. I had come on slightly earlier than I expected, and went wild when McMillan crashed my second ball to deep cover. That was to be our fourth and final wicket of the game.

Following the loss to New Zealand, we were under some pressure to beat Canada and Kenya. And it intensified after what soon became known as the 'Fredalo' incident, when Andrew Flintoff ended a long night by capsizing a pedalo in the sea by our hotel. Five of the other players were out late as well and word somehow got back to the England management. The rumour was that a nightclub they visited – little more than 200 yards from the hotel – saw the chance of some cheap publicity by offering photos to the newspapers. But there were so many holidaymakers in the Gros Islet area where we were staying, including dozens in our own hotel, that it was almost impossible to keep anything to ourselves.

The first I knew about what happened was the following morning, the day before our game against Canada. We were suddenly called in for a team meeting and told to write on a board the time we had gone to bed. Duncan Fletcher made his feelings known and it is common knowledge that fines were imposed. As far as I am concerned, what people do in their own time is not any of my business. I know how much all of the squad wanted to do well in the Caribbean. This was a matter between the management and the players concerned.

There is no doubt that the business affected the general mood. I didn't detect any sort of rift between those who were out and those who weren't, but I'm sure we can all think back to school-days, for example, when things go quiet for a while after a teacher has had a go at the class. You don't like to see your mates in trouble. I know that I felt a bit downbeat for a few days and I know that Freddie was devastated at being suspended for the Canada game and told that he would not stand in as captain if Michael Vaughan was injured again. I thought he responded superbly in training the next week when he steamed in to players, including Vaughan and Paul Collingwood, in the nets.

Fortunately we beat Canada fairly comfortably. I dread to imagine the headlines if we'd slipped on that particular banana skin. It was also on the Sunday that we heard of the death in Jamaica of Bob Woolmer. As the days went on, the story became more and more sinister and unpleasant. We never thought about flying home – the future of the event was a matter for the ICC, not for us – but it put the 'Fredalo' incident into a more appropriate context. The original idea that somebody may have been murdered because of cricket seemed mind-boggling and I didn't like the suggestion that it could have had something to do with match-fixing. I barely knew Bob, but that left me in a minority among the squad. All of us had seen him at the opening ceremony less than a fortnight before. It came as a relief when his death was finally attributed to natural causes.

Woolmer's death was still the biggest talking point by the time we made it through to the Super Eights. From St Lucia we went on to Guyana, where we beat a determined and improving Ireland side. I must share quite an embarrassing story from this leg of the trip. Because my room was starting to get quite cold, I thought it would be a good idea to turn off the air conditioning overnight. Bad move. Next morning the condensation was so heavy that the floor was damp and some of my kit literally dripping wet.

From then on the tale of our competition was 'nearly, but not quite'. Against Sri Lanka we lost on the last ball and then we reached a fantastic position against Australia – 164 for 2 in the 30th over with Ian Bell and Kevin Pietersen batting like a dream. If we had won even one of those two games we would have gone through to the semi-finals and then, who knows? At Antigua, we actually pushed Australia harder than any other side over the whole seven weeks. It was like hitting the rewind button and going back to the Ashes – we had a really bad period, lost a lot of wickets and couldn't recover.

The Sri Lanka game produced the most exciting finish of the competition. I watched as nervously as anyone as Paul Nixon and Ravi Bopara pulled us back from a desperate position with some incredible shots. I'm sure that Ravi will become a top-class one-day batsman. He can manoeuvre the ball between fielders, while some of Nixon's reverse-sweeps took my breath away, even though I'd seen him play those shots time and time again. It came as a special relief to me when Ravi lined up to face Dilhara Fernando's last ball. I had been padded up and shaking at the thought of having to go in next. We needed three to win, but Fernando played a very clever trick as he pulled up in his delivery stride, watching

Ravi's footwork to see whether he would back away and where he intended to place the ball. We were a bit annoyed at his gamesmanship in the dressing room, but no doubt we would have done the same.

In the end Bopara was bowled by Fernando. When you lose by such a narrow margin – two runs – you replay every single ball in your own mind. I tried afterwards to think of my fielding – could I have saved a run here or there by being a little bit quicker to the ball or throwing flatter? And how did I bowl – did I give away runs too easily? A loss like this was as bad in its own way as the really heavy defeats we suffered in Adelaide.

It came down to the penultimate game against South Africa at Bridgetown. The Kensington Oval had been virtually rebuilt and it was the best of the grounds we played in. The stands were named after the great West Indies players and in the field between balls I tried to piece together a team from all the stars who were being honoured. I imagined those names – Sobers, Greenidge, Haynes, Marshall and Garner among them – playing on the same acres of grass. That sent a chill down my spine.

The sad part was that we couldn't be out there for longer. Andrew Hall had carved through our batting with reverse swing, and they passed our 154 in less than 20 full overs. My own two overs went for 24. And there my World Cup ended. Dropped for the 'dead' game against West Indies, I thought back to the farewells to Shane Warne, Glenn McGrath and Justin Langer in Australia as another great player, Brian Lara, bowed out this time. I remembered back to my conversation with him in that bar in Barbados eight years earlier when he said that we might face each other one day. Yet another 'nearly, but not quite'.

Overall, I thought that I bowled pretty well, especially against Bangladesh when I took three wickets. Admittedly there was nothing flash about my bowling. I don't have a doosra like Muttiah Muralitharan or a googly like Brad Hogg, the two leading spinners in the tournament. Daniel Vettori was another guy who impressed me. He is a good comparison because we are both orthodox slow left-arm. He is a very subtle bowler who uses the crease well to change his angle. That kind of thing comes with experience. I tried to do things the way I knew: simply, as accurately as I could manage and with variations of pace. This wasn't the place to experiment. I was also happier with my fielding and I never thought of myself as a liability to the side.

Even though I had passed the first anniversary of my debut, I still had an incredible amount to learn. At the same time I knew that one era was ending for England, with Duncan Fletcher stepping down as coach. He gathered us round into a tight group at training a couple of days after the South Africa game to say that he had handed in his resignation. We could see the tears in his eyes as he spoke and it became a very sad few minutes as we all shook his hand. I just said to him, 'Thanks, coach, you've helped me and good luck.'

I guess people didn't see that emotional side of Duncan, and it was written many times that his ability to stay on an even keel helped to make him such an effective coach. But he is a human being, like all of us, and he has his highs and lows. He was very angry in St Lucia after the late night, and after the second one-day defeat in Adelaide when he felt he had to apologise to supporters for the performance. I also remember the delight on his face when I took my first Test wicket, Sachin Tendulkar. I know he took a lot of criticism for leaving me out of the first two Ashes Tests, but I always backed his judgement. The idea that he held back my England career is silly. How can that argument stack up when he picked me in the first place after I was a few months out of university? I would have been fine if he had decided to stay on, but results were disappointing over the winter and he may have felt that he'd just had enough.

I could relate what happened to something I learned in a sports-management module while I was a student at Loughborough. Theory runs that winning is difficult, but to win for a second time is even harder. Having won the Ashes in 2005, it was always going to be harder in 2006–07 because Australia had seen the strategy we applied to make us successful. I can remember both their coach John Buchanan and captain Ricky Ponting describing how they learned from England and adapted their own game. Which is why, as I wrote in the last chapter, we have to make sure that we now learn from Australia in time for 2009.

They had an amazing winter, adding the World Cup to their 5–0 Ashes win. For me, they were easily the best side in the tournament because they had all bases covered. They could score runs quickly against the new ball when the power-plays were in operation, work it around in the middle and then hit out at the end. Their seamers all bowled very intelligently and Brad Hogg probably enjoyed the best two months of his life. There wasn't a weak link in the XI, or probably in the squad, given that their reserve batsman, Brad Hodge, hit a hundred. Sri Lanka were the next best side and then South Africa and New Zealand just behind. Whatever people think of the format and the length of the tournament, it resulted in the top four sides reaching the semi-finals and produced the final that people seemed to want to see.

I was back in Luton by the time Australia and Sri Lanka contested the 51st and last game. Yes, it was good to be back home – not least because I landed on my 25th birthday. My parents had arranged a party to celebrate with friends, family and the home cooking that I'd begun to wonder whether I would taste again.

They had also bought a great present, a Nintendo games console, which allowed me to play virtual sport instead of having to worry about the real thing – at least until I reported back to Northampton with the 2007 season already in full swing.

To be honest, I only dipped in and out of the final. Even I, with my deep love of the game, was ready for a break. Put yourself in my shoes. After our winter, did I really want to watch Adam Gilchrist hit balls into stands? I'd had enough of that first-hand. No, I switched off the television long before the end and missed the farce of Sri Lanka having to bat out three overs in near darkness against the Australia spinners because the umpires had misread the rules. I don't think I missed a lot there.

11

A NEW ERA

THE arrival of a new boss can make a lot of people apprehensive, but I wasn't the least bit worried when Peter Moores was chosen to replace Duncan Fletcher as the England coach. I did not know Moores too well, but I did have one very happy memory from our brief acquaintance: he was the man who passed me on to David Graveney when I heard about my first call into the Test squad in 2006. At the time he was director of the National Academy. We did not spend much time together then because I was independent from his group. But even in those three days at Loughborough I gained a very positive feeling about the way he went about his work. As the 2007 season continued I realised that my first impression was spot on.

The striking features about Moores are his enthusiasm and the amount of energy he brings to the squad. If that sounds like mumbo-jumbo, I can explain it easily. When a guy is happy and active, and has lots of ideas, it rubs off on people around him. You can also draw energy from a big, supportive crowd, or from a player who scores a hundred or takes some wickets. On the opposite side, a man who is downbeat and cynical, who knocks down suggestions from everybody else but never has any of his own, can create a negative atmosphere around him. It stands to reason that, in sport, a lot of these positive vibes come from actually winning, but I think it works like an ever-expanding circle.

A successful team is a happy team, and because it is happy it has more chance of winning again.

Like most people, I can be a bit slow and sleepy first thing in the morning. But whenever I see Moores at breakfast he is so bright and breezy that he seems to have been up for hours already. He almost always breaks into a big smile and says something like, 'Hello there, Monty.' I am usually in such a dozy state that I can barely grunt anything in reply.

One of the big advantages to me was that Moores had been a wicketkeeper before moving into coaching. The men behind the stumps always have a good insight into bowling because they get a front-on view and are often the first to spot when the action is not quite right. Moores built up a great deal of experience in his playing career with Sussex, and during the summer I spent a lot of time bowling to him just to make sure that everything remained in good working order. Even from the dressing room during play he noticed little things – perhaps if I was bowling a shade too quickly, which can be a weakness of mine, or not giving the ball enough air. I sense things, but Moores can see them and, between us, I think we have worked pretty well so far.

His choice of Andy Flower to replace Matthew Maynard as assistant also helped. As I learned from the experience of playing against Essex early in my career, Flower was a brilliant player of spin in four-day and one-day cricket. He gave me an insight into the way a batsman thinks and his approach to playing slow bowling on different pitches. With David Parsons still involved as the ECB spin coach, I had every base covered when it came to preparing for the Test series against West Indies.

It was natural that Moores would be compared with Fletcher, and I suppose the 3–0 win against West Indies confirmed that we were ready for a change. As far as I know, Fletcher was a big supporter of Moores and a lot of what they say is the same. That ought not to be surprising – the basics of cricket, which I try to stick to, are the same whoever is in charge. The difference is probably in the way they go about the job. Fletcher liked to stay in the background at training. He was always there if you wanted him, but otherwise he would watch quietly and bide his time before making his suggestions. Moores, on the other hand, is a visible presence. He likes to get involved and bounce ideas around.

One of the fielding drills he introduced was described as 'happy slapping' in the press, and got some bad publicity when Steve Harmison bruised a finger. But it is great fun and a really good way of working on balance and agility. Splitting into pairs, the aim is to touch your opponent's knee and then retreat quickly so that he doesn't touch you back. You need a low centre of gravity and quick reflexes to win. We first tried it before the First Test against West Indies at Lord's and, inevitably, it became very competitive. I was up against Harmison and Matt Prior and soon found that my big hands and long fingers gave me an advantage. I could touch the others easily but they didn't have the reach to respond. Somebody said that I was like Mr Tickle, a character in Roger Hargreaves's Mr Men series for children, whose long, rubbery arms allow him to span huge distances without moving his body. Mr Tickle would be a good man to field on the boundary.

Moores also has an amazing way of giving slip-catching practice. Usually, one man throws the ball towards a batsman who then guides it to the fielders. I don't know if Fletcher used to nick a lot of balls when he played in South Africa and Zimbabwe, but he could place the ball as though he had it on a rope. Moores does it differently. He throws the ball with his right hand against a bat held in his left, and then turns his wrist to direct it towards first, second or third slip. You have to react very quickly because you cannot follow the ball along its path from the thrower. Although giving catches like this looks very easy, Paul Collingwood could not get a ball anywhere near the fielders when he tried it at Headingley. The players and the crowd were in hysterics.

Of course, I am no expert at slip catching, but I now try to take part in practice at least once during the two days building towards a Test match. I have found it a good way to work on getting sharper and anticipating the ball coming towards me – at slip there is far less time to react than at long leg or mid-on. During the Fourth Test against West Indies at Chester-le-Street I did actually get to field in the slips for the first time. They were down to their tail and Michael Vaughan wanted to put everybody in attacking positions. 'If you get a catch now, the crowd will go mad,' he told me. Unfortunately the chance never came my way, although I will admit that I felt a bit nervous as I crouched down, wondering how much time I would have to react.

The First Test began less than a month after our last game in the World Cup. I had played a pair of four-day matches for Northamptonshire in the meantime and felt that I needed those games more than an extra week or so of rest. It was important to get used to bowling once more on soft pitches where the ball does not bounce as much as it had done in the Caribbean. Besides which, the intense schedule of international cricket means there are few openings to represent your county once the programme gets under way. I enjoy the opportunities to play for North-amptonshire when they come along, and one of my ambitions is to take the field for them in a one-day final at Lord's.

After the disappointments of the Ashes and the World Cup, and with a new coach in charge, we were desperate to get the season off to a winning start. Unfortunately, the weather inter-vened just when the First Test was heading towards an exciting finish. We had set West Indies 401 to win, a huge task for them but possible given the talent in their batting line-up. The fact that they had scored 89 for 0 from only 22 overs suggested that they would have gone for the runs rather than trying to block out for survival. That said, we knew we were in a stronger position and would have backed ourselves to take all ten wickets on the final day, given the chance.

I will always remember this game because I managed to get my name carved onto the famous Lord's honours board in the dressing room by taking 6 for 129. Somebody quickly looked into the fate of spinners at the ground and worked out that the last one to claim six wickets in a first innings at the ground had been none other than my great influence Bishan Bedi as far back as 1974. Just so that I was up there immediately, instead of having to wait for the engraver, our fitness coach Nigel Stockhill and physio Kirk Russell wrote my name on a long piece of brown tape and stuck it onto the board. I could hardly wait to return later in the season to see the proper inscription, placing me alongside other bowlers to take five or more wickets in an innings for England. There is another board for batsmen who score hundreds and, with five of our batsmen reaching three figures, including Matt Prior on his debut, it was a wonder that Stockhill and Russell didn't run out of tape.

Cricket history means a lot to me. I would be exaggerating if I said I could name all the England captains in turn, but I have read a few books and appreciate the long line of players who have represented the country. Very, very few get this far in the game, and I have the greatest respect for everyone who has done so. During the World Cup the editor of *Wisden* named me as one of his five Cricketers of the Year and I knew straight away the importance of that nomination. Awards like that, and the honours board at Lord's, go way back into the nineteenth century. You cannot help but feel proud at being linked with great players.

When I first went into a Lord's dressing room with the Combined Universities side, I read in awe the list of players commemorated, some of them long gone, some still alive. It is incredible to think that in a hundred years' time another young spin bowler will sit in the same place and do the same thing. I had a quiet chuckle to myself when I imagined all those players, yet to be born, thinking, 'M.S. Panesar – I wonder what he was like.' The mind really does boggle at times.

What the board does not show is how I took my wickets. Five of them were given out lbw, which became quite a big talking point in the media. I had been trying to get closer to the wicket when I bowled to increase my chances of getting leg-before decisions. That way, the natural curve of the ball would take it towards middle rather than off stump, and because I was bowling pretty much wicket to wicket, anything that went on with the arm would probably hit the stumps. Even so, some umpires are reluctant to give a batsman out if he shapes to play forward with his bat behind his pad, because they believe there is an element of doubt. That can be very frustrating, but Asad Rauf showed brilliant skill in his judgement because Hawk-Eye proved him right in all five cases. Rauf is relatively new to the international panel but I think he has a big future because he makes so many right calls in pressure situations.

On a seaming pitch like the one at Lord's, the role of the spinner is bound to change and the two games for Northamptonshire stood me in really good stead. The ball can grip off the surface, but it will not fizz through. Batsmen have that little bit of extra time to react. You can still create pressure with accuracy and dot balls, but I had worked out for myself that I needed to make the slight adjustment to my landing point at the crease to be more effective.

Lord's can be a difficult ground for batsmen and bowlers because there is an eight-foot slope from one side to the other. It goes left to right downhill looking from the pavilion, and some players struggle to keep their balance. As a spinner, it can work in my favour at either end. From the Nursery End, the incline takes the ball away from the right-hander, adding to any spin I can impart. But from the Pavilion End it means the ball is more likely to go straight on.

The other highlight, for me, was meeting the Queen and Prince Philip. In the dressing room before we all went out to line up I worked myself into a panic, flapping around and firing out questions to nobody in particular: 'What do I say? What do I say? What do I call her?' I get a bit tongue-tied at the best of times, which is perhaps why some of the things I say on TV would look a bit funny if they were written down in print. I think it might have been Andrew Strauss who put an arm round me and told me that I wouldn't be required to say anything more than 'hello, Ma'am'.

'Don't worry,' he said. 'She's not going to ask about your arm ball.'

She did little more than shake my hand – I was amazed at how small it was compared with mine – but Prince Philip had more of a word. 'Ah,' he said. 'I remember when you came into the side a year ago, and here you are still in the team. Well, it's great to see you.' Five minutes later we were back playing cricket, another priceless experience over.

After the game, Ramnaresh Sarwan, the West Indies captain, said that his side were not especially worried about me because I had not taken my wickets with spin. I guess that was fair comment. Balls had skidded on rather than turned square.

Perhaps the fact that batsmen had played outside the line suggested they thought it would spin a bit more than it did. Sarwan also said that the batsmen would aim to take me on through the rest of the series. I was quite happy to read his comments. If, from now on, they were playing for no spin, it ought to be easier to take the edge. And I also saw it as a victory of a kind that they were having to re-think their approach.

Every game has the potential to bring out something new and the Second Test at Headingley was no different. This one made the record books because the fourth, and thankfully final, day was the coldest recorded at a Test match in England. The temperature dropped to 7.4 Celsius but, as one of those out there in the field, I would have put it even lower. I always wore at least two jumpers and in my pocket I carried a little sachet full of powder that magically warms up when you rub it. Whoever came up with the invention deserves a knighthood.

I bowled seven overs in the match. Somebody said it was the easiest match fee I'd ever earned. When I did come on I was about to hand umpire Rudi Koertzen my second jumper when he said, 'Are you sure you don't want to keep that on?' I bowled one over in my shirt sleeves before taking his advice. Gripping the ball was not so easy in the conditions, but I challenged myself to see whether I could still be effective. The task became gradually easier and I managed to dismiss Dwayne Bravo, my only wicket, with a quicker one, which I think took him by surprise.

Our seamers were outstanding, especially Ryan Sidebottom on his first appearance since 2001. West Indies may not be the side that everyone remembers from the 1970s and 1980s, but to bowl them out for 146 and 141 was a tremendous achievement. It was something of an on-off game because of the weather, but I was really impressed with the way that Sidebottom, Steve Harmison and Liam Plunkett came out firing immediately after every break. Usually it can take a couple of overs to get back into the swing. I had a little bit of sympathy for West Indies because Shivnarine Chanderpaul missed the game with injury and Sarwan proved unable to bat after hurting his shoulder in the field. He did not play again on the tour. But, then again, we did not have Andrew Flintoff at all. These things have a way of balancing out across time.

We did have Michael Vaughan. Amazingly, this was the first time that I had played under his captaincy in a Test match. It was inevitable that he would be the subject of most interest from the media in the build-up, and not all the comments were flattering. But his story should be an inspiration not just to youngsters but to anybody in the professional game who is recovering from serious injury. Less than a year earlier, Vaughan had been told that his knee would not allow him to play again. Yet here he was scoring a hundred on his comeback – and on his home ground. Such an achievement speaks more than any number of words, but I would like, one day, to be able to talk to him about his experiences during that long period away from the action, to discover where he found the mental strength to fight his way back.

When I think about what he must have gone through I wonder whether I have had things easy in my own career. All right, I learned to play on what was basically a park and did not go to a private school with state-of-the-art facilities, but I came into the England side relatively early and, touch wood, have not suffered serious injury. If anything does happen, I will use Vaughan as a role model to keep going through all the recovery work and never, ever give up. Having led England in the 2005 Ashes, it was not as though he needed to play now to leave a legacy.

Headingley is unique, as far as I know, because the main stand doubles up for cricket on one side and rugby on the other. Facilities are shared and the dressing room is towards the rugby side of the structure. It means that you cannot see the play from inside and the viewing area outdoors is a very small section directly next to the press box. There is not room for everyone to sit down so you find that players watch from different places. I actually saw part of Vaughan's innings on a small television in a room used by the media for their lunch. But once he started to get to 80 and 90 we gradually made our way from our separate spots out onto the cramped balcony to make sure we were all there together when he reached his hundred. We were all there, too, in the dressing room when he got out not long afterwards, ready to pat him on the back and say 'well done'. Vaughan's innings was the perfect example of an individual performance giving energy to the rest of the side.

It takes a lot to keep Kevin Pietersen out of the limelight, but Vaughan's innings managed to do exactly that – even though Pietersen's 226 was the highest for England in 17 years. I am convinced that he will score 300 in a Test innings before the end of his career. He is not just a great batsman, but he can score so quickly that he will make the time to hit those runs. With that extra gear he could sprint from 200 to 300 in little more than an hour once he is set. It has already got to the stage where people expect him to score runs every time. He is a player who brings spectators into the grounds. At Headingley he played a really mature innings. He accelerated and then slowed down a few times, depending on the bowling. The key word is 'control'. He always seems to be hitting balls where he wants them to go no matter what the bowling.

For the rest of us it is a case of picking up what we can, where we can. All players have favourite grounds. Lord's must be mine, even though the pitch is flat, and I was also struck by most of them in Australia. I liked Brisbane with its big stand and Melbourne for its sheer size all round. Perth, too, made an impression because it felt very open and airy even with thousands of people packed into the stand. At this point I ought to include Northampton. Unfortunately, not even the most loyal members would describe our Wantage Road base as pretty. Speaking as a spinner, I can at least say that the pitch has a beautiful appearance.

Then there are lucky grounds, and there is no doubt about Old Trafford topping my list. I arrived there at the start of June thinking back to the eight Pakistan wickets I had taken in 2006, and left a week later with my first ten-wicket match haul for England in the bag. The last spinner to do this was Phil Tufnell, a hero of mine with a brilliant natural loop. More importantly, our 60-run victory meant that we had taken an unassailable 2–0 lead in the series. The Ashes and the World Cup were now well and truly behind us.

My figures were 16.4–5–50–4 in the first innings and 51.5–13–137–6 in the second, so with 68.3 overs in the match nobody could say that it was easy money this time. West Indies made it hard work, especially the fit-again Chanderpaul who batted for almost nine hours during the match. Reports said that I bowled with more over-spin than usual, but really the extra bounce was due to the hardness of the pitch rather than anything extra that I managed to impart to the ball. I am like a lot of spinners in that I would rather have a pitch with bounce than turn. Ideally, of course, I would have both, but you shouldn't be greedy in life. If the ball spins slowly, good batsmen can react quickly enough to play the ball off the pitch. Batting becomes harder when the ball rears quickly from what would be a normal length.

The surface at Old Trafford was as hard as solid concrete. For the first time in my life umpire Aleem Dar had to signal that I had bowled a bouncer when a ball shot past Chanderpaul at head height during the second innings. I know that he is quite small, but that is something I never thought would happen. Some spin bowlers down the years, including Shane Warne and Phil Edmonds, have bowled bouncers as a deliberate tactic. I guess it could be used as a surprise every so often to try to peg the batsman on the back foot if he is wanting to come down the pitch.

With such a helpful pitch it was inevitable that we would create a lot of opportunities which, in turn, would lead to a regular stream of appeals. Things get very exciting in the middle when you feel you are close to taking a wicket and, in the second innings, with West Indies chasing a massive 455, we could afford to go on the attack all the way through. I like to play enthusiastically even when we are up against it and I must admit that I probably went slightly over the top on the final day. People commented on the number of appeals and Aleem Dar had a word at one point just to remind me not to celebrate before I asked the question. The rules do not allow this because it is seen as a way of trying to intimidate the umpire. But it was far from the formal warning reported in some circles. Aleem was smiling and what he actually said was, 'I know you're excited, just take it easy.'

He knew that I was not trying to put him under extra pressure. To me, that would be counter-productive. Why would a bowler want to get on the wrong side of an umpire? There are few secrets in international cricket these days and umpires know what I am like. The celebrations when I take a wicket are not an act. They are a release of energy and joy, and that sometimes kicks in when I am convinced a batsman is leg-before or has nicked one through to the keeper. I don't think anybody would really want me to contain my enthusiasm. Without that competitive edge I would be only half the bowler that I am.

There is an ICC Code of Conduct, which applies to international matches, with a system of penalties including fines and suspensions for bad behaviour. The fact that I was not charged confirms that any offence was very minor. Aleem made his point, I took note and we got on with what had become a fantastic game. Had I shown any dissent, it would have been a different matter. I have always accepted the word of the umpire and, as I said earlier, under the kind of pressure we all felt on that final day at Old Trafford, it is amazing that they get so many decisions right. Peter Moores and Michael Vaughan were both happy with my approach. Vaughan said to me afterwards, 'Go out there, have some fun and express yourself. If I think you're going too far, I'll let you know.'

Aleem made a funny remark when I asked him for the ball as a souvenir for taking the six second-innings wickets. He looked at me with a stern face and said, 'Only if you promise to behave next time.' I didn't know how to reply, until he burst out laughing and threw me the ball. I try to get the ball every time I take five or more wickets and my collection, although still small, is beginning to build up nicely. I mark them all with a thick felt-tipped pen so that I know which is which. Somebody suggested that I get a cabinet made to display them, but it would still look quite empty at the moment. There is a long way to go before I can start thinking in those terms. But I do get them out from time to time and spin them around in my hands, thinking back to each of my wickets in that particular innings. They are special to me and carry great sentimental value.

West Indies blew hot and cold during the series. I think that the Old Trafford Test showed that more than anywhere. In the first innings they lost their last six wickets for 13 runs, yet second time around they reached 394, the highest total of the match, in really difficult conditions. Chanderpaul's unbeaten 116 in almost seven hours ranks as one of the best defensive innings I have seen, given the way that the ball was bouncing and spitting or hitting a crack and shooting through low.

If I had to pick a favourite wicket I would struggle to choose between two. In the first innings I managed to get one to turn sharply to Darren Sammy, which he could only glove to slip. Then, in the second innings, I found another. Denesh Ramdin took it high on the bat to give Paul Collingwood another catch. Actually, there is a third contender because I also completed my first caught and bowled in Test cricket when Sammy drove a ball back to my right. Sammy looked even more surprised than I felt – which is saying something. As a bowler you really do just thrust your hands instinctively in the direction of the ball. If it sticks, you pretend it was under control all along.

As at Old Trafford the previous year, I spent a long time in partnership with Steve Harmison. He was really hostile at times in the second innings. We are a better side when he is on song because he can ruffle up batsmen with his pace and bounce. There was no better example than the way he blasted out Jerome Taylor and Fidel Edwards. I think it is slightly unfair to complain about inconsistency because none of the out-and-out fast bowlers in the world get it right every single time. Brett Lee, Fidel Edwards and Shaun Tait can be expensive, but you have to balance that against their wicket-taking potential.

By lunch on the fifth day West Indies had reduced the target to below a hundred, but with seven of their wickets down we were confident we would be able to take the other three as long as we kept putting the ball in the right areas. That has become a bit of a cliché but, like many clichés, it is used so often because it is true. We were very relaxed during the break – in fact, from my experience, we've never been any different under Vaughan. The pressure was on West Indies because we were still in front. They had done really well to stay in the game, but it would still take a great effort to keep going and actually win. Harmison struck very soon after lunch when Taylor could only fend off a ball to Alastair Cook, and we were up and running again.

The final wicket arrived when Ian Bell took a brilliant instinctive catch to his right at short leg. Corey Collymore had got a bottom edge onto his pad trying to defend. It went to the third umpire, but I knew it was legitimate straight away – although after what had happened earlier I didn't want to be seen celebrating before the final decision. I am very lucky in the England side because Bell and Cook are both superb fielders around the bat, Bell in particular. It comes down to bravery, fast reflexes and good hand-eye coordination. In most sides the position of short leg is given to the junior player and I always find it funny to see Bell there, because when I first played for England at Under-19 level, he was my captain and could choose any spot on the field. It is actually an important position for a spinner and I always develop a relationship with the man there. Sometimes when he takes the helmet, Bell will say, 'Don't bowl a long hop now, Monty.' With the banter that goes on, it can often seem like there are two wicketkeepers out there offering encouragement with their little comments and claps of the hands.

We decided as a team to save our big celebration for after the Fourth, and final, Test at Durham. I went away feeling really happy with my bowling and my figures, but stressed in my *Daily Mail* column that I was still far from the finished article. Even without thinking, I came up with four spinners – Muttiah Muralitharan,

Harbhajan Singh, Anil Kumble and Daniel Vettori – who were better than I was, and had more experience. It would have been five, of course, had the great Shane Warne not retired a few months earlier. I didn't feel I was being over-modest. I might have taken ten wickets in a match, but conditions had been very favourable. Things were bound to be different in the next match, which is why I was overjoyed to take five wickets in an innings for a sixth time and add another ball to my collection.

As expected, the Riverside pitch was slower and did not offer a lot of spin. The whole of the first day was washed out and we bowled only 40.4 overs on the second. The seamers did the bulk of the work in the first innings with Chanderpaul, again, batting for hour after hour without offering a chance. He does not fit into the West Indian tradition of hitting the ball on the up and thrilling crowds, although his approach is entirely different in the one-day game. To me, he is more like a typical Indian batsman who likes to play late. He uses his wrists and very quick hands to work the ball into spaces, often at the last moment, when you think you have finally got through his defence.

He looks unusual at the crease, almost crab-like, but there are so many different styles in international cricket that you quickly get used to the occasional odd stance. Certainly, by the time we got to Durham, I don't think there was anything he could have done to surprise us. He may set himself up outside leg stump, but with his trigger movements he is bang in line by the time he puts bat to ball. I would describe him as a brilliantly skilful player whose statistics over more than a decade mean that he deserves to rank in the next group below the real greats such as Brian Lara and Sachin Tendulkar.

Whether I prefer to bowl to Chanderpaul or Rahul Dravid rather than Shahid Afridi or Adam Gilchrist is a difficult question. I have taken hammerings from both of that second pair, so I know how destructive they can be. The other side of the coin is that they give you a chance by being so adventurous. My favourite players are those who come out to bat looking tentative. Maybe that comes from being out of form, a lack of experience or because they think that the pitch is against them and they are going to get the killer ball at any moment.

Being a spinner does require a certain attitude. We have to be the most patient players in the game. Just imagine how it feels to be whacked into the stand by Gilchrist or Afridi. You can shrink almost physically because the crowd will be cheering and shouting for a repeat. Tens of thousands of people want you to fail and your opponent to succeed. But you are not like a fast bowler who can get his own back by ruffling up the batsman with a few sharp bouncers. Sometimes you feel like the puny little kid being bullied in the school playground – except there is no teacher to run to for sympathy. You just have to will yourself to keep going and think how silly the bully will look when you get him out with a ball at around 50 mph.

Aggression was not on the West Indian agenda going into the final day of the series. They were three wickets down and still behind overall, but we knew that if we kept our discipline we might be able to frustrate them into making mistakes. Matthew Hoggard made the breakthrough by removing Chris Gayle, and Chanderpaul could only watch as wickets fell at the other end. The Collingwood–Panesar combination that worked successfully at Old Trafford struck again when Marlon Samuels pushed forward and edged to slip. But my favourite wicket came four overs later. Nothing against Denesh Ramdin, but I was just really pleased with a ball that dipped, pitched on middle-and-leg and hit his off stump. It reminded me of the ball that had bowled Younis

Khan a year earlier, which I think is the best I have ever delivered.

At the presentation ceremony I was surprised and thrilled to be named as man of the series for the first time. With 23 wickets, I was the leading wicket-taker on either side, but I thought that Ryan Sidebottom might be close, having made such a brilliant return after six years out, while Alastair Cook again batted very consistently. I've been asked a few times what I do when I am given a bottle of champagne, bearing in mind that I am teetotal because of my faith. Do I break it open for the others in the dressing room or take it home to give to a friend? The truth is that I keep the bottles, unopened, as souvenirs. I guess people who like the taste of champagne will say that the drink is being wasted. But I think of those bottles, and the contents, as trophies of my success. They are almost as special as my collection of cricket balls. And, no, I have never been tempted to crack one of them open and take a sip out of curiosity. It wouldn't feel right.

A day or so after the game, the latest ICC rankings put me joint sixth among bowlers in the world. Muttiah Muralitharan was on top. I have not seen the computer program, but I do know that the calculations go beyond averages and the number of wickets taken. The quality of the opposition is also taken into account. Five wickets against Australia, for example, would be worth more than five wickets against Bangladesh. There is also what is called a decay factor, so that recent performances are given greater weight than those in the distant past. The ratings ought to be accurate, but I do wonder how a batsman or bowler can climb a significant number of places on the basis of a single good performance. During the winter, when many of the countries are playing at the same time, the list resembles a pop chart with climbers, fallers and new entries.

In terms of popularity, I was now getting at least as many messages as when I came back from Australia. More and more of them seemed to be from women. So many emails were posted on my website complaining that all the clothing lines were aimed at men that we decided to design a couple of T-shirts specifically for the fairer sex. One of them said 'MmmmmMonty' and the other simply 'I Love Monty'. I don't think I've blushed so much in my life as when I saw the first batch from the factory. Needless to say, it wasn't long before my mates found out and the ribbing started. One of them described me as 'Monty Panesar, sex symbol and cricketer' – which promptly sent my face red for a second time.

As England players we receive all sorts of invitations. Most of them I cannot accept because of time, but one arrived during the West Indies series that I was determined to accept at any price: an invitation to attend the premiere of *Die Hard* 4.0 at the famous Empire in Leicester Square, not long after the Durham Test. Bruce Willis is my favourite actor and I love the *Die Hard* series. I like a good action film and I think he has a great image in that dirty vest. The film lived up to all my expectations and the one regret was that I didn't get to meet Willis himself. I am not a big autograph collector these days, but I would definitely have plucked up the courage that night if I'd managed to get near him.

12
INDIAN SUMMER

A UTOGRAPH collecting seemed to be on the minds of some of my friends in the weeks that followed. India were due to take the place of the West Indies and that meant coming face to face again with Sachin Tendulkar. It seemed that everybody I knew wanted me to ask for his signature or a little piece of memorabilia. I tried to explain that it isn't part of being an England player to pester an opponent for autographs. Again, though, I thought back to that day in 1996 when we all cheered him on in Luton, and the early mornings a few months earlier when we sat together in front of the television to watch him bat in the World Cup in Asia. My mates all want me to do well, of course, but Tendulkar remains the big hero. I lost count of the number of messages I received during the series along the lines of 'Sachin's going to get you.'

There was a bit more sympathy from relatives back in India, and especially from my Uncle Kaka. He follows my career particularly closely from the Punjab and it is always a joy to exchange some very friendly banter. It amazes me how quickly he finds out when I take a wicket and he is always ringing with the reaction from over there. I sometimes wonder how people find time to work, as they always have a very detailed knowledge of cricket. They are very proud, to the point that I think Uncle Kaka can recite my career figures better than I can. As he says, he can't lose when England play India.

I have a natural connection with India, but they are fantastic opponents for any spin bowler. Not even the Australians present the same challenge, because Indian batsmen are raised on slow, turning pitches. It is hard enough bowling to them in conditions that might offer help, let alone in England during a wet summer. At least my career had moved on since I made my Test debut in Nagpur. By now I felt more at home with England and had the confidence of a few wickets under my belt. But I still recognised that they were brilliant players. India were not due to return to England for a Test series until 2011, so there was a chance that crowds would be getting their last sight of Tendulkar, Rahul Dravid, Sourav Ganguly and V. V. S. Laxman. I couldn't believe that some critics suggested these players were past their best. They all looked plenty good enough to me.

As well as playing in the First Test itself I was desperate to go back to Lord's to see my name on the famous honours board after my six wickets in the West Indies match back in May. I felt humbled to see my name actually engraved on the wood and it made that performance feel all the more real now that it was recorded properly, not just inked on a strip of tape. During the next week I kept looking at the board to make sure that I was still there. In fact I was a bit worried at one point that some of the guys would notice what I was doing. For as long as I am lucky enough to play for England at Lord's, it is sure to serve as a personal inspiration. Meanwhile, in the museum behind the pavilion, the MCC had found a place for the signed shirt that I had donated after the innings.

Unfortunately we could not quite get our second series of the season off to a winning start. We knew that rain was on its way on the last day and just couldn't take the final wicket we needed to go 1–0 up. But it must have been a very close-run thing. As the light was fading, I hit the last man Shantha Sreesanth on the pad with an arm ball that I was very confident would go on to hit the stumps. I've seen pictures since of my appeal and it looks as though my eyes are bulging from my face – first in expectation, then in disappointment.

Umpire Steve Bucknor is famous the world over for the thought he puts into every decision. An age seemed to pass before I knew he had finally rejected my claim. It was getting very tense in the middle because the dark clouds were moving closer. By that stage, Michael Vaughan was bowling at the other end as he did not want to risk the light being offered to the batsmen against our pace bowlers. I guess that Bucknor wanted to be 100 per cent sure, knowing that a raised finger would have finished the game. At the end of the over I asked why he had given it not out. He said that it might have missed off stump. We will never know. It looked good to me, but then I am hardly an unbiased witness and Bucknor is one of the best in his trade.

Once we went off I think we knew deep down that our chance had gone. A few of the players took it in turns to go onto the balcony to see if the rain was getting lighter or the clouds were starting to break up in the distance. But one glum face followed another as they re-entered the dressing room. It reminded me of the Ashes Test at Melbourne the previous winter, when I thought I had a good leg-before shout against Andrew Symonds early in his innings. Instead, he continued towards his maiden Test hundred and no doubt now looks back on a breakthrough innings. Australia, as we all know, went on to win the game.

I just think that some things are meant to be. The combination of a rejected appeal and rain starting to fall a few minutes later makes me believe that a higher authority did not want us to win at Lord's. Cricket has helped to teach me to accept disappointment and remain philosophical rather than get angry and disenchanted. I want to win as much as the next man; I think my celebrations whenever I take a wicket show the commitment and determination. But I never get upset if an appeal is turned down. You just have to turn around, clear your mind and try again. Setbacks are sent down as challenges to your character.

In any case, it did not feel as though we had wasted an opportunity at Lord's. We simply ran out of time after playing really well in the gaps when the weather allowed. I don't know of anybody who thought that India would have hung on without the rain. There was nothing more we could have done, and I don't agree that we should have bowled our overs quicker on that final day. If we had raced through, then would Michael Vaughan have been able to set the fields he wanted? Mahendra Singh Dhoni deserves a lot of credit for the way he stuck out defiantly for over three hours, showing that he is more than just a brilliant hitter. He played the situation so well for his side and did more than anybody to save that game.

Given the poor forecasts, I was surprised that we managed to play as much as we did. During one of many breaks, Daniel Radcliffe, who plays Harry Potter in the films, visited our dressing room. I asked him whether he could wave his wand to keep the rain away from the ground. No doubt he hears jokes like that every day of his life, but he is a very polite, happy guy who also happens to be a big cricket fan. So much so that he wanted to spend his 18th birthday watching the game before heading off into the West End for his celebrations. Andrew Strauss for one was very excited when he found out that Radcliffe would be around. He wanted him to sign the new book – supposedly for his son. I enjoy the special effects in the films and I told the actor that I would love to have a go at Quidditch – although I'm not sure I would be quick and smart enough to catch the Golden

Snitch. Like me, he turned out to be a big Tendulkar fan. Earlier, he had queued unrecognised among the public to get Tendulkar's autograph.

My special memory of the game certainly involved Tendulkar. For the second time, I managed to get him lbw. The dismissal was almost a carbon copy of what had happened in Nagpur as a ball pitched on off stump and continued with the arm. When I come to list my favourite moments in cricket I don't think this will quite match my first wicket but, given the venue of Lord's, it may rank fairly close. Needless to say, I rushed around in celebration and received plenty of messages that night from mates asking what I thought I was doing. 'I don't know – you tell me,' I had to say. It was only when I saw a replay that I realised how pumped up I was. As well as it being Tendulkar it was also an important wicket in the context of the game because we were trying to get through India for a second time.

It was strange to think, after what he had written on the ball at Nagpur – 'never again' – that he fell in a similar fashion. I did not have a particular plan to set him up with the arm ball after turning a few away from the bat. From what I can gather, one or two people in the media start to roll their eyes when I talk about putting the ball in the right areas, but that same phrase gets repeated because it is the key to bowling well. I hoped that if I put the ball in the right areas – sorry – for long enough, then he might make a mistake. That it came against another one going straight on with the arm was coincidence. And, no, I didn't ask for the ball this time.

Injuries to Matthew Hoggard, Steve Harmison and Andrew Flintoff meant that I was the most experienced member of our bowling attack. I could hardly believe that when somebody pointed it out, as it was only my 18th appearance. Anil Kumble in the

India side had more caps than all of our bowlers put together. But Ryan Sidebottom, Jimmy Anderson and Chris Tremlett managed to dismiss India for 201 with a great first-innings effort. By the end of the series they had put a lot of pressure on Harmison and Hoggard for places. With Stuart Broad also on the fringes of the side, the selectors had a strong pool of bowlers for the winter and beyond.

Around this time I was doing quite a bit of work for npower, the sponsors of Test cricket in England. The promotional side was something new to me, and I found it very good fun. As part of their advertising campaign I had to dress in a dark business-man's suit and pose with an umbrella and a bowler hat. Though I say it myself, I looked every bit the dapper gent heading for a day on the stock market – a career move, by the way, that is very unlikely to happen, even with my interest in numbers. I was flanked by a couple of the blonde npower girls who are now a conspicuous feature at Test matches in their vivid red and green uniforms. The image was reproduced at something close to life size and used in cardboard, stand-up form in an attempt to attract spectators to the npower stalls at the grounds. As part of the same campaign, they also filmed me landing a ball on a pound coin, which went spinning out of the shot. I then went to collect the coin and waved it at the camera to make the link with money being saved. The short clip was shown on the big screen during drinks breaks and so on, often to the amusement of the rest of the team. 'Why can't you be as accurate as that in the real games?' Ian Bell asked me. I must admit that it took a few takes before I got it right.

Tours are so compact these days that the home side always tries to catch the tourists early when they may not quite be accli-matised. Where India were concerned, their experience meant that they knew what to expect. Maybe they would have been more vulnerable in the first half of the summer. Having said that, the terrible rain meant that it seemed like May even when we were heading towards August. I felt for the people who were forced to leave their homes because of the flooding in parts of the country and I was struck by the terrible pictures of the Worcester ground, a place that I knew, as the water levels rose and rose to such damaging levels.

Those problems ought to place cricket in context, but any sense of proportion was lost during the Second Test at Trent Bridge. Given all the column inches in the newspapers and talk on television and radio it is bound to be remembered – bizarrely – as the game where a couple of jelly beans found their way onto the crease. Zaheer Khan took offence, waved his bat at Kevin Pietersen and the publicity machines began to roll. As far as I am concerned, the sweets must have got there by accident. At worst, as Michael Vaughan said, it was a little prank intended to lighten the mood during a drinks break. As I don't field close to the bat I cannot shed any more light on what happened. I do know that we lost the Test match, and that our defeat had nothing to do with jelly beans.

I thought that a lot of the criticism we received was unfair. Like India, we play aggressively but we also play fairly. We encourage each other and occasionally a comment is directed at a batsman. But I did not think there was anything worse about this game than others. The only physical contact came when Shantha Sreesanth brushed against Vaughan. Sreesanth was fined half of his match fee for that. Cricket is hard fought, but we know how far we can go and recognise that we have to set the right example to young players. If people heard everything that was said via the stump microphone I think they would be surprised at how mundane and mild we all are.

There is nothing wrong in trying to unsettle a batsman – as long as it does not become nasty. You are looking for a reaction. Often it does not matter what that might be, as long as it takes his concentration away from his natural thoughts. You can sow seeds of doubt by talking among yourselves about technique. A player who is inexperienced or suffering a dip in form may be particularly vulnerable. In other cases it can backfire because it might strengthen a player's resolve. We are all human beings with emotions and sometimes a comment might touch a nerve. I must admit that in my case I get lost in the cricket banter and attempts to undermine me often sail over my head. Bowlers have a good chance against me without having to say much.

One of the best sledgers I have come across is Lance Klusener at Northamptonshire. He is a tough man who is not afraid to take any flak in return. If he is bowling and he feels he has the upper hand he might ask the batsman where he wants the next ball to pitch, or whether he wants it a bit quicker. The idea is to force a mistake. Another weapon is to glare at a batsman if he has played and missed. Sometimes I will stare for an extra second or two, but I don't think I look menacing enough to sustain that ball after ball. Anil Kumble can just about manage to look threatening – he's been described as a slow bowler with the mindset of a nasty fast one. He is actually a really gentle and devout man off the field. As a rule, spinners do not frighten batsmen into giving up their wickets.

Matt Prior took a lot of the criticism at Trent Bridge. Much of it was unfair. Along with the captain, the wicketkeeper is the focal point of the team, so he is bound to be the noisiest player. Most of what he said was not even directed towards the opposition. On this occasion we spent 160 overs in the field after being bowled out for 198 on the first day. As a bowler myself I can say that I welcomed every bit of encouragement as the Indians were stretching their lead into a formidable advantage. Players suffer ups and downs in their careers, and I guess it is impossible to be popular all the time. But I was surprised at what seemed to be a backlash against Matt so soon after his debut hundred at Lord's.

The toss had a big impact on the result, but that should not take anything away from India. They batted and bowled superbly. The ball always swings at Trent Bridge and their left-armers Zaheer Khan and R. P. Singh exploited the movement to perfection with clever changes of position at the crease. They were both prepared to go around the wicket to our right-handers and still managed to swing the ball away, against the angle. Ryan Sidebottom was amazing for us and I cannot remember a game where one bowler has beaten the bat so often for such little reward. His complexion goes pink very quickly and at one point his face resembled a beetroot as he was so frustrated. When he screams out loud it is purely to release the anger that builds up, not to intimidate batsmen.

Tendulkar and Sourav Ganguly played really well in difficult conditions but the key partnership was between Dinesh Karthik and Wasim Jaffer for the first wicket. They were the two relatively unheralded batsmen in their top six, but they both did a really good job in the three Tests. Their opening stand of 147 this time supplied the platform and from then on it was a question not of whether India would take a first-innings lead, but whether they could build towards something decisive, knowing that they had to bat last.

We managed to strike either side of tea on the second day; I had Karthik first ball after the break when he edged to short leg via his pad, attempting to play through midwicket. I also managed to tempt Rahul Dravid into pushing to short extra cover, a triumph for Michael Vaughan's field placings. And there may have been some irony in the fact that I claimed Sreesanth as my fourth wicket of the innings – if only I'd managed that a week or so earlier at Lord's. But we could never quite set a domino effect in motion, where wicket followed wicket in quick succession. Instead, we finished 283 runs behind on first innings and with little prospect of being saved by the weather. We needed to bat brilliantly to survive.

Being able to watch the top players go about their business is one of the best parts of being around the England side. I've mentioned earlier the way that Kevin Pietersen paced his double hundred against West Indies at Headingley. There was another example in the way that Michael Vaughan batted at Trent Bridge. As captain, he managed to forget about all of the controversy surrounding behaviour and the difficult situation in the game. He just batted and batted in his own way without any fuss, simply hitting the balls he wanted to hit to the places he wanted to hit them and refusing to move outside his own bubble. I watched quietly from the dressing room and never once saw him ruffled. That is what I think of as mental strength. It took a piece of bad luck to end the innings when he was bowled via an edge onto his thigh pad, which trickled onto the stumps.

We held out for nearly eight hours in all and Chris Tremlett gave India a little bit of a fright before they knocked off the 73 runs they needed. In a situation like that you wish for a miracle to happen, but failing that you can try to strike a blow for the next game. A wicket taken is never wasted because it gives the bowler confidence and the batsman something to think about. I had played with Tremlett at Under-19 level several years before, so I knew how he causes problems with his height and bounce.

There isn't a nasty bone in his body, but that doesn't make him any less effective. When conditions are in his favour he can inflict serious damage on good batting sides, and when there is not as much help from the pitch he is still hard to get away.

Around this time I received some good news resulting from work for Walkers crisps. I had agreed earlier in the summer to promote a new chilli and lemon flavour created especially for the Asian market. It was an honour to be used by such a big company familiar to everybody in the country. Walkers have had links with the Leicester area since the days of Queen Victoria and they are well aware of the Asian connections in the city these days. They thought that a series between England and India would be a perfect time to launch their new product. It must say something for the popularity of cricket that they thought I was recognisable enough to be their public face. One of their people told me that the new flavour had become their best-seller in its first week. I hope that the partnership can go on and on, as it has with Gary Lineker. Some of their television adverts have been really funny.

As with all commercial work, it is important not to overlap with my cricket. I am only too aware that if I start to get ideas above my station and believe that I don't have to practise any longer, then my figures will deteriorate and even small companies will not want to be associated with my name. Mike Martin, my manager, always says that if I look after my cricket then everything else will fit into place. Those are very wise words indeed.

There was certainly no room for distracted minds once we arrived at The Oval. Our task was straightforward: win the Third Test, or lose our unbeaten home record stretching back to 2001. Again, we suffered a pretty big blow half an hour from the start when Rahul Dravid called correctly and decided to bat first. The toss was not the be-all and end-all, because India still had to play really well, but I think we probably all knew that by bowling first and with the likelihood of having to chase against Anil Kumble on the final day, our task had just got harder. We were coming to the end of our Test season and were about to face our biggest challenge.

India gave us no let-up. They kept us in the field for 170 overs, spanning almost two full days. It was a brilliant innings, because although only Kumble scored a hundred they stitched together partnership after partnership. When you field first in a Test match you have that initial period of high concentration and great enthusiasm and excitement. By the afternoon you need to work hard to keep that up – again, the encouragement of your team-mates is important. A wicket re-energises the side in the field. That is one reason why a new batsman is vulnerable early on. But in this innings India did not lose wickets in quick succession. Whenever we thought we had made ground, they kept pushing us back.

It is hard to describe the equivalent of spending so much time in the field. Other than a paper round when I was younger, I don't have much experience of working outside cricket. People think that our sport is not physically demanding, but simply being on your feet for three two-hour blocks in a day can be draining – and that is without the running in to bowl and the sprinting across the outfield to cut off boundaries. Then there is the sheer mental fatigue of concentrating intensely for so long, knowing that every move you make may be scrutinised by the crowd and the cameras. This particular occasion also coincided with some rare warm weather. I will never see playing for England as anything but a privilege, but when you are tired out and Mahendra Singh Dhoni is starting to open his shoulders on a dream batting pitch, you have to remind yourself of how lucky you really are. You have to be strong and keep looking the captain in the eye, effectively telling him that you want to bowl and you think you can make the breakthrough. Test cricket does exactly what it says on the tin. It really does test you in many, many ways.

By the end of the innings I was shattered. My figures were 45–5–159–2 and India had racked up 664, the highest total in any game between the two countries. There cannot have been many cases where Sachin Tendulkar is replaced at the crease by Kumble, and the situation gets worse for the opposition. But Kumble went on to score his maiden Test hundred on his 118th appearance and, at the age of 36, showed what can be done by working hard enough for long enough. It is very revealing to go through his career record game by game to see how many overs he has bowled for India. You will see 30 in an innings, 40, 50 and even 60. He deserves his success, and his joy at completing his century was visible to everybody. Afterwards, he said that the pitch must have been very flat for him to achieve the feat, a statement underlining his modesty. If he can do that, then why can't I make a big score one day?

There were plenty more examples of strength during the game. For Alastair Cook and Andrew Strauss to see out the last overs of the fourth day having spent so long in the field during the game took incredible resilience. Set 500 to win in 110 overs, we had it all on to survive, and a wicket or two at that point would have given India great encouragement going into the last day. I think the fact that our opening pair held out on the Sunday evening played a large part in our saving the game. Although India only needed a draw, they were playing to win the series 2–0 and would have fancied their chances of taking ten wickets overall.

Rahul Dravid was criticised for not making us follow on 319 behind, but by batting again he probably removed any lingering chance of a fightback. If we had posted 500 in good time in our second innings and set India something close to 200, they would have been under pressure, especially given the late success of Chris Tremlett at Trent Bridge. Our target of 500 was all but impossible. No side has ever come close to scoring as many to win a Test match. And don't forget that Test cricket has been around for 130 years. Did we ever think about a chase? Well, if we had gone into lunch on the fifth day with all ten wickets in hand, then perhaps we would have had a go in the afternoon and reassessed our position at tea. Realistically, it was just not on. You can never compare the asking rates in Test cricket with those in one-day games because the rules on wides are far more lenient and there are no fielding restrictions. If India thought we were getting close, they could have bowled a couple of feet outside off stump and defended the boundaries.

We may have lost the series but the character we showed in avoiding defeat at The Oval will stand us in good stead in the future. Unbeaten runs have to end some time. When that happens I think it is good to look back and see what has been achieved between the two points. I did not come into the side until the winter of 2005–06, so I am not the best person to make a comparison. But I did think, by the end of the 2007 season, that we had the makings of being a really good side with plenty of young players getting better, an inspirational batsman in Kevin Pietersen and a great captain, Michael Vaughan, who defied medical experts by even playing again, let alone scoring hundreds. It felt a strange series to lose. I thought that the sides were very evenly matched. We were so close to winning at Lord's, and we might have been successful had we won the tosses at Trent Bridge and The Oval. There was no shame or embarrassment on our part. As for the messages I received from relatives in India, they all said how much they had enjoyed following the series.

My own return of eight wickets from the three games at an average of 50.37 was perhaps a bit disappointing. Remember what I said about the ICC rankings resembling the pop charts? Within the space of a few weeks I had slipped to 15th position on their computer, although I didn't feel a better or worse bowler than when I had stood at number six a couple of months earlier. As always, the experience of bowling to such wonderful players of spin will stand me in good stead for the long term. It may be easier when India's great batsmen retire, though I think the game as a whole will lose something when Sachin Tendulkar decides that the time has come to step down. With the love of cricket in India they will never be short of players, but Sachin will be an impossible act to follow.

Working on this book has given me a structure to look back through my own life. The Oval was my 20th Test appearance for England. I still wonder how it has happened to a boy who basically learnt to play the game on a park. I have worked hard to improve, but I have also been very lucky. Mike Hussey, a top batsman, had to score around 15,000 runs before he was given a chance to play for Australia. England picked me after half a full season for Northamptonshire, less than a year after I completed my degree.

The continuing Monty Mania is also hard to fathom. At Northamptonshire they had a special Monty Zone during Twenty20 games so that people who wanted to dress up in big false beards could all sit or stand together. And earlier in the season one of the players even put on a Monty mask for the team photograph because I was away at the World Cup. I still chuckle sometimes when I look into the stands and see people in fancy dress.

I smile to myself, too, when people say that I am different. I consider myself to be very normal indeed. I do not know how it feels to be anything else, not to wear the patka, have a beard and follow my faith. No doubt the beard will turn grey and I will wear a turban, like my father, but otherwise I do not expect much to change. I feel so proud when Sikh people I have never met before stop me in the street to say that their mates at work call them by the nickname 'Monty'. I have heard that so many times now. I will never push my beliefs on anybody. A lot of them are personal to me in any case. But it makes me so happy when I hear Sikh people say that I have given Sikhism some recognition in England.

On the field, one thing I can guarantee is that my enthusiasm will never die. I do not feel the game in my body unless I am excited and have that passion. Every time I take a wicket for England I feel such a rush of energy. For those few seconds I still feel an ecstasy that I can hardly describe. That's where the celebration comes from. And when those seconds are up, you never get them back. The wicket is gone and you have to work hard for the next one to experience that wonderful, wonderful buzz. That is part of the incentive to bowl.

My last wicket for England will be celebrated like my first – or my second, to be more accurate, because Sachin Tendulkar was such a special way to get off the mark. I am not even going to dare predict when that might be. If the England selectors never pick me again, I will be grateful to have played as much as I have – 20 times more than I ever imagined when Hitu Naik was banging on my door to make me go out into the cold and work on my bowling.

My ambition is simply to keep on improving. I would like to become established in all England teams, one-day and five-day. I was a little bit disappointed to be left out of the squad for the ICC World Twenty20 in South Africa. David Graveney, the chairman of selectors, spoke to me about the decision. He said that it was partly to give me a rest after all the cricket I had played and with so many games to follow during the winter and beyond. I think I am strong enough to cope with the workload demanded by the international schedule, but I also know that I have to keep working on my batting and fielding to offer a second skill to the one-day side.

And beyond playing? You know, that is something I really haven't thought about. Some players go into the media when they retire. I am not sure that is for me. It would make sense to put my degree to good use, if only to get something back for all those dark nights spent cramming to pass the exams. I enjoy working with computers, but technology changes so quickly that I may need to go on a few refresher courses. Anyway, what was that about not looking too far ahead? For as long as I feel able, I intend to keep playing cricket. Let's hope that I don't have to think about a new career for several years to come.

CAREER RECORD

Compiled by Victor Isaacs

Monty Panesar in Test Cricket

Test Career Record (2006–7) – *up to and including Third Test v India at The Oval*

M	I	NO	Runs	HS	Avge	Overs	Maids	Runs	Wkts	Avge	Best	5wI	10wM
20	28	11	124	26	7.29	765.3	162	2249	73	30.80	6-129	6	1

1. v India at Nagpur 1-5 March 2006 - match drawn
    Toss: England
    England 393 (P.D. Collingwood 134) & 297-3 dec (A.N. Cook 104)
    India 323 (M.J. Hoggard 6-57) & 260-6 (W. Jaffer 100)

1st innings	lbw b S. Sreesanth	9
2nd innings	did not bat	
1st innings	42-19-73-2	S.R. Tendulkar lbw 16
		M. Kaif b 91
2nd innings	16-2-58-1	R.S. Dravid b 71

2. v India at Mohali 9-13 March 2006 - lost by 9 wickets
    Toss: England
    England 300 (A. Kumble 5-76) & 181
    India 338 & 144-1

1st innings	c R.S. Dravid b A. Kumble	0
2nd innings	not out	0
1st innings	19-3-65-1	W. Jaffer c Flintoff 31
2nd innings	11-0-48-0	

3. v India at Mumbai 18-22 March 2006 - England won by 212 runs
    Toss: India
    England 400 (A.J. Strauss 128) & 191
    India 279 & 100

1st innings	not out	3
2nd innings	not out	0
1st innings	26-7-53-1	A. Kumble lbw 30
2nd innings	4-1-15-0	

4. v Sri Lanka at Lord's 11-15 May 2006 - match drawn
   Toss: England
   England 551-6 dec (M.E. Trescothick 106, K.P. Pietersen 158)
   Sri Lanka 192 & 537-9 (D.P.M.D. Jayawardene 119)
   1st innings   did not bat
   1st innings   did not bowl
   2nd innings   27-10-49-2   W.U. Tharanga   c Jones   52
                                 K.C. Sangakkara   c Jones   65

5. v Sri Lanka at Edgbaston 25-28 May 2006 - England won by 6 wickets
   Toss: Sri Lanka
   Sri Lanka 141 & 231 (M.G. Vandort 105)
   England 295 (K.P. Pietersen 142, M. Muralitharan 6-86) & 81-4
   1st innings   lbw b S.L. Malinga   0
   2nd innings   did not bat
   1st innings   2-0-7-1   S.L. Malinga   lbw   26
   2nd innings   28-6-73-2   K.C. Sangakkara   c Collingwood   18
                                 T.T. Samaraweera   st Jones   8

6. v Sri Lanka at Trent Bridge 2-5 June 2006 - Sri Lanka won by 134 runs
   Toss: Sri Lanka
   Sri Lanka 231 & 322 (M.S. Panesar 5-78)
   England 229 & 190 (M. Muralitharan 8-70)
   1st innings   not out   0
   2nd innings   lbw b S.T. Jayasuriya   26
   1st innings   5-3-3-0
   2nd innings   37.1-13-78-5   W.U. Tharanga   c Cook   46
                                 S.T. Jayasuriya   lbw   4
                                 M.F. Maharoof   b   6
                                 S.L. Malinga   b   22
                                 M. Muralitharan   c Strauss   2

7. v Pakistan at Lord's 13-17 July 2006 - match drawn
   Toss: England
   England 528-9 dec (A.N. Cook 105, P.D. Collingwood 186, I.R. Bell 100*)
   & 296-8 dec (A.J. Strauss 128)
   Pakistan 445 (Mohammad Yousuf 202) & 214-4
   1st innings   not out   0
   2nd innings   did not bat
   1st innings   27-3-93-0
   2nd innings   27-7-60-2   Faisal Iqbal   c Cook   48
                                 Mohammad Yousuf   lbw   48

8. v Pakistan at Old Trafford 27-29 July 2006 - England won by an innings and 120 runs
Toss: Pakistan
Pakistan 119 (S.J. Harmison 6-19) & 222 (S.J. Harmison 5-57, M.S. Panesar 5-72)
England 461-9dec (A.N. Cook 127, I.R. Bell 106*)

1st innings	not out	3		
1st innings	7.4-3-21-3	Mohammad Yousuf	c Jones	38
		Faisal Iqbal	c Jones	3
		Shahid Afridi	c Pietersen	15
2nd innings	27-4-72-5	Imran Farhat	c Bell	34
		Younis Khan	lbw	62
		Mohammad Yousuf	st Jones	15
		Inzamam-ul-Haq	c Cook	13
		Faisal Iqbal	c Trescothick	29

9. v Pakistan at Headingley 4-8 August 2006 - England won by 167 runs
Toss: England
England 515 (K.P. Pietersen 135, I.R. Bell 119, Umar Gul 5-123)
& 345 (A.J. Strauss 116)
Pakistan 538 (Younis Khan 173, Mohammad Yousuf 192) & 155

1st innings	not out	5		
2nd innings	not out	5		
1st innings	47.4-13-127-3	Inzamam-ul-Haq	hit wicket	26
		Mohammad Sami	c Harmison	19
		Danish Kaneria	c Trescothick	29
2nd innings	17.5-4-39-3	Taufeeq Umar	c Cook	11
		Younis Khan	b	41
		Inzamam-ul-Haq	st Read	37

10. v Pakistan at The Oval 17-20 August 2006 - England won by concession
Toss: Pakistan
England 173 & 298-4
Pakistan 504 (Mohammad Yousuf 128)

1st innings	b Umar Gul	0		
2nd innings	did not bat			
1st innings	30-6-103-1	Umar Gul	lbw	13

11. v Australia at Perth 14-18 December 2006 - Australia won by 206 runs
Toss: Australia
Australia 244 (M.S. Panesar 5-92) & 527-5dec (M.E.K. Hussey 103, M.J. Clarke 135, A.C. Gilchrist 102)
England 215 & 350 (A.N. Cook 116)

1st innings	not out	16

2nd innings	b S.K.Warne	1		
1st innings	24-4-92-5	J.L. Langer	b	37
		A. Symonds	c Jones	26
		A.C. Gilchrist	c Bell	0
		S.K. Warne	c Jones	25
		B. Lee	lbw	10
2nd innings	34-3-145-3	M.L. Hayden	c Collingwood	92
		M.E.K. Hussey	c Jones	103
		A. Symonds	c Collingwood	2

12. v Australia at Melbourne 26-28 December 2006 - Australia won by an innings and 99 runs
Toss: England
England 159 (S.K. Warne 5-39) & 161
Australia 419 (M.L. Hayden 153, A. Symonds 156)
1st innings: c A. Symonds b S.K. Warne   4
2nd innings c M.J. Clarke b B. Lee   14
1st innings   12-1-52-0

13. v Australia at Sydney 2-5 January 2007 - Australia won by 10 wickets
Toss: England
England 291 & 147
Australia 393 & 46-0
1st innings   lbw b S.K. Warne   0
2nd innings run out (A. Symonds)   0
1st innings   19.3-0-90-2   A. Symonds   b   48
                              S.K. Warne   st Read   71
2nd innings did not bowl

14. v West Indies at Lord's 17-21 May 2007 - match drawn
Toss: West Indies
England 553-5 dec (A.N. Cook 105, P.D. Collingwood 111, I.R. Bell 109*,
M.J. Prior 126*) & 284-8 dec (K.P. Pietersen 109)
West Indies 437 (M.S. Panesar 6-129) & 89-0
1st innings   did not bat
2nd innings not out   3
1st innings   36.1-3-129-6   D. Ganga   lbw   49
                              D.S. Smith   b   21
                              R.R. Sarwan   lbw   35
                              S. Chanderpaul   lbw   74
                              R.S. Morton   lbw   14
                              C.D. Collymore   lbw   1
2nd innings 3-0-13-0

15.   v West Indies at Headingley 25-28 May 2007 - England won by an innings and 283 runs
Toss: England
England 570-7 dec (M.P. Vaughan 103, K.P. Pietersen 226)
West Indies 146 & 141
1st innings: did not bat
1st innings 1-0-1-0
2nd innings 6-1-20-1   D.J. Bravo   c Plunkett 52

16.   v West Indies at Old Trafford 7-11 June 2007 - England won by 60 runs
Toss: England
England 370 & 313 (A.N. Cook 106, D.J.G. Sammy 7-66)
West Indies 229 & 394 (S. Chanderpaul 116*, M.S. Panesar 6-137)

1st innings	not out	14		
2nd innings	c C.H. Gayle	b D.J.G. Sammy	0	
1st innings	16.4-5-50-4	D.S. Smith	c Bell	40
		D.J.G. Sammy	c Collingwood	1
		J.E. Taylor	c Strauss	0
		C.D. Collymore	c Collingwood	4
2nd innings	51.5-13-137-6	D.S. Smith	c Cook	42
		R.S. Morton	lbw	54
		D.J. Bravo	c Cook	49
		D. Ramdin	c Collingwood	34
		D.J.G. Sammy	c and b	25
		C.D. Collymore	c Bell	0

Match highlights: *Man of the match*

17.   v West Indies at Chester-le-Street 15-19 June 2007 - England won by 7 wickets
Toss: England
West Indies 287 (S. Chanderpaul 136*, R.J. Sidebottom 5-88) & 222
(M.S. Panesar 5-46)
England 400 (P.D. Collingwood 128, F.H. Edwards 5-112) & 111-3

1st innings	b D.B.L. Powell	4		
2nd innings	did not bat			
1st innings	13.1-2-34-1	C.D. Collymore	lbw	13
2nd innings	16-2-46-5	R.S. Morton	b	7
		S. Chanderpaul	b	70
		D.J. Bravo	c Sidebottom	43
		M.N. Samuels	c Collingwood	2
		D. Ramdin	b	4

18.   v India at Lord's 19-23 July 2007 - match drawn
      Toss: England
      England 298 & 282 (K.P. Pietersen 134)
      India 201 (J.M. Anderson 5-42) & 282-9
      1st innings   lbw b S. Sreesanth   0
      2nd innings   lbw b R.P. Singh   3
      1st innings   8-3-22-0
      2nd innings   26-7-63-2   S.R. Tendulkar   lbw   16
                                  R.P. Singh   b   2

19.   v India at Trent Bridge 27-31 July 2007 - India won by 7 wickets
      Toss: India
      England 198 & 355 (M.P. Vaughan 124, Z. Khan 5-75)
      India 481 & 73-3
      1st innings   c V.V.S. Laxman b Z. Khan   1
      2nd innings   c K.D. Karthik b A. Kumble   4
      1st innings   33.3 8 101 4 K.D. Karthik   c Cook   77
                                  R. Dravid   c Bell   37
                                  R.P. Singh   lbw   0
                                  S. Sreesanth   lbw   2
      2nd innings   did not bowl

20.   v India at The Oval 9-13 August 2007 - match drawn
      Toss: India
      India 664 (A. Kumble 110) & 180-6 dec
      England 345 & 369-6 (K.P. Pietersen 101)
      1st innings   lbw b A. Kumble   9
      2nd innings   did not bat
      1st innings   45-5-159-2   Z. Khan   c J.M. Anderson   11
                                  S. Sreesanth   c M.P. Vaughan   35
      2nd innings   18-1-58-0

First-Class Career Record (2001–7) – *up to and including Third Test v India at The Oval*

M	I	NO	Runs	HS	Avge	Overs	Maids	Runs	Wkts	Avge	Best	5wI	10wM
64	83	30	430	39*	8.11	2508.5	605	7244	246	29.44	7-181	16	3

Debut: Northamptonshire v Leicestershire at Northampton 23 August 2001

Monty Panesar in One-Day International Cricket

One-Day International Career Record (2006–7) – *up to and including 3rd ODI v West Indies at Southampton*

M	I	NO	Runs	HS	Avge	Overs	Maids	Runs	Wkts	Avge	Best	4wI	Econ
19	7	3	23	13	5.75	152	9	681	17	40.05	3-25	-	4.48

1. v Australia at Melbourne 12 January 2007 - Australia won by 8 wickets
   Toss: England
   England 242-8 (50 overs) (K.P. Pietersen 82)
   Australia 246-2 (45.2 overs) (R.T. Ponting 82*)
   Batting   not out   0   (0 balls)
   Bowling   10-1-46-1   M.L. Hayden   c Nixon   28

2. v New Zealand at Hobart 16 January 2007 - England won by 3 wickets
   Toss: New Zealand
   New Zealand 205-9 (50 overs) (J.M. Anderson 4-42)
   England 206-7 (A. Flintoff 72*)
   Batting   did not bat
   Bowling   10-0-36-1   D.L. Vettori   lbw   11

3. v New Zealand at Adelaide 23 January 2007 - New Zealand won by 90 runs
   Toss: New Zealand
   New Zealand 210 (50 overs) (J.D.P. Oram 86, A. Flintoff 4-21)
   England 120 (37.5 overs) (D.L. Vettori 4-24)
   Batting   c N.J. Astle   b S.E. Bond   6   (12 balls)
   Bowling   9-0-44-1   R.L. Taylor   c Collingwood   15

4. v Australia at Adelaide 26 January 2007 - Australia won by 9 wickets
   Toss: England
   England 110 (34.3 overs) (M.G. Johnson 4-45)
   Australia 111-1 (24.3 overs)
   Batting   not out   0   (7 balls)
   Bowling   5-0-19-0

5. v New Zealand at Perth 30 January 2007 - New Zealand won by 58 runs
   Toss: New Zealand
   New Zealand 318-7 (50 overs) (L. Vincent 76, R.L. Taylor 71)
   England 260-8 (50 overs) (E.C. Joyce 66)
   Batting   did not bat
   Bowling   10-2-35-2   C.D. McMillan   st Nixon   11
                              B.B. McCullum   c Strauss   19

6.   v Australia at Sydney 2 February 2007 - England won by 92 runs
    Toss: England
    England 292-7 (50 overs) (E.C. Joyce 107)
    Australia 200 (38.5 overs)
    Batting   did not bat
    Bowling   10-0-64-1   N.W. Bracken   b   21

7.   v New Zealand at Brisbane 6 February 2007 - England won by 14 runs
    Toss: England
    England 270-7 (50 overs) (P.D. Collingwood 106, S.E. Bond 4-46)
    New Zealand 256-8 (50 overs) (S.P. Fleming 106)
    Batting   did not bat
    Bowling   8-1-38-1   L. Vincent c Flintoff   31

8.   v Australia at Melbourne 9 February 2007 - England won by 4 wickets
    Toss: Australia
    Australia 252 (48.3 overs) (M.L. Hayden 82, R.T. Ponting 75)
    England 253-6 (49.3 overs) (P.D. Collingwood 120*)
    Batting   did not bat
    Bowling   10-0-44-2   R.T. Ponting   c Collingwood   75
                             B.J. Hodge   lbw   5

9.   v Australia at Sydney 11 February 2007 - England won by 34 runs (D/L)
    Toss: England
    England 246-8 (50 overs) (P.D. Collingwood 70)
    Australia 152-8 (27 overs)
    Batting   did not bat
    Bowling   2-0-15-0

10.   v New Zealand at Gros Islet 16 March 2007 - New Zealand won by 6 wickets
    Toss: New Zealand
    England 209-7 (50 overs)
    New Zealand 210-4 (41 overs) (S.B. Styris 87*)
    Batting   did not bat
    Bowling   10-0-47-1   C.D. McMillan   c Dalrymple   27

11.   v Canada at Gros Islet 18 March 2007 - England won by 51 runs
    Toss: Canada
    England 279-6 (50 overs)
    Canada 228-7 (50 overs)
    Batting   did not bat
    Bowling   10-1-35-1   A.M. Samad   lbw   36

12. v Kenya at Gros Islet 24 March 2007 - England won by 7 wickets
     Toss: Kenya
     Kenya 177 (43 overs) (S.O. Tikolo 76)
     England 178-3 (33 overs) (E.C. Joyce 75)
     Batting   did not bat
     Bowling   8-0-28-0

13. v Ireland at Providence 30 March 2007 - England won by 48 runs
     Toss: England
     England 266-7 (50 overs) (P.D. Collingwood 90)
     Ireland 218 (48.1 overs) (A. Flintoff 4-43)
     Batting   did not bat
     Bowling   10-1-31-2   A.C. Botha   c Flintoff   18
                               K.J. O'Brien   lbw   12

14. v Sri Lanka at St Peter's 4 April 2007 - Sri Lanka won by 2 runs
     Toss: England
     Sri Lanka 235 (50 overs) (S.I. Mahmood 4-50)
     England 233-8 (50 overs)
     Batting   did not bat
     Bowling   8-0-45-0

15. v Australia at St Peter's 8 April 2007 - Australia won by 7 wickets
     Toss: England
     England 247 (49.5 overs) (K.P. Pietersen 104, I.R. Bell 77)
     Australia 248-3 (47.2 overs) (R.T. Ponting 86)
     Batting   not out   1   (2 balls)
     Bowling   9-0-48-0

16. v Bangladesh at Bridgetown 11 April 2007 - England won by 4 wickets
     Toss: England
     Bangladesh 143 (37.2 overs)
     England 147-6 (44.5 overs)
     Batting   did not bat
     Bowling   7-2-25-3   Mashrafe Mortaza   b   13
                               Mohammad Rafique   c Strauss   0
                               Abdur Razzak   c Collingwood   15

17. v South Africa at Bridgetown 17 April 2007 - South Africa won by 9 wickets
     Toss: England
     England 154 (48 overs) (A.J. Hall 5-18)
     South Africa 157-1 (19.2 overs) (G.C. Smith 89*)
     Batting   c M.V. Boucher   b A. Nel   2   (28 balls)
     Bowling   2-0-24-0

18. v West Indies at Lord's 1 July 2007 - England won by 79 runs
     Toss: West Indies
     England 225 (49.5 overs) (I.R. Bell 56, F.H. Edwards 5-45)
     West Indies 146 (39.5 overs) (S. Chanderpaul 53)
     Batting   lbw b R. Rampaul   1
     Bowling   8-0-29-1   D.B.L. Powell   lbw b Panesar   1

19. v West Indies at Trent Bridge 7 July 2007 - West Indies won by 93 runs
     Toss: West Indies
     West Indies 289-5 (50 overs) (C.H. Gayle 82, R.S. Morton 82*)
     England 196 (44.2 overs) (O.A. Shah 51, D.B.L. Powell 4-40)
     Batting   lbw b R. Rampaul   13
     Bowling   6-0-28-0

Twenty20 International Career Record (2006–7) – up to and including v West Indies at Sydney

M	I	NO	Runs	HS	Avge	Overs	Maids	Runs	Wkts	Avge	Best	4wI	Econ
1	1	0	1	1	1.00	4	0	40	2	20.00	2-40	-	10.00

1. v Australia at Sydney 9 January 2007 - Australia won by 77 runs
    Toss: Australia
    Australia 221-5 (20 overs)
    England 144-9 (20 overs)
    Batting   run out   1   (2 balls)
    Bowling   4-0-40-2   A.C. Gilchrist   b   48
                              M.E.K. Hussey   st Nixon   18

One-Day (List 'A') Career Record (2002–7) – up to and including 3rd ODI v West Indies at Southampton

M	I	NO	Runs	HS	Avge	Overs	Maids	Runs	Wkts	Avge	Best	4wI	Econ
28	12	7	59	16*	11.80	239	12	1057	29	36.44	5-20	1	4.42

INDEX

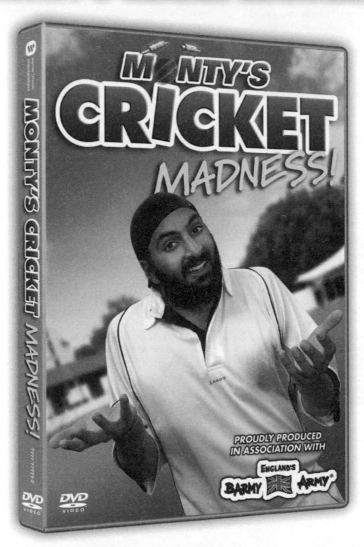